ABRAMELIN
LUNAR ORDEAL

AN ALTERNATIVE MAGICAL JOURNEY

About the Author

Frater Barrabbas Tiresius is a practicing ritual magician who has studied magic and the occult for over forty years. He believes that ritual magic is a discipline whose mystery is unlocked by continual practice and by occult experiences and revelations. Frater Barrabbas believes that traditional approaches should be balanced with creativity and experimentation and that no occult or magical tradition is exempt from changes and revisions.

Frater Barrabbas also founded a magical order called the Order of the Gnostic Star and is an elder and lineage holder in the Alexandrian tradition of Witchcraft.

ABRAMELIN
LUNAR ORDEAL

AN ALTERNATIVE MAGICAL JOURNEY

FRATER BARRABBAS

Chicago, Illinois

Abramelin Lunar Ordeal: An Alternative Magical Journey © 2025 by Frater Barrabbas. All rights reserved. No part of this book may be reproduced in any manner whatsoever without written permission from Crossed Crow Books, except in the case of brief quotations embodied in critical articles and reviews.

Paperback ISBN: 978-1-959883-83-8
Library of Congress Control Number on file.

Disclaimer: Crossed Crow Books, LLC does not participate in, endorse, or have any authority or responsibility concerning private business transactions between our authors and the public. Any internet references contained in this work were found to be valid during the time of publication, however, the publisher cannot guarantee that a specific reference will continue to be maintained. This book's material is not intended to diagnose, treat, cure, or prevent any disease, disorder, ailment, or any physical or psychological condition. The author, publisher, and its associates shall not be held liable for the reader's choices when approaching this book's material. The views and opinions expressed within this book are those of the author alone and do not necessarily reflect the views and opinions of the publisher.

Published by:
Crossed Crow Books, LLC
6934 N Glenwood Ave, Suite C
Chicago, IL 60626
www.crossedcrowbooks.com

Printed in the United States of America.
IBI

Other Books by the Author

Other Books by Frater Barrabbas

Mastering the Art of Ritual Magick (Crossed Crow Books, 2024)
Disciple's Guide to Ritual Magick (Crossed Crow Books, 2024)
Liber Nephilim (Crossed Crow Books, 2024)
Mastering the Art of Witchcraft (Crossed Crow Books, 2024)
Sacramental Theurgy for Witches (Crossed Crow Books, 2024)
Transformative Initiation for Witches (Crossed Crow Books, 2024)
Talismanic Magic for Witches (Llewellyn, 2023)
Elemental Powers for Witches (Llewellyn, 2021)
Spirit Conjuring for Witches (Llewellyn, 2017)
Magical Qabalah for Beginners (Llewellyn, 2013)

Forthcoming Titles

The Magical Notary Art (Crossed Crow Books)
Liber Artis Archaeomancy (Crossed Crow Books)

Dedication

This book is dedicated to Frater Arjuna, Frater Calixtus, and Frater Discipulus Merlini, who were there thirty years ago with me in the Order; Frater Anubis, a faithful and talented associate; Scott Stenwick, an important mentor; my wife Joni, who taught me how to write books; Lynxa, my feline muse; and to all my readers who wanted this book with its ritual lore to be published.

Acknowledgments

Many thanks to Blake and Wycke Malliway of Crossed Crow Books; to Tony Mierzwicki, who gave me good advice and excellent guidance about the Sacred Magic; and to many others who have supported my alternative path working and trail blazing over the decades.

CONTENTS

Note by the Author..*xv*
Introduction and Preface to the Abramelin Lunar Ordeal.................*xvii*

PART I
HISTORY AND AUTHENTICATION OF THE LUNAR ORDEAL

Chapter One
ABRAMELIN LUNAR ORDEAL:
SACRED OGDOADIC TABERNACLE • 1

Chapter Two
IS ACHIEVING THE KNOWLEDGE AND
CONVERSATION OF THE HGA IMPORTANT? • 14

Chapter Three
ALTERNATIVE USE OF THE BORNLESS OR HEADLESS
ONE INVOCATION AS THE HGA • 19

Chapter Four
WINTER 2009 ABRAMELIN LUNAR
ORDEAL WORKING • 33

Part II
RITUALS AND CEREMONIES ASSOCIATED WITH THE LUNAR ORDEAL

Chapter One
ORDEALS OF TRANSFIGURATION, SUPER-ARCHANGELS, AND RITUAL TECHNOLOGY • 41

Chapter Two
CIRCLE CONSECRATION RITES • 63

Chapter Three
ARCHETYPAL GATE RITUAL FOR INVOKING THE CHERUBIM, SERAPHIM, AND ELEMENT GODHEADS • 73

Appendix I
THE CALL OF INVOCATION OF THE TETRAMORPHIC GODHEAD • 85

Appendix II
IMAGO OF THE EIGHT SUPER-ARCHANGELS AND FOUR ELEMENT GODHEADS • 87

Chapter Four
OGDOADIC GODHEAD VORTEX RITUAL • 92

Chapter Five
TRIPLE TETRAHEDRAL GATE RITUAL • 102

Chapter Six
BORNLESS ONE INVOCATION RITE OF STELLAR GNOSIS • 111

Chapter Seven
ALCHEMICAL HIEROMANY RITE OF UNION • 135

Chapter Eight
BORNLESS RING CONSECRATION RITE • 148

Chapter Nine
BORNLESS ASSUMPTION OF GREAT POWERS RITE • 152

Chapter Ten
BORNLESS ENVISIONING RITE • 157

Part III
DIARY ENTRIES FOR THE ORDEAL FROM AUTUMN 2009 TO SPRING OF 2011

Note from the Author
DIARY ENTRIES FOR THE ORDEAL WORKING FROM NOVEMBER 2009 TO MAY 2011 • 169

Chapter One
BEGINNING OF THE ORDEAL: PREPARATIONS AND CONSECRATIONS (11/18/2009) • 170

Chapter Two
ABRAMELIN LUNAR ORDEAL: FIRST WEEKEND, ATTRIBUTE OF EARTH (11/23/2009) • 173

Chapter Three
ABRAMELIN LUNAR ORDEAL: SECOND WEEKEND, ATTRIBUTE OF AIR (11/30/2009) • 177

Chapter Four
ABRAMELIN LUNAR ORDEAL: THIRD WEEKEND, ATTRIBUTE OF WATER (12/7/2009) • 182

Chapter Five
ABRAMELIN LUNAR ORDEAL: FOURTH WEEKEND, ATTRIBUTE OF FIRE (12/14/2009) • 187

Chapter Six
INVOCATION OF THE OGDOADIC ELEMENTAL GODHEAD OF WATER (12/27/2009) • 193

Chapter Seven
ABRAMELIN ORDEAL AND BORNLESS ONE
INVOCATION: FINAL ACTIONS (01/01/2010) • 200

Chapter Eight
SUMMARY AND CONCLUSION OF THE ABRAMELIN
LUNAR ORDEAL WORKING (01/11/2010) • 206

Chapter Nine
SOME THOUGHTS ABOUT THE ABRAMELIN
LUNAR ORDEAL (03/01/2010) • 208

Chapter Ten
DISCOVERY AND DEVELOPMENT OF
THE MISSING RITUAL (11/10/2010) • 211

Chapter Eleven
PLANS FOR WORKING THE FINAL
RITES OF ALO (03/06/2011) • 212

Chapter Twelve
PHASE ONE OF FINAL ABRAMELIN LUNAR
ORDEAL WORKING (04/25/2011) • 214

Chapter Thirteen
PHASE TWO OF FINAL ABRAMELIN LUNAR
ORDEAL WORKING (05/17/2011) • 220

PART IV
CONCLUSION AND INSIGHTS ABOUT THE
ABRAMELIN LUNAR ORDEAL

Chapter One
SEEKING ALTERNATIVES AND BREAKING
WITH TRADITIONS • 229

Chapter Two
JOURNEY AND DEVELOPMENT OF
THE LUNAR ORDEAL • 233

Chapter Three
ULTIMATE DESTINATIONS—WHERE DOES THIS PATH LEAD US? • 236

Appendix III
ABRAMELIN MAGIC SQUARES: CONFIGURATION, CONSECRATION, AND USE • 239

Bibliography *249*
Index *251*

Note by the Author

Nearly fifteen years ago, I performed a different version of the Abramelin working and posted the edited diary entries into my blog. I claimed to have developed a completely new and different approach to acquiring the Knowledge and Conversation with my Holy Guardian Angel, or K and C of the HGA, as it is called, which created quite a stir in the various Internet social circles inhabited by ceremonial magicians. I had already established myself as something of a rebel and iconoclast, and this further cemented that opinion. There had been an informal congregation of individuals who claimed to have completed this working despite the tedious nature and the requirements of lengthy self-imposed isolation that it required. They could be found in various Internet and Facebook groups and formed an exclusive club of exalted practitioners. Since I had developed my own version of this working and broke with that tradition, they considered my claim of having succeeded with the overall objective dubious at best—scandalously fraudulent at worst. I found myself criticized and defamed wherever these individuals met.

Others requested that I give them the lore so that they could scrutinize it, or at least test my hypothesis. I felt that giving away my developed lore without any acknowledgement or consent was something I was loath to do. I instead made this lore available to my brothers and sisters of the Order of the Gnostic Star and more or less turned my back on these external requests. While some of these appeals could have been sincere, I was not willing to share with individuals that I didn't know or who wouldn't appreciate the work I had done to develop this ordeal. I thought about writing a book, but I didn't get around to doing it at the time since there were many tasks at hand other than writing a lengthy book about this working.

What I did was to write up a series of documents and articles that would help anyone in the Order figure out how to perform this ordeal. I also made myself available to them if they ever needed help getting this working started. Many of the members had this documentation and the rituals, so they could, if they wished, move forward with performing this rite. I never heard that anyone attempted this working, although several used the Bornless One invocation rite. It is indeed an advanced working, and so it is not for beginners or even someone knowledgeable and moderately experienced. This working is for someone who is mature in their magical work and adept in their metaphysical understanding. This is a working for someone who has the ability to perform highly charged invocations of the Seraphim and Cherubim, the Element Godhead, and a completely revised version of the Bornless One invocation rite. However, I cannot determine if someone is able to perform this working comfortably or if it would be a challenge that could be beyond them. That will have to be something that a magician who seeks to work this ordeal judges for themselves.

Those documents, rituals, and diary entries that I made available to members of the Order were the perfect foundation for writing a book about this ordeal. Therefore, some years later, I took the task of assembling this material upon myself, editing and adding to it to produce a book that would make this Lunar Ordeal available to the public for the first time. I have pulled together, refined, rewritten and revised the Abramelin Lunar Ordeal so that it can be useful to the greater occult community. I had my reasons for developing this working years ago, and I can now share that perspective and the ritual lore that is a major functional part of it. Here, then, is the story of an alternative journey to undergoing and experiencing the phenomenon of the K and C of the HGA. Because I successfully performed these rites years ago, I have a high degree of confidence that you will find it useful and perhaps even greatly rewarding.

—Frater Barrabbas

Introduction and Preface to the Abramelin Lunar Ordeal

Back in 2009, when I developed my own version of the Abramelin working and scheduled to kick it off in the late autumn of that year, I became a kind of Abramelin psychonaut. I had been contemplating this kind of working for a few years prior to that time, and, in fact, I had always been fascinated with the grimoire *Book of the Sacred Magic of Abramelin the Mage* translated and published by S. L. MacGregor Mathers.[1] It was a mysterious hardcover book filled with amazing magical squares, and the ordeal to activate them was legendary amongst the elite of the practitioners of ceremonial magic. However, that ordeal was quite difficult, if not almost impossible, for most people to perform. Many had attempted it and failed, due to the length of that working and the dedication it required.

Mathers' edition was translated from a later French copy to which he had access, and it required the adherent to perform hours of religious contemplation, expiation, prayer, and personal abasement for days.[2] Additionally, a special tabernacle was required to be built with a sand floor and eastern- and western-facing windows through which one would talk to the spirits. That version followed a regimen consisting of six months of preparation. An earlier and more complete German sourced version, translated by Steven Guth and edited by Georg Dehn, that surfaced only recently called for a year and six months of continuous liturgical practices.[3] That period was based on a solar cycle, whether for a solar half-year or a year and half bracketing the religious celebrations of Passover and the Feast of the Tabernacles, which are six months apart.

---

1 Mathers, S. L. MacGregor, *The Books of the Sacred Magic of Abramelin the Mage* (L. W. De Laurence Inc., 1948).

2 Davies, Owen, *Grimoires: A History of Magic Books* (Oxford University Press, 2009) p. 180, states that the manuscript was from the collection from the early eighteenth century in the Bibliotheque de l'Arsenal in Paris. This is the same collection where the famed *Grimoire of Armadel* came from.

3 Dehn, Georg and Steven Guth, *The Book of Abramelin: A New Translation* (Ibis Press, 2006) p. xxiii, identifies the source of two documents, dated 1608, for this version of the book as coming from the library of Duke August in the town of Wolfenbüttel near Hanover, Germany.

Mathers' version called for a period of one month to be sequestered, and the Guth-Dehn version called for a period of three months. The length of this ordeal and special requirements for the tabernacle ensured that few had the resources or the time to perform such a working. It was a regimen that fit perfectly with a fifteenth-century middle-class merchant but is beyond the ability of most modern practitioners. That was inherently the test and challenge that this working presented to anyone who aspired to plumb its mysteries and acquire the use of the potent collection of magical squares. A person had to slowly retire from the world for the period leading up to complete sequestration, where they left this material altogether to complete the ordeal. However, it was the mystique and reputed potency of the magical squares that were uniquely part of this grimoire, along with the realization and dialogue with one's Holy Guardian Angel and the mastery of a list of Goetic demons and their servitors that made it so attractive to magicians of the twentieth century. Few other such grimoires dealt with the preliminary requirements to achieving spiritual and magical mastery.

Aleister Crowley attempted to accomplish the goal of knowledge and conversation with his Holy Guardian Angel using the Abramelin working at Boleskine cottage in Foyers, Scotland in November 1899. He was unable to complete the operation, giving various excuses that a truly dedicated adherent probably would have ignored. He attempted it a second time and also failed to achieve the goal of K and C with his HGA.[4] It was after these failures that he began to experiment with a very obscure ritual fragment that Mathers had uncovered, which was called the Bornless One rite.[5] He also sought to perform other ceremonies to achieve what he considered to produce similar results to that of the Abramelin working. Apparently, he was able to activate the magic squares that are contained in that grimoire, since he was sensitive to anyone perusing his personal copy and releasing unimaginative forces into the world.[6]

Others over the decades since Crowley assert to have successfully completed the Abramelin working, and many of them were likely telling the truth while others have likely fabricated their claim. Since this was a highly subjective operation, there wasn't an ability to validate anyone's accomplishment. Still, this has given some individuals a kind of imprimatur of excellence, showing that they have achieved what even Crowley had failed. It has become a kind of club, with individuals promoting their vaunted achievement as a mechanism to separate the sheep from the goats, distinguishing individuals who were truly vested magicians from pretenders or those who had not

---

[4] Bogdan, Henrik, *Ars Congressus Cum Daemone: Aleister Crowley and the Knowledge and Conversation of the Holy Guardian Angel,* University of Gothenburg, Entangled Religions 14.3, accessed December 24, 2023, er.ceres.rub.de/index.php/ER/article/view/10265/9934.

[5] Crowley, Aleister, "Liber Samekh," *Gems from the Equinox,* Israel Regardie, ed. (Weiser, 2007) pp. 325–353.

[6] Dehn, Georg, and Steven Guth, *The Book of Abramelin: A New Translation,* (Ibis Press, 2006) pp. xviii–xix. Lon Milo Duquette, in his forward, talks about how Crowley frightened Grady McMurdy when he was caught opening up Crowley's copy of Mathers' version of the *Book of Abramelin* the Mage. Crowley believed that the book itself had magical powers.

achieved this great goal. However, Crowley had proved that performing this ordeal was not the only way to achieve this sacred objective, which was something that I paid close attention to when studying his writings. Developing an alternative to performing the long and grueling Abramelin working was something with precedence that could be done based on Crowley's writings.

I had a hard copy of Mathers' version of the Sacred Magic of Abramelin for many years, and I still possess it today. I read it thoroughly, thought a lot about it for a while, and then put it away as unfeasible for me. What had attracted me to that singular book was the infamy attached to it, and the fact that Alex Sanders himself had boasted about working and achieving it.[7] Once out of college, I was a nine-to-five working stiff struggling to get a career started, so taking a month off was practically impossible. I instead continued to develop my own system of magic and spent a lot of time developing the ritual that had appeared in the later versions of the Golden Dawn material, entitled "the Invocation of the Bornless One." It was, unfortunately, a corrupted version of the original, saddled as it was with the imaginings and embellishments of Mathers. Crowley had his own version that was a better magical representation, but it, too, had many embellishments associated with Thelema and Crowley's magical and spiritual perspectives. I used both versions to develop my own personalized ritual. My experiences working with this ritual were quite profound, and performing it seemed to bring me to a closer approximation of my own HGA.

When the Guth-Dehn version of the *Book of Abramelin* came out in 2006, I happily purchased a copy of it and read it from cover to cover. This version was from a more complete set of source manuscripts and was much more culturally and religiously Jewish than Mathers' edition. That made it much more authentic, but the period of the working was slated at eighteen months instead of six, and the period of sequestration was three months instead of one. That discovery made any plans to use the more authentic method completely unrealistic for me, placing it even more beyond my reach. That was a disappointing moment for me, but not unexpected. I had long ago consigned this elaborate and demanding working to something that I would admire but never actually perform.

Learning that the working spanned the liturgical dates of the Passover and the Feast of the Tabernacles and was based on a solar cycle got me thinking. Since I was a Witch and a ritual magician, and the lunar cycle was more significant to me than the solar cycle, could I somehow replace the eighteen-month solar cycle with a similar lunar cycle? As I thought about it, the two religious events would be replaced with the new moon and full moon. That would mean that the working would span a period of around forty days instead of eighteen months. However, by shortening the period of the working, I would need to fill it with much more intensive rituals and practices so that the shorter period would produce a powerful and profound transfiguration. Of course, making such a change would be in violation of the tradition established by the grimoire and its following, but I felt that since many individuals had performed the six-month version instead of the

---

[7] Johns, June, *King of the Witches: The World of Alex Sanders* (Coward-McCann, 1969) pp. 65–68.

eighteen-month version without any trouble, making such a change would not invalidate what I was seeking to accomplish.

It is with these thoughts that I came up with the invocation of the highest and most powerful angelic intelligences that I could summon—namely the four Cherubim and Seraphim—and use them as the foundation for this ordeal. Many religious traditions and authorities agree that the Seraphim and Cherubim represent the highest level in the angelic hierarchy, but they do not agree as to the names of these angels or that there are four of them. I made some decisions and selected four angels whose names were not found in other lists and felt that four was a number that would fit with the four Hebrew letters of the Qabalistic Godhead. I decided that invoking these angels, two each weekend, and then pulling the manifested energies and intelligences set at each watchtower and angle together into a vortex with the elected Element Godhead in the center would generate a powerful, magical environment, a veritable magical tabernacle within which to perform the greater ritual mysteries.

Also around this time, I bought the book *Greek Magical Papyri in Translation* (known by its initials as the *PGM*) edited by Hance Deiter Betz,[8] and found within it the original version of the Bornless One invocation rite, known in the book as the "Stele of Jeu the hieroglyphist" or the Headless One summoning rite, which was actually the empowerment phase used before performing a magical exorcism.[9] Using that work, I was able to perfect the version of the Bornless One invocation rite that I had taken from the Golden Dawn and Crowley. I had also, by this time, produced a version of this rite that performed a Qabalistic ascent through the four Worlds of Assiah, Yetzirah, Briah, and Atziluth. These four layers were part of what I called the powers of the four masters or fathers, named the Tetrapatronis. Yet it was at that azimuth in the world of Atziluth that the Bornless One invocation rite was to be performed in an inner temple, which was the fifth level. I had determined that this format of the Bornless One rite would function as the inner mystery rite of the Super-Angelic tabernacle vortex.

There were additional rituals that I needed to develop in order to complete this working, some of which I had already developed and others that I needed to research and produce. The Triple Tetrahedral Gate Ritual, also known as the Ascension Gate, uses the western and eastern gateways joined to a third that fuses them both together with a gateway whose points are the north, south, and zenith or Ultrapoint of the magic circle. These three gate structures open the operator up to the highly charged Ascension Gate which produces a transformative wave that draws them beyond the domains of earth, astral, and spirit to the absolute plane itself. This ritual is the key to the process of transfiguration and, used in conjunction with the Bornless One invocation rite, it establishes a conduit between the operator, their Holy Guardian Angel, and the Absolute Godhead.

Since I was able to do detailed research on the *PGM*, I found three additional rituals to perform along with the Bornless or Headless One invocation. These rituals were

---

8   Betz, Hans Dieter, ed., *The Greek Magical Papyri in Translation: Including the Demotic Spells*, second edition (University Chicago Press, 1996).

9   *Ibid*, p. 103.

derived from specific spells found in the *PGM* and added much to the empowerment and transfiguration generated by the Bornless One rite. A number of the spells in that collection consecrate and charge a special magical ring, which can be used to wield the powers of a series of workings or a specific godhead. I felt that this would function as the ideal link between the operator and the Bornless One or HGA. This rite is performed in the quiet period between establishing the Ogdoadic tabernacle and the performance of the Bornless One invocation rite. I later deduced that it functioned as the wedding ring to be worn during the alchemical wedding ceremony that I derived later in the ordeal process.

Additionally, I found two other spells that I used to craft the Assumption of Great Powers rite and the Envisioning rite. The Assumption rite is used to assume the powers and authorities, and to quicken the manifestation of the Bornless One as the Higher Self. It is performed just a day after the Bornless One invocation rite. The Envisioning rite takes a total of three days to perform, requiring three masses to be said with an accompanying incantation, known as the "Hidden Stele and Death Delivering Stele" from the *PGM*.[10] The Envisioning rite gathers the powerful visions that the operator experienced while performing the ordeal and projects them into the magic mirror to receive visions from the Higher Self or HGA of their near and ultimate destiny.

One additional ritual that was not included in the originally derived set was the Alchemical Hieromany rite of Union. It is supposed to be performed immediately after the Bornless One invocation and before the Assumption and Envisioning rites. Because I had not developed this ritual as part of the overall ordeal working, the achievement I had acquired seemed to be missing something important. My HGA or Higher Self did not meld itself with my own consciousness, so it still seemed to be frustratingly apart from me—close yet still somewhat distant. I experienced the full manifestation of my HGA, but I did not experience union with it.

The Hieromany Rite of Union is based on the seven-part symbolic allegory of the Chemical Wedding of Christian Rosenkreutz and as an alchemical formula for deriving the unified perfected state of the Philosopher's Stone, which is a kind of archetypal fusion of opposites, and this formula, when performed after the Bornless One invocation rite, ensures that the HGA and the operator consciously merge into a single magnificent being.

Since I had not performed that rite as part of the Abramelin Lunar Ordeal, I suffered for nearly a year before I finally developed this ritual. I then performed it alongside redoing some of the climactic rites of the ordeal to aid in bringing everything together. I have made certain that this ritual now has its proper place and sequence in the ordeal, which will make that process more fulfilling and complete. It was the mystical direction of the HGA that helped me to discover this missing ritual and performing it to bring my work to its completion. When I reveal the diaries that are a part of this working as I performed it nearly fifteen years ago, you will see that the ordeal itself was extended into the following year, whereas, if performed as it should be, the working would be completed in around forty days, with the Envisioning rite performed during the following full moon.

---

10 I will cite the exact locations of these sections of the *PGM* when the rituals themselves are presented.

As you have no doubt noticed, I have alternated between referring to the target entity of this working as the Holy Guardian Angel (HGA), the Bornless or Headless One, and the Higher Self. All three of these entities are one and the same as they are defined in this working. I know that there is some disagreement as to the nature of the HGA and the Bornless One or Headless One as a distinct Deity and not necessarily identified as one's higher self. I refer to the Higher Self as the Deity within one, which is our inherent godlike nature. This is also known as the *Atman* in Indian philosophy of Vedanta, and it taught that there is no difference between the Atman and the *Brahman*, which is its attribute of the Absolute Godhead. Thus, there could not be anything higher than the Deity within one, and this godhead is directly and indivisibly connected to the ultimate Godhead—there is no difference between them. While Vedanta takes this approach to deny the possibility of duality, the nature of Christianity speaks of a Holy Guardian Angel assigned to each living person separate from God. This perspective allows for a kind of duality that can only be resolved if the HGA is tied directly to the Deity within one. Therefore, I feel confident that my explanation and perspective accorded to these metaphysical attributes is the correct one.

Of course, there is a lot more detailed information contained in this work that will explain the background to this ordeal and the various concepts and rituals used to achieve the ultimate climax of the working—the K and C with the HGA, perhaps better stated as the manifestation and conscious awareness of the Deity within, or the illumination of the Higher Self. How I came to develop this ordeal, and why I felt that departing from the traditional approach was important and necessary, needs to be explained in a clear manner. This decision was not an impulsive one, and the development of this lore occurred over a couple of decades, especially my rendition of the Bornless One invocation rite. I feel that all of the components that one would find and experience in the much longer solar-based ordeal are intensified and condensed to occur within the cycles of the lunar period, from new moon to full, to new and then again to full: a full forty-two days from start to finish.[11]

Now, I am not advocating that the Abramelin Lunar Ordeal is somehow better than the traditional ordeal, whether the six-month or eighteen-month version is used. In fact, I am not advocating that you should replace any other traditional versions with my version. What I am advocating is a different and I believe more practical approach than the traditional version. It might be similar in some ways to the traditional version—or at least I think it is—but the two different approaches will undoubtedly produce two different results.

Those who have successfully achieved their K and C with their HGA, whichever methodology used, deserve respect for what they have achieved and the labor they have expended to achieve it. I am completely willing to give those adherents the respect due to them. However, similar to Crowley, I believe that the same or similar results can be achieved using a different methodology. All that is required to make any approach legitimate are

---

11   Consider that one and half lunar cycles would be twenty-eight days and fourteen days, which added together would be forty-two. However, my ordeal actually occurred over forty-one days.

the experiences and ultimate results of that working. It is a wholly subjective experience, and one that cannot ever be completely corroborated by a peer group. Anyone could lie and fabricate their experience, but perhaps those who have undergone it might detect a fraudulent claim in the telling; then again, it might not be detected. However, because of the subjectivity involved, it is likely that even those who use the same practices might find themselves experiencing something quite different.

This book is about one of those different approaches to gaining the knowledge and conversation with one's Holy Guardian Angel. That is the objective of this working, and I can say without any doubt or hesitation that it does achieve that objective. Would it have been different if I had used one of the traditional workings? Perhaps, but unless or until I perform the long version, I will never be able to answer that question. What I can say is that I am completely and thoroughly satisfied with the results produced by my version. What I did fifteen years ago is still having a profound effect on me to this very day.

Abramelin Lunar Ordeal is divided into three parts. The first part contains all of the background that is needed for someone to fully understand what this ordeal does, why it works, and what it should achieve. The second part contains all of the ritual lore required to perform this ordeal fully and completely. There are a few rituals that are not included, such as the Mass rite and the Benediction rite; these can be found in one of my previous books, *Sacramental Theurgy for Witches*, which should give to the adherent the necessary liturgical rituals to continually sacralize the tabernacle—an important task. Each ritual has an introduction that will help to describe the ritual pattern and how it functions.

Part three contains the diary entries that I wrote describing my personal experiences when I performed this ordeal back in 2009 and into 2010. I think that the combination of background documentation, rituals and explanations, and diary entries from when I performed this working will give you, the reader, a comprehensive exposure to this ordeal. My objective is to make this Lunar Ordeal working one that you can acquire, plan, and perform as part of your ultimate spiritual and magical objectives.

Therefore, let us proceed to examine the metaphysical explanations and how this ordeal was conceived and developed. I know that you will find it very rewarding, revealing, and exciting, which will lead to the next part, where we discuss the actual rituals used in this ordeal. I am quite certain that you will see the value of my approach and be inspired to perform it. It will also prove whether or not my ordeal and the lore it contains is useful and produces the results that I claim it will produce. I would be eager to know your results when you perform this ordeal, and then perhaps when there are several (or more) of us, we can start our own exclusive club of Abramelin Lunar Ordeal adepts.

PART I

History and Authentication of the Lunar Ordeal

CHAPTER ONE

ABRAMELIN LUNAR ORDEAL: SACRED OGDOADIC TABERNACLE

I wrote this introduction to the Abramelin Lunar Ordeal in March of 2011 for members of the Order of the Gnostic Star. It was an overview of the ordeal working, but it did not contain all of the information required to make the explanations and functions of this working wholly sensible. I have therefore decided to include this document, but also to add additional information so that it will be complete and more comprehensive. Much has occurred since I wrote this text, and the years have added a more seasoned perspective to this lore.

INTRODUCTION AND JUSTIFICATION

I have been puzzling over the Abramelin magical system for over thirty years, ever since I got my first hard bound copy of the tome *Book of Sacred Magic of Abramelin the Mage*, translated by MacGregor Mathers. The book was reputed to be written by a historically obscure person: a Jewish man named Abraham (referred to as Abraham the Jew) who lived in the town of Worms in Germany during the early fifteenth century. I previously deduced that there was a very advanced Jewish occult community in that town, since another important work was written there nearly one hundred years earlier, called *Sepher ha-Raziel* or the *Book of Raziel*. So, the *Book of Sacred Magic* was part of a plausible historical line of occultism and ceremonial magic. It's fairly certain that there was a sharing of lore between Christian and Jewish occultists, so it is one of the areas where Jewish magic and occultism was appropriated and used by Christians.

One of the main features of the *Book of Sacred Magic* is that it contains a very long and intense preparatory ordeal that many magicians have attempted and failed to complete. Aleister Crowley was reputed to have attempted this working twice at Boleskine cottage in Scotland, and Alex Sanders was also supposed to have performed the ordeal and completed it; there are numerous others as well. The ordeal is arduous and difficult

*The classical Holy Guardian Angel as depicted in
The Road to Jerusalem by Gustave Dore.*

because it spans a period of eighteen months,[12] using the two sacred Jewish holidays of Pesach (Passover) and Sukkot (Feast of the Tabernacles) to break the year into six-month periods. Three of these six-month phases represent the stages of the Abramelin working.

The final working in this ordeal is performed after the second Sukkot, where the magician summons into manifestation their Holy Guardian Angel through the grace of God and by means of a successful but long period of fasting, expiation, purification, consecration, devotional prayer, and contemplation. There is little in the way of tools that are required for this working (a special wand, incense brazier, balm, lamps, at least two different robes, a headband, and a cincture), but building a special prayer room with windows facing east and west, an outdoor arbor, and a floor covered by sand or potentially an outdoor tabernacle may have posed a daunting series of preparatory tasks.[13] Once the prayer room is completed and the other required items are obtained, the ordeal basically consists of a regimen of devotional prayer, frequent ablutions, expiation, contemplation, and various forms of abstinence (renunciation).

However, performing this rigorous regimen for eighteen months would guarantee that something would certainly happen, even if it wasn't what the magician sought at the start of the ordeal.

Many magicians have attempted this working, but few have questioned the necessity of its arduous discipline and practices. The supposed outcome of the ordeal is the manifestation of the Holy Guardian Angel, yet that event only begins a long process of spiritual mastery and indenture. It's done for the exclusive purpose of mastering the good spirit (the HGA), commanding the unredeemed spirits (demons), and unleashing the power and potency of hundreds of magical squares contained in Book Four of the grimoire. The key is to have access to the Holy Guardian Angel, without which the rest of the magic is pointless and incapable of being realized.

This preparatory work represented the bulk of the practices and contained no actual magical rituals. There were the magical squares—the list of demonic servitors—but how to activate the squares and command the demons was omitted. The author assumed that the adherent (his son, Lamech) would be taught everything needed when and if he successfully manifested his Holy Guardian Angel. Without that angelic helper, everything in the book would be useless and inactive. From the standpoint of the *Book of Sacred Magic of Abramelin,* the ordeal is just the initiation rite for becoming a magician; the rest of the specific ritual lore would be provided and expounded upon by the HGA. It would seem, then, that the HGA acted as a kind of lofty magician's familiar spirit and

---

12 Mathers' version of the Book of Abramelin has only six months or three phases of two lunar cycles for the duration of the ordeal. However, Mathers' version is from a later French manuscript that was very corrupt. I suspect that the six months duration is a modification that did not exist in the original. I am using the duration of the ordeal from the German edition, which appears to be more authentic.

13 Mathers' edition also has the requirement of a virginal male child to accompany the practitioner the first time the Holy Guardian Angel is summoned. The role of the child is to act as an innocent and unbiased channel, but this is completely omitted from the German edition, and I suspect that it is a superfluous addition.

was a required component of this magical tradition. Many magicians have desired the powers and abilities associated with the fabulous and mysterious magic squares that are a hallmark of this system of magic, but few had the time, resources, or ability to achieve the basic requirements for the ordeal.

So that is the essential conundrum underlying this system of magic. The bar for success was placed very high for the would-be apprentice magician to pass over, so few actually managed to complete it. I suspect that was the purpose of the ordeal: to separate the true magicians from the pretenders. The ordeal also required a strict discipline of piety, renunciation, and spiritual devotion that many would have understood back then, but few (if any) could comprehend now, centuries later. Abraham the Jew makes allowances for those who might have businesses or be required to work in order to survive, yet the times have dramatically changed since then and this system of magic hasn't changed. We are talking about a magical system that was derived in the early Renaissance, a time which held a completely different mental outlook and way of life than today's modern world. There simply isn't an opportunity to retire from the world for the last six months of the ordeal unless the magician is independently wealthy and can support a monomania for several months without interruption.

Since the central ordeal to the *Book of Sacred Magic* is so rigorous and difficult, I have decided to forgo this regimen and find other activities and practices that are more immediately rewarding and capable of being sustained while living in the twenty-first century. I have a job and a career, a home, a relationship, friends, and family that require much of my time. What time I have left over is given to my magical and occult studies. But I don't have time to devote eighteen months to perform a powerful ordeal, and I can't function in semi-retirement for the last six months. It would seem that the Abramelin system of magic is a tradition that I can admire and study, but not one where I could possibly perform even the basic initiatory ordeal. I have had to put this book and its system aside for other more pressing activities and studies, but it's always on the periphery of my mind, tantalizingly near yet out of reach, waiting to be resolved.

Recently, I have been examining the power and potential of lunar-based magic and its associated mysteries. I put the entire Elemental and Talismanic systems of magic squarely into the matrix of lunar-based magic. Of course, Talismanic magic makes use of the twenty-eight lunar mansions, and Elemental magic uses the Moon and Sun to imprint a powerful timestamp onto the magical working so as to assist it in focusing changes into the present world. Both of these approaches have worked marvelously well, and in fact, after performing a series of these rites in June, July, and August of 2007, they are still aiding and rewarding me with renewed and unexpected sources of money. Certainly, these kinds of magic work very well through the use of the lunar mysteries. However, I had not attempted to apply any other magical system to the lunar cycle—that is, until I began to re-examine the Abramelin Ordeal.

Since purchasing the newest version of the *Book of Sacred Magic*, which was translated from a completely intact pair of German manuscripts by Steven Guth and Georg Dehn,[14] and giving it a thorough study, I have found myself rethinking the ordeal's entire

---

14 See Dehn, *op. cit.*

structure.[15] Previously, if you wanted to perform this ordeal, there wasn't any ability to make substitutions since the timeline appeared to be firmly determined, which is what made the ordeal so effective and difficult. The regimen of prayer and contemplation was not particularly demanding, nor were the tools required, although the requirement for the prayer room might be difficult for some (which might be where some substitutions could be made). However, the timeline was based on the religious holidays of the Passover and the Feast of the Tabernacles, roughly six months apart in the Jewish calendar. One might even substitute these Jewish holidays with Christian ones, such as Easter and maybe Michaelmas, but that would be the extent of the possible alternatives.

Yet this ordeal is decidedly solar-based, since each of the three phases is six months in length. I began to ponder that since I am neither Jewish nor Christian, and since my faith is an earth-based spirituality, why would I follow a solar cycle for this kind of ordeal? Why not a lunar-based cycle? Since a lunar cycle takes only twenty-eight days to complete, breaking it in half and building an ordeal that would cover three phases, or one and a half cycles, of the moon would be quite appropriate. Similar to the traditional Abramelin working, there would be three phases, but instead of using an annual sacred holiday like the Passover as the starting point, I would start at a point in the lunar cycle that would connote *beginnings*, and that would most certainly be the new moon. Then, the ordeal would span the lunar cycle of new moon to full moon, to new moon again, and finally to full moon once more. The duration of the lunar ordeal would last approximately forty to forty-two days. This period of time seems analogous to the ubiquitous forty days and nights of the Old Testament, which is used to denote an archetypal duration. It would seem that the period of one and half lunar cycles is just as auspicious as the solar cycle of eighteen months, not to mention that it would have the added power of being very significant to someone who practices an earth-based spirituality.

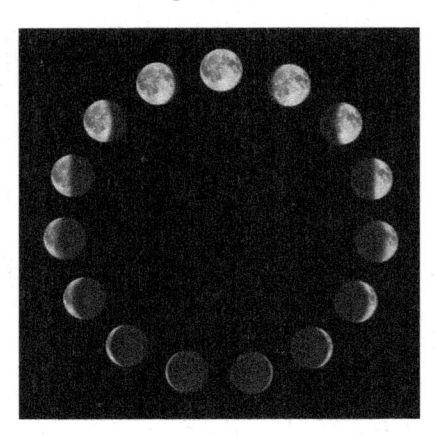

---

15 This edition of *The Book of Abramelin* seems to have a number of variances with the version published by Mathers. There is no mention made of the Passover and the Feast of the Tabernacles in the ordeal, so it would seem Mathers' version has been sanitized of all Jewish traces. Also, many of the magic squares are incomplete (160 out of 242), there are nine missing squares, and an entire book is missing from the Mathers edition. Since that version appears to be a later incomplete French manuscript, I suspect that we can rely on the German manuscript to be more definitive and authentic of this system of magic.

So, I would substitute the three phases of the solar cycle with the three phases of the lunar cycle and establish a timeline that would be quite doable for a person in the post-modern world of the twenty-first century. That being said, I was quite pleased with the new structure of the ordeal, but I began to see other possibilities as well. The regimen of devotional prayer, expiation of sins, contemplation, fasting, and ablutions performed in ever-more rigorous fashion represented the only activity that the practitioner engaged in for months, only increasing in intensity and frequency as the ordeal approached its final weeks.

Since I am already initiated and functioning in a spiritually transformed state, and I am quite capable of performing rituals and ceremonies during the shortened Lunar Ordeal, I have decided to completely modify and change the regimen of the ordeal to make it even more powerful and demanding in the area of applied rituals. What I decided to do was to merge the Invocation of the Bornless One, as derived from the Golden Dawn system, with the Abramelin ordeal to produce a working that would, at its climax, assist in invoking the Holy Guardian Angel as an attribute of the magician's absolute self, or the God/dess Within. Other workings also emerged in my thoughts, and an entire ritual magical ordeal took form.

Is the Bornless One the same as, or at least closely analogous to, the Holy Guardian Angel? Now that's a question that any knowledgeable occultist would ask. The key word that links them is found in the term *Augoeides*, which was used in the Golden Dawn and Theosophical circles to denote the luminous radiance of the self as godhead. It has cognates in the related terms *Daimones* (Greek), *Atman* (Sanscrit), *Genius* (Latin), and the Holy Guardian Angel. The source of this term is obscure, but it seems to have originated in the writings and thoughts of the Neoplatonists, most notably Iamblichus and Porphyry, but was promulgated by theurgists in late antiquity. To quote a reliable source:

> *Augoeides (Greek, "shining image") is a term that has had various definitions within Western occult tradition over the past two thousand years. The Greek Neoplatonic writers of the late Roman period first used it to refer to the Body of Light or the transformed spiritual body worn by the initiate who had overcome the materialism of the physical world.*[16]

An examination of this term would seem to link it even more closely to that aspect of the Self called the "Higher Self" or "Absolute Self," and it would therefore be more bonded to the individual than what was believed of this term in the Middle Ages.[17] Aleister Crowley himself referred to the Holy Guardian Angel as the personal godhead Augoeides, and I think that we can safely assume this to be correct. Therefore, it would

---

16 "Augoeides," The Mystica Online Encyclopedia, www.themystica.com/augoeides/. Accessed December 24, 2023.

17 Not to be confused with any aspect of the self that is associated with the ego or persona. A better term would be "the self as godhead."

seem that the invocation of the Bornless One would represent a magical process used to summon the highest aspect of the self as deity, and that this operation would be quite similar to the invocation of the Holy Guardian Angel. Some may dispute this linkage, but I believe that it is adequately supported by past usage and associations.[18]

This leads us to examine the nature of the revised ordeal that I am proposing to establish, and to carefully examine its various steps. The following is a detailed analysis of this newly devised Abramelin Lunar Ordeal, which takes around forty days to complete and is actually much more ritually demanding and intensive than the original solar ordeal.

The prerequisites are that this new ordeal should be performed only by an adept, analogous to the sixth or seventh degree of the E.S.S.G. or Order of the Gnostic Star.[19] This level of ability requires that the magician is capable of performing a magical Mass on a weekly basis and performing the Archetypal Gate rituals, as well as the newly formed version of the Invocation of the Bornless One. The magician would have to be competent at performing magical evocations and all of the rigors that such a discipline would require. I suspect that if someone who does not have these requirements were to undertake this ordeal, then nothing or, at worst, complete personal disaster would be encountered through the misapplication of this ordeal. Of course, someone outside of the Order and its initiatory structures will be able to determine if the rituals and practices are beyond their ability to perform.

ABRAMELIN LUNAR ORDEAL

The Lunar Ordeal requires six to seven weeks of intensive magical workings. It begins at the advent of the new moon and proceeds without interruption or deviation for the duration of the ordeal. If one begins this working, then it must be completed; once started, it must be performed entirely and without interruption.[20] I suspect that there might be repercussions that would occur for an aborted ordeal, and the extent of those repercussions would depend on how far into the ordeal one progressed before quitting. If you don't have the time or resources to perform this ordeal through all three phases of ritual work, then I would advise you not to begin. All the rituals that are to be used in this ordeal must be completely understood and familiar to the magician.

---

18 See Crowley's articles "Liber Samekh" and "Liber VIII." "Liber Samekh" associated the HGA with the Bornless One, and "Liber VIII" proposes an alternate form of the Abramelin ordeal that lasts ninety-one days.

19 This represents a higher octave than seeking K and C of the HGA, since the plan was to use it to forge a gateway across the Greater Abyss. The Bornless One rite can be used to produce a transfiguration at either point in one's development. In the GD, this rite is used to cross the lesser abyss that leads to becoming an adept.

20 The fifth weekend may require a break from the activity, depending on the lunar phases. For an early start, the magician will actually get ahead of the lunar cycle and have to wait to complete the final two workings during the final full moon.

Basic practices and requirements for this period of the working are as follows.

- **Daily meditation:** performed at least once or twice a day (at waking, and then before retiring). These practices should use yogic practices of asana, pranayama, mantra, and mandala to establish the proper mind-state, then contemplation on the intent of the working, as well as seeking a special kind of illumination or grace from the Deity.
- **Partial fasting:** eat lightly and often—avoid excessive meals. Eat less meat than usual or become vegetarian (eating dairy, eggs, vegetables, and fruit).
- **Keep a special journal:** note down everything, from dreams and musings to the actual results of the ritual workings.
- Weekends are reserved for at least two major magical workings. These times must be reserved and not be used for anything else. Saying the magical Mass and other liturgical ceremonies (a Benediction) will generate the proper atmosphere and energy for these workings; this would include a circle consecration rite. Also, one should spend at least an hour or more meditating before performing the ritual working. I would recommend that the ritual workings be performed on either Friday and Saturday night, or Saturday and Sunday night. I would not recommend skipping a day between the weekend workings.
- Special emphasis should be placed on observing the phases of the moon, particularly when they change. These times should involve some degree of meditation and focused awareness, particularly if they occur during the waking period.

The first part of the ordeal covers four weeks, representing the full cycle of the moon from new to full and then back again to new. During the weekend ritual workings, the magician will invoke the four Seraphim and Cherubim for the four Elements, starting with Earth, then Air, Water, and finally, Fire. This activity will require separate ritual workings for each Super-Archangel invoked, so for each of these four weekends, two invocations will be performed on separate evenings. The Archetypal Gate Ritual will be used to invoke the Super-Archangels.

Performing an invocation of just one of these powerful angels during a period of three to six months would be more than adequate for any aspiring magician. However, I am proposing invoking all eight of these entities in a single period of a month! You can easily see why this would be a very intensive series of workings, and also why it would be prudent to not start this ordeal unless one were intent on completing it.

Invoking all eight of these angels means that the magician is seeking full and total illumination, and the combination of Seraphim and Cherubim would inspire and teach the magician all that is required to achieve this end. Not completing the ordeal would show a high degree of superficiality and insincerity, which might set up a very terrible backlash or wave of retribution since these entities do not suffer fools gladly and have the power to punish as well as grant requests. If the magician is not fully convinced of the "rightness" of this ordeal, then they may receive a warning from the very first angel invoked, and such a warning should be immediately acknowledged and obeyed. If, on the other hand, the magician receives blessings and grace from all eight of these angels, then that would clearly indicate that one is prepared and ready to meet the challenges of the next two weeks. That was my experience when I invoked all eight of these Super-Archangels.

The fifth weekend has nothing scheduled, so it would be a time of rest, meditation, and contemplation. It is also a time when the magician can charge and consecrate the magical ring, which is used in the Bornless One invocation rite to establish a material link between the Bornless One and the magician. It's also necessary to have this break point to catch up on any other required work that might be done. The break usually occurs because the lunar cycle may start early in the week with the first working weekend, which will cause the workings to get ahead of the actual lunar cycle. It's critically important that the final working be performed exactly on or just prior to the full moon.

Prior to the advent of the sixth weekend, the magician performs an intensive meditation session for four evenings, focused on each of the Four Elements and the pair of Seraphim and Cherubim. The first night is focused on the Super-Archangels of Earth, then the next night is Air, the next night Water, and the final night is Fire. The magician focuses on the sigils of the Seraph and the Cherub separately, communing with that entity for a full immersion and deep trance-based meditation session. The purpose for these deep meditation sessions is to connect with all of the eight Super-Archangels before attempting to pull them together into a single unified being as the emissaries of the Element Godhead.

The sixth weekend continues the activity of the previous four, and the magician uses the Archetypal Gate Ritual to invoke an Element Godhead to act as the central and unifying entity to the ogdoad of angelic spirits. This is the first step taken for the sixth weekend, and it is quite critical to the whole operation. It's assumed that the magician will discover which Element Godhead to invoke by successfully invoking the previous eight Super-Archangels, or that information might be communicated in some other fashion. The magician may further qualify that central entity and even make it representative of one's personal Godhead, but the qualification does not replace the basic Qabalistic Element Godhead; it only augments it.

The next evening's working for the sixth weekend is where all of the previous entities and structures are brought together into a complete synthesis. This is where the magician establishes the holy ogdoad of four Seraphim, four Cherubim, and the Elemental Godhead. This is done through the artifice of the magical structure of the octagon. The four Seraphim and the four Cherubim are each summoned and set to one of the four watchtowers, and the attributes of the Elemental Godhead are set to each of the four angles. The Elemental Godhead is summoned and focused on the Ultrapoint, and all nine points are drawn together to form an octagonal vortex. Over this vortex structure is set the Triple Gateway, the Double Gateway with an Ascension Gate. Then all of these entities and forces are drawn together as the collected focus of the Ultrapoint is drawn down into an inner circle and into the heart and soul of the magician, where they perform a deep trance.

The basic premise of the Triple Gateway is to establish three concurrent gateway ritual structures: the western gateway into the underworld, the eastern gateway of ascending into light, and then, over that, a Gateway of Ascension. The Gateway of Ascension would cross the western and eastern points of the circle, engaging the seldom-used points of the North, South, and Ultrapoint, ultimately drawing all of the points of the three gateways together into a grand gateway. The purpose for this ritual is to establish the mystery system of the three phases of the Lunar Ordeal, which represents a trigon of the moon, the focus of the ordeal. This ritual is called the Triple Tetrahedral Gate Ritual, and the companion rite is called the Ogdoadic Godhead Vortex rite. Both are to be used on the second evening of the sixth weekend.

The completion of the workings for the sixth weekend brings the ordeal to the point of the first quarter phase of the moon. This is the last major phase before the full moon occurs and completes the ordeal. The final weekend can be either just before or just after the full moon—even to the point of the next lunation cycle type. When I worked this ordeal, the moon was full before the seventh weekend, so I had to begin that Monday for the three-day climax to the working. This pattern will always occur in some form because one and a half lunar cycles occupy forty-two days of a seven-week period.

The final three days that include the Bornless One invocation should be planned so that the final day is either on or before the full moon. During this period, the magician should be completely sequestered and abide by the instructions of the traditional Abramelin Ordeal. What this consists of is the following steps, which must be strictly followed.

On the first morning, rise at dawn and perform an intense atonement exercise consisting of periods of prayer, anointing the forehead with oil and ash from the censer. Perform an all-day meditation session consisting of intermittent prayer accompanied with full sequestering (no visitors, cell phone calls, TV, or Internet) and a complete fast until sunset, then eat a meal of bread and water. Sleep in the temple. Repeat this pattern for the second day without the oil and ash but washing the face and head. Just before sunset, perform an intense prayer summoning the HGA to appear. The Triple Tetrahedral Gateway rite should be performed on the evening of the second night of this vigil.

The first of two nights of the final three days of the working is where the magician begins by drawing down the Element Godhead into themselves and assuming all of that power, authority, and majesty prior to actually performing the Bornless One invocation rite. The magician will then perform the Triple Tetrahedral Gateway rite a second time to ensure that the Element Godhead is present for the next and final working. Thus, all of these entities and forces are joined as the collected focus of the Ultrapoint is drawn down into an inner circle and into the heart and soul of the magician, where one performs a deep trance and begins to verbally summon the Bornless One. After this rite, the magic circle is not sealed, and the magician spends the evening alternately dozing and meditating until the next day.

On the morning of the third day, perform complete ablutions, wear a clean white robe, and break the fast with bread, fruit juice, fruits, and cheese. A solemn high Mass is said in the morning, and the magician should adhere to a meditation vigil and partial fast consisting of bread, fruit juice, fruit, and cheese. Intense cleansing ablutions are also performed to prepare for the final evening of work.

The third evening is where the magician performs the newly revised Bornless One rite in its entirety. This is immediately followed by the Alchemical Hierogamy rite of Union, which fully completes the ritual working process for the Abramelin Lunar Ordeal. The next day, or at a convenient time, the Assumption of Great Powers rite is performed. These three rituals may each take more than three or four hours to perform, so it is possible that completing them within a single evening might be more than the adherent is capable of doing. It is possible, then, that they might consider performing the Hierogamy rite on the morning of the next day after a period of sleep, and then the Assumption of Great Powers at some convenient time afterwards.

Once all of these rites are accomplished, what remains of the working schedule consists of an evening of meditation and deep trance, sleep, and incubation in the temple, and another Mass the next day, this time with special prayers and emphasis to the Great Goddess as a form of thanksgiving. If the working spilled over into the next day, then the Mass would be performed, followed by the Hierogamy rite and the Assumption rite. Then, the magician seals the temple and avoids entry into it for at least a week (seven to nine days).

After several days, the magician re-enters the temple, says a Mass, sets the magic circle, and then performs once more the Triple Tetrahedral Gateway rite. At the climax of that ritual, they charge a specially made book containing all of the magical squares of the Abramelin system, as well as other sigils and characters (like those from the Grimoire Armadel). This book will be blessed by the HGA and fully activated. The magician then would only have to re-enter the Triple Tetrahedral Gateway to access the internal spiritual chamber of the Bornless One and seek to unleash the powers of one or more of the squares or sigils. Once unleashed, a magic square can be used at any time or place, or even kept on the magician's person in the mundane world. The Bornless One would also teach, guide, and give assistance in mundane matters to the magician.

On the following full moon, the magician will perform the fourth rite in the Bornless One rite series, called the Bornless One Envisioning rite. This is where the magician, fully vetted with the Bornless One, will perform a divination task that will project one's highest will (i.e., the Personal Destiny set by the Deity) into the material world. Preparation includes determining what that destiny consists of and what mundane steps the magician is expected to perform to fulfill it. During the month between the invocation and assumption of the Bornless One, the magician will have hopefully determined the nature of that mystery.

A synopsis of this ordeal would be as follows:

1. Begin ordeal on the advent of the new moon.
2. **First weekend:** invoke the Seraphim and Cherubim of Earth.
3. **Second weekend:** invoke the Seraphim and Cherubim of Air.
4. **Third weekend:** invoke the Seraphim and Cherubim of Water.
5. **Fourth weekend:** invoke the Seraphim and Cherubim of Fire.
6. **Sixth weekend:** invoke the Elemental Godhead, establish the Ogdoadic Tabernacle, and open the Triple Gateway.

7. **Final three days:** re-open the Triple Gateway, perform a vigil, and perform the Invocation of the Bornless One.
8. A new ritual working was added to the final three days, and that is the Alchemical Hierogamy rite of Union, which follows the Invocation of the Bornless One. Once that rite is completed, then the magician performs the Assumption of Great Powers rite.
9. Ancillary workings include the unleashing of the Abramelin grimoire (seven to nine days) and the Bornless Envisioning rite (next full moon).

This is the revised version of the Abramelin Lunar Ordeal and all its various steps and tasks. The magician who undergoes this ordeal should remember that they are performing this ordeal under completely different circumstances than the original, whether consisting of the six-month working, the eighteen-month solar cycle version, or the three-phase double lunar version. Since claiming to have successfully completed this ordeal carries with it a certain notoriety or fame, the magician who completes the Abramelin Lunar Ordeal should always state that they have undergone a modified version of this working and not claim to have performed the traditional one. I strongly advise this, since it would be disrespectful to those who have undergone the traditional ordeal and also quite misleading, which is not faithful to the aim of this revised version.

Keep in mind that not everyone would agree with this revised version, and that others who are highly respectful of tradition wouldn't see it as being the same thing. There is certainly a place for those who would seek to perform the traditional ordeal and for those who have found alternative approaches. So we, as magicians, celebrate both the traditional approach and creative re-interpretations. I, for one, chose to seek an alternative path.

A NOTE ABOUT THE GOETIC DEMONS AND THEIR SERVITORS

In the original book, there is an ancillary set of tasks that consisted of summoning and mastering the unredeemed spirits, namely the demonic kings and their dukes, and that these same demons gave servitors who operated the many magic squares. It is my belief that summoning demons and gaining servitors from them is magically superfluous. This is just my opinion, of course, yet since I have rewritten the entire ordeal, I can also modify the manner that the magical squares are deployed.

Some have found this linkage between the magic squares and the demons troubling, and some have sought to white-wash or explain it away as some kind of cathartic ordeal. Yet in all versions of the book, it is quite plain that the purpose of invoking and manifesting the HGA is to gain mastery over the demons, seek from them servitors to perform tasks directly, or use the demons to empower and activate the magic squares. It's also possible to seek additional magic squares from the HGA or the demons. The magic of the Abramelin system is powered by demonic spirits existing in a rigid spiritual hierarchy, even if they are completely dominated and mastered by the magician through the assistance of the chosen Godhead and the HGA.

It's my belief that the HGA, who is like a personal godhead for the magician, can do all of these tasks. If one is successful in invoking the HGA into some form of manifestation, then there is little need to command demons to do certain tasks. The power of the magician's magic, the depth of their wisdom, and the strength of their will, fortified and magnified greatly by the HGA, will enable them to perform any working or accomplish any possible objective. The Abramelin book dictates that the magician should not summon the HGA unless absolutely required.

My theory is that the HGA would become ever-present to the magician who successfully invoked it into manifestation, and that the magician would function almost like an avatar, having the vision and depth of a godhead acting through their conscious mind. It could be easily argued that such a great accomplishment would allow the magician to find a route to complete enlightenment and union with the Godhead, and that all of the other operations may seem irrelevant or even grossly petty to such a mind-state. So, for this reason, I doubt needing the supernatural intercession of demons to perform magical feats—they should be possible by the magician's will, fortified as it is with the power, wisdom, and majesty of the Augoeides.

One thing that I need to clearly state is that when I performed this ordeal back in 2009, it was not as fully determined and outlined as I have written it in this section. Since I was developing this ordeal and performing it for the first time, it was subject to changes and modifications as I was performing it. What I have written here is the final form, which was not fully evident to me when I first started the working. This is also certainly true because I had omitted an important ritual simply because I had not understood the need for it—namely, the Alchemical Hierogamy rite of Union. I did not perform that rite until April 2011, when I was able to incorporate it into the ordeal. What seems like a straightforward sequence was anything but straight, but that is the nature of developing a new, elaborate working. The only way to know if a magical working is complete is to perform it and then analyze the experience.

However, I can verify that the sequence of rituals employed in this ordeal is now complete, even though I had to undergo some trauma for eighteen months before I was able to rectify and fully validate the pattern. It is a bit ironic that I was not able to complete the full ordeal until eighteen months had passed, since that is the number of months that the full Abramelin ordeal is supposed to take. Still, the completed pattern will take around forty to forty-two days to complete from start to finish. That is far more compact than the ninety days, six months, or eighteen months associated with the two Abramelin traditional workings or Crowley's version.

CHAPTER TWO

IS ACHIEVING THE KNOWLEDGE AND CONVERSATION OF THE HGA IMPORTANT?

WHAT MIGHT THROW A BANANA PEEL into the whole conversation about the Holy Guardian Angel and the Abramelin working that seeks to manifest it is wondering if the whole process is worth all the writings, claims, efforts, and hype that it appears to receive in various ceremonial magical circles. That is the million-dollar question, and it needs some kind of cogent and clear answer. If achieving this goal serves no real purpose, then even the ink used to write this book has been wasted. I will try to answer this question, both from a theoretical perspective and drawn from my own experience.

This question is probably why some magicians in the blogosphere have recently stated that they think the huge importance placed on a magician achieving knowledge and conversation with their Holy Guardian Angel is rather overblown. It has become something of a badge of honor for some; still, I find myself agreeing more with the pundits' opinion than that of the promoters. If the basic opinion is that a magician must perform the traditional Abramelin working to accomplish this end, then I believe the pundits are correct. However, I would stress that some cautionary insights be included in the argument.

While it seems to have become something of status symbol for individuals who claim to have undergone the traditional Abramelin Ordeal, the actual achievement represents something that harkens back to antiquity and has an ancient provenance. In those times, the signature achievement of any sorcerer or Witch of repute was that they had acquired, in some manner, a familiar spirit. Whether you call it a person's Genius, Higher Self, Indestructible Spirit, Over-Soul, Augoeides, Eudaimon, or Holy Guardian Angel, it is, in my opinion, variations on the theme of possessing a familiar spirit. I think that all of these entities are one and the same, although not everyone would likely share my point of view.

Since it was believed that humans alone could not affect the destinies of their community or nation, and that even their abilities to alter their own fate was either limited or nonexistent, possessing a spiritual intermediary was considered an important magical acquisition. This fact is well-documented in various historical documents and collected folkloric beliefs. This is the basic tenant that is promoted in the Spirit Only model of magic, which has a large group supporting the approach today. For those who seek to reconstruct the grimoire traditions of the late Renaissance, this approach is considered optimal and the use of the traditional Abramelin working is integral to that system. However, there are many models of magic, used either separately or in combination, and only a few of them require some kind of functional spiritual intermediary.

Anyone who has perused the spells listed in the *PGM* will quickly discover that there were quite a number of different techniques for acquiring the vaunted familiar spirit. This is likely still true today, despite there being systems of magic that do not require any kind of spiritual intermediary. The variety of spells in the *PGM* shows that achieving this quest had many different approaches and methodologies, and we would be led to believe that the modern variants would be as varied, if not more so. While some purists may thumb their noses at anyone who had claimed to achieve the K and C without performing either the six-month or eighteen-month Abramelin working, I believe that there are as many ways of achieving this important goal as there are magicians currently practicing the Western Mystery Tradition. Of course, that assumes that achieving this goal is relevant to the type of magic that the ritual magician might perform.

The Bornless One invocation rite (à la Crowley or the Golden Dawn), the Abramelin Lunar Ordeal, the Pyramidos rite and Liber Samekh (again, of Crowley), the rite of Beatification (as found in Liber Juratus), the rites of conjuring of a spirit guide, family animal totem, departed ancestor, or nature ally (as found in various earth-based religions), and numerous other rites represent the same analogous trial, which is achieving the intimate companionship of a spiritual mediator. The most direct and simplest of them is assuming a specialized godhead, which is a primary practice in modern Pagan and Witchcraft traditions. Over time, such practices develop a powerful alignment with the assumed Deity, eventually causing it to manifest and fully integrate with the operator. While some of these rites might not immediately bring about the manifestation of a spiritual intermediary, they have the potential through repetition or provident auspices to achieve this goal.

We won't spend any time here discussing my belief that there should be some kind of mechanism or peer group assessment to validate that a magician has indeed succeeded in this quest other than just taking their word for it. As I have stated previously, the ordeal is very subjective, and even if individuals practice the same operation, they may have completely different experiences. Presently, it seems like many individuals are claiming to have undergone the traditional Abramelin ordeal without providing any proof that they did indeed undergo it. Still, it seems to me like there are far too many who are making this claim for it to be credible, but woe betide anyone who would contradict or challenge the claimants to somehow prove their claims. That, of course, is another topic for another time, if we would even want to consider it.

Another point about this whole magical methodology is that acquiring a familiar spirit was one of the first steps that any credible magician would undertake in order to be considered a legitimate sorcerer-for-hire. It would seem that having this spiritual aid was what separated the adepts from the would-be dabblers, and I think this is still a valid consideration. Achieving this quest doesn't represent the end of all quests for the magician; instead, it represents the very beginning of a more serious practice of ritual magic.

In other words, it is just one of many steps to becoming an adept magician, so it is neither a mark of prestige nor uniqueness. It represents that the magician has the ability to mediate the world of spirits with the mundane world and to enact changes in both worlds. A magician with a familiar spirit could also be assumed to have access to inner plane contacts, since they would be able to make important spiritual associations through the intermediation of that spirit agent.

So, it would seem that this achievement, although important, should never be perceived as some kind of exclusive club for purist aficionados of the Abramelin system of magic. While I honor those who have taken the time and effort to perform the original Abramelin ordeal, I don't believe that their achievement somehow makes them better than any other magician. In fact, having undergone my own version of this working, I would have to say that it is as much a burden as a status symbol. This is because it requires the magician to operate in a larger spiritual field than just working magic for their own selfish and independent needs. If you don't see the person who claims to have undergone this working also engaging with their spiritual and magical community (and even their local mundane community), making themselves available to teach, help, and give consolation to other people, then it is likely that their achievement is still not completed. I even find myself stumped and compromised when it comes to engaging with my fellow humans, where generosity and compassion are thwarted by suspicion and paranoia. That kind of behavior and thought process goes against the whole basis of achieving a form of magical enlightenment.

Unlike the adherents of the "grimoire-only" crowd, I know that there are many ways of achieving this goal, and each ordeal should actually be unique and tailored to the magician and their path. To my way of thinking, successfully mastering a custom path is much more legitimate and authentic than just following what is written in some book or grimoire. We are all impacted by our choices, but one path or choice is not necessarily superior to another for everyone.

BURDEN AND OBLIGATIONS FOR ACHIEVING THE HGA

In my social journeys where I meet and talk with various magicians and occultists, one theme that seems to be consistent—especially with a few of my friends who have successfully completed the Abramelin working—is that the aftereffects of this achievement can be quite underwhelming and a burden to constantly give meaning to years after the fact. Make no mistake: the completion of this working, as monumental as it is, is only the beginning, and the struggles and spiritual expectations are usually far greater than what is typically believed or expected. Sometimes the whole work seems unjustified, and other times it is more than rewarding. This makes this achievement a complex life event, and it is not one that can be easily explained or distilled to someone who hasn't undergone it.

Is Achieving the Knowledge and Conversation of the HGA Important?

A couple of magicians even confided with me that they are struggling to find meaning to the massive commitment of time and resources associated with their ordeal, whether it is days, weeks, months, or years after their successful completion of the working. They wonder what it was they achieved, and labor with the difficulty of integrating that achievement into their mundane activities and daily lives. Achieving the knowledge and conversation of the Holy Guardian Angel is actually more of a kind of assimilation, like having your mind partitioned into a lower and higher domain, which are seldom connected or aligned. The ultimate quest is to unite them into a single mind and a single being, but that is quite difficult to establish at all times, so there are peak moments of brilliance and clarity and other times of darkness and confusion. It is never a happy ending or a blissful existence without pain, doubt, and remorse for having completed this working. It is really a terrible responsibility to maintain that connection and enhance it over a lifetime.

I can tell you quite clearly that I have, overall, failed to maintain the perfect moment that I experienced at the conclusion of my Lunar Ordeal. However, any expectation that promoted an idea of permanent and blissful union with the Deity through the HGA was doomed to be a disappointment. I did not understand this fact when I was developing and formulating this operation, but I understand it all too well now. It is the nature of enlightenment that it happens briefly and profoundly, and then after that brief moment, the light goes out, and life resumes its normal and banal progression. It is the responsibility of the magician to seek reconnections with that internal godhead now fully realized for the first time, and to ultimately cause a merging between it and oneself so that there is no division. That responsibility becomes more onerous as the distance from that pivotal event slips away, becoming a poignant but shadowy memory. It is therefore important for the magician to revisit parts of this working every few years so as to attempt to recapture some its fading glory, and I have found that at intervals of three, seven, and ten years, it is important to acknowledge that event and reconnect with it. This is something that the Lunar Ordeal can easily allow with the distinct and separate suite of rituals. It might be more difficult to do it with the traditional Abramelin working.

So, after revealing this somewhat disappointing outcome to the working, what benefits are there in its successful completion? First and foremost, the operator is able to meet with their Godhead and perceive the infinite domains that connect the One with everything. That vista and its associated vision are priceless, since they continue to teach and instruct, to guide and protect the operator for the rest of their lives. I also found that this single moment of enlightenment has profoundly shaped my life and set the course of my personal destiny, which I am continually in the process of working. Writing this book and publishing it for my reading public is certainly one of the tasks that I undertook as part of my self-revelation in the Abramelin working, and there are others as well.

That profound moment of light shined brilliantly on my soul, and it forever changed me for the better. Since I am certainly flawed, imperfect, and seemingly frail and mortal, I cannot maintain a perfect alignment with my internal Godhead, but I never cease trying and will ultimately come to a point in my path where I will find a state of functional union with my Higher Self, however that works out. That moment of transfiguration was worth all of the effort by itself. Everything else that was supposed to be part of the Lunar Ordeal has become nothing more than a novelty to me now.

A greater irony is that the magical squares that I sought to activate and wield as singular materialized powers have never been used, although as activated powers residing in my spiritual being (and my liber spiritus), they have likely made differences in my life unbeknownst to me. They are just part of the spiritual and magical garment that I wear after having achieved a momentary union with the One. I liken my condition to the Grail Knight Perceval, who experienced the full manifestation of the mystery of the Grail and then had to journey through many years of difficulty and conflict to finally achieve it the second time and fully understand its meaning and importance. The ordeal of K and C with the HGA is lot like that quest, or any quest for extreme spiritual transformation.

I must, therefore, say that pursuing this operation is a good, noble, and profound task that an adept magician should, at some point in their career, pursue with single-minded ambition. Performing this working in whatever tradition or methodology is worth the resources and the effort. The outcome, if successful, will change the operator forever, but the long-term results from that working will entail greater and heavier responsibilities than if they decided not to pursue this path. It will also transform a seasoned and experienced magician into an adept with a specific purpose and destiny in the world. It takes the operator to a place where will-based magic and the seeking of material-based goals becomes meaningless and superfluous. It matures the magician and places them on a higher plane than they had previously occupied. If this is what you seek, then the Abramelin working is what you need to perform.

Additionally, there are a number of different methods and traditions that one can choose to undergo this ordeal, and mine is just one of many. I am hoping that what I will present in this book will help you to build your own ritual-based technology and elect the lunar cycle as your pathway. I believe that you will not be disappointed at the results of this working once you have determined your own methodology and developed it into a working ritual ordeal. Yet, we still need to examine the nature of the so-called Bornless or Headless One and its associated invocation rite so you can be apprised of its magical technology and how it can work as a surrogate for a traditional six-month or eighteen-month Abramelin working.

CHAPTER THREE

ALTERNATIVE USE OF THE BORNLESS OR HEADLESS ONE INVOCATION AS THE HGA

WE HAVE ALREADY MADE THE POINT that the Bornless One invocation rite can be used as a surrogate for the rite of obtaining the K and C of the HGA, and that it stands as an alternative to the traditional Abramelin working. However, this rite has its own history and foundational lore as found in the collection *Greek Magical Papyri in Translation*, or *PGM*.[21] I felt that it was important to cover the history and function of this ritual since it represents the core ritual for the Abramelin Lunar Ordeal.

I wrote a few articles about this ritual in my blog, and I am assembling them with additional commentary in this chapter. I will try to cover all bases and fully examine this ritual just short of analyzing its ritual pattern, which we will leave for Part II of this book.

DEFINING THE RITE OF THE HEADLESS ONE FROM THE *PGM*

Perhaps one of the most compelling rituals that I have ever studied or attempted to perform is known as the Bornless rite, which I have called the "Bornless One invocation rite." It's part of the extended Golden Dawn lore but has little or no documentation accompanying it. In fact, it doesn't even fit in with the rest of the extended Golden Dawn rituals and writings; it's just there, alone, and seemingly completely out of context. However, it was not at all ignored, since the invocations that it uses are remarkable, powerful, and highly relevant even today. It is most likely the crown jewel of the Golden Dawn tradition, but the question remains: where's the rest of the jewels that go with it, and where is the crown? These questions have been in my mind for years, but there really wasn't any ability on my part to answer this question because it wasn't until a few years ago that I discovered the source material for this ritual. I admit that I have been

---

21 Betz, *op. cit.*

a bit slow in making that connection, since other magicians have been examining the source material for over a decade or more.

Aleister Crowley was quite taken with this ritual as well, since he published a version of this rite for his order, the A. A., which is called Liber Samekh. This article has been used and studied for quite some time. However, whether Crowley knew the source of this ritual, or like me, accepted it as is (with modifications and reworking) is unknown. He does mention revising the ritual with corrected versions of the god-names and barbarous words of evocation, but careful examination shows that he may not have known the actual source of this ritual.

Later occultists identified where the ritual came from, although I am at a loss to state exactly who first made this discovery (was it Stephen Flowers?). Needless to say, I didn't discover it myself until I checked my assumption that the ritual was taken from the Leyden Papyrus located in the British Museum. Of course, I didn't find it there, and further research revealed a much larger work that was both obscure and significant, and that is the now the famous *Greek Magical Papyri in Translation*, released in an edited format by Hans Dieter Betz. The translations have been accomplished by many different scholars since the scrolls were first discovered in the early nineteenth century.

The Greek Magical Papyri have their own unique history that is quite interesting. According to sketchy historical records, the different sections of papyrus were originally a single massive scroll, buried in the tomb of some unknown important and wealthy person in Thebes, perhaps sometime in the second century of the common era. This tomb was discovered and illegally entered, and its contents pilfered by professional tomb robbers, the kind that have been stealing the contents of tombs great and small since dynastic times. The massive scroll, however, was deemed to be worth less than the artifacts and eventually found its way to Cairo to be sold along with a myriad of other stolen artifacts to European collectors who had ready cash for such priceless pieces.

When all this occurred is unknown; however, the scroll was sold to a foreign collector named Jean d'Anastasi, who was an ambassador to the Egyptian pasha in Alexandria, and from there, the collection of papyri found their way to several European museums in the 1820s, where they continue to be examined and studied to this day.[22] Apparently seeking to maximize his profits, d'Anastasi cut the papyrus scroll into smaller sections. Each of these museums had their own section, and each, apparently, thought that their section was unique. It wasn't until almost the end of the nineteenth century that scholars, by accident, noted that the different sections of papyri were in fact from the same massive scroll. They began to translate and pull the different sections together so that, at least in translation, the great work is once again whole—or at least more so than it was previously.

This collection of scrolls contains perhaps the only extant copy of magical practices and spells as they were supposedly used in Egypt in antiquity. It's possible that the collection spans a long period and the original collector pulled together a very heterogeneous batch of magical spells, recopying them into a scroll that was apparently continually added to. The text is written predominantly in Greek, but other parts are written in Coptic and

---

22 Betz, *op. cit.*, pp. xli–xliv.

even Demotic. The spells incorporate magical ideas and practices from all over the known world, including Greek, Egyptian, Jewish, Persian, Chaldean, Christian, and Gnostic god names, techniques, and materials. The magical spells are representative of what magic probably was like from that time, incorporating the religious beliefs, practices, and esoteric notions of all of the peoples of the Graeco-Roman world. This shouldn't be too surprising, since other rare sources of magical writings (Hermetic, Gnostic, or Christian) show a decidedly heterogenous mixture of nearly every religious creed and belief in antiquity. However, these rare glimpses show that magicians were anything but strict sectarians and would use whatever worked for them.

These spells cover the gamut of typical magic, such as various kinds of divination, love spells, money and buried treasure spells, curses, healing spells, exorcisms, the creation of magic artifacts, and the summoning of spirits, whether gods, powerful entities of obscure origin, or even spirits of the dead. Yet the most intriguing thing found in all of these spells is the collection of powerful and barbarous words of evocation, a seemingly plethora of what historians call *verba ignota* (unknown words). Some of the magic words are obvious corruptions of identifiable god names from various religions; others are more obscure and even indecipherable. But even after all these centuries, these words of power and magic, when properly pronounced and intoned, still have a remarkable effect, so this is the value that these spells have as words of power.

The Bornless rite was taken from one of these scrolls, pulled from its source context and given a name remotely like its original. The section of scroll that it was liberated from is known to scholars as *PGM V,* lines 96 through 172. The full-blown ritual is actually an exorcism, where the magician invokes their highest godhead in order to authoritatively order the spirit out of the body of the victim. The name of this godhead is the *Headless One,* which functions as a rubric for the spell. It could be surmised that Mathers, having been introduced to the British museum's section of the scroll and an 1850s translation of it, expropriated the interesting part of the ritual to be used in the advanced lore of the Golden Dawn. It may have been his intention to liberate other parts as well, perhaps to build a magical system based on what was practiced in antiquity, but this never occurred, and the Bornless rite was stored alone with other bits of ritual lore until Aleister Crowley published his own version of it in the book *Goetia.* Some editions of the Golden Dawn published by Israel Regardie had this ritual in its original form included; other editions omitted it for unknown reasons. Needless to say, this is what the practitioners of modern ritual magic have to work with—at least until recently.

A question about the name that the Golden Dawn chose for this rite has rankled a number of occultists, who have said that the original title for this ritual is the "Headless One," which is not the same thing as the Bornless One. However, I have a theory that would explain why the title of Bornless One is actually a good one. In Hebrew, the word "head" can have the additional meaning of "beginning." An example is the first word of Genesis, which in Hebrew is *Brashet.* This word means "in the beginning"—or, literally, "in the head," since "rosh" means head. Similarly, Rosh Hashanna— beginning of the year (New Year)—is literally "head of the year." I suspect that the Hebrew word *Rosh* has cognates in Arabic and even Hamitic languages (such as Egyptian). So perhaps, with that being said, the Greek translation of *Headless* might actually be from the original Egyptian, which would have meant "without beginning" or "bornless," similar to the Greek *Autogenes,* "self-begotten," which is a powerful Gnostic name for an aspect of the Godhead. I believe that the term Headless has this meaning and is comparable to Autogenes. But that's just my opinion. The proof would be to trace the word to either Coptic or Egyptian and see if it's used in a similar manner to the way it's used in Hebrew and Arabic.

After learning about the real source of the Bornless One rite and purchasing a copy of Hans Dieter Betz's book, I decided that I should at least look over all of the rituals in that massive tome to see if there were any other rituals that might be useful. If one could expropriate one very powerful ritual from it, then why not repeat the exercise, especially since I had a resource that was much larger than Mathers had over a hundred years ago. So, I looked over the collection of spells and began to pick anything that really grabbed my attention, knowing that such an exercise would have to be done many times in minute detail to give the massive collection a fair assessment.

So, I performed this exercise, going over all of the known spells in the Greek Egyptian Papyri collection. I found several excellent additional sources that can be used as additional lore to the Bornless rite, producing what I think would be a complete set of rites for that type of magic. What I found required some extensive rewriting and reinterpreting, but it was not any more difficult than what the Golden Dawn did 120 years ago to produce the Bornless One rite. I am quite tickled by the whole process and that I found additional useful ritual lore, and I am looking forward to adding more rituals to the lore of the Order.

Has anyone else done magical work with this extensive collection of rituals and spells? The answer is, of course, "yes," but no one that I am aware of has actually thought of adding companion rites to the Golden Dawn Bornless One rite. Other authors have done the task of reclamation to make some of this lore available to practicing magicians, most notably Tony Mierzwicki's book *Graeco Egyptian Magic* (which I very highly recommend). Then there is the book *Hermetic Magic* by Stephen Flowers, a lesser work in my opinion, but also of value to the practitioner.

These books assemble a workable system of magic from the extant source materials, but I do wonder why no one else has come up with the idea of looking for additional rituals to accompany the Bornless rite. Certainly, GD students and high magic practitioners have known about the source for the Bornless rite for some time, but no one thought of producing additional lore. The loneliness of this rite begs for additional companion rites, or at least that is how I interpret it. I guess no one else saw the insularity of the Bornless rite or thought about extending it as a greater working but me.

I would, therefore, assume that the Bornless rite is part of a suite of rites that would include rituals to assist the magician in assuming the spirit of the Bornless One. Other tasks would include consecrating a magical ring, which would act as a powerful link to deploy the magic of that assumption. A rite of envisioning would also be appropriate—one that would allow the magician to perform a kind of active divination, projecting their true will into the present or future, and so fulfilling the will of the godhead.

So, to recap, I have deduced the following rituals to be part of the Bornless One suite of rituals, making for a total of four rites in all. In addition, I have also decided to merge the Abramelin ordeal with the Bornless rite but perform it using one and half lunar cycles instead of the traditional six or eighteen months. I would also perform the Bornless One rite as a climax to that ordeal and not at the two to four times a day that Aleister Crowley proposed in Liber Samekh. This is the list of rituals:

1. Bornless rite and the temple stairway of four Qabalistic Worlds and Ante Chamber of Ultimate Spirit (this is already done)
2. Assumption of the Bornless One and vestment of powers and wisdom of the Monad (extension of the existing Bornless rite)
3. Consecration of the Magician's Ring (the ring is used as a physical link to the Bornless spirit)
4. Rite of Envisioning (Bornless Spirit vision quest)

These rituals were taken from *PGM IV* (the Paris Papyrus), *PGM VII*, and *PGM XII*, and they were completed in early 2009 as part of my objective to develop the Lunar Ordeal. Much of this material hasn't been used in over two thousand years, but it is still very valuable and quite powerful, requiring only extraction and integrating them into a modern ritual structure. I have also found that Stephen Flowers has identified some of the magic spells in his book, but since I am using them to create companion rites for the Bornless One, they won't be used in a similar manner at all.

Reclamation has many different approaches. Some might seek to reconstruct the rituals in some manner, perhaps skipping the animal sacrifices and other dubious practices, and others will just pull out the words of power and use them in an analogous rite. I respect both of these approaches and, in fact, my workings tend to give justice to both since I am more faithful to the actual original use and purpose of these spells.

QUESTION OF BORNLESS OR HEADLESS ONE

My occult research and studies have been focusing on the writings of a very knowledgeable and brilliant German Professor of Egyptology by the name of Jan Assmann. His translated books on Egyptology and, oddly, modern monotheism (and its price to the post-modern world) are all quite inspiring to me, although probably not in the way that Professor Assmann had in mind when he wrote these books. He is a contemporary scholar, so I am not trying to read the writings of someone from the nineteenth or early twentieth century whose scholarship is missing a century or more of archeological discoveries. Dr. Assmann's writings are current and include a lot of the most up-to-date discoveries in the field of Egyptology. I will be discussing some of the things he has written in my future articles, since what he is saying about modern religious theology is also quite interesting and insightful.

While Dr. Assmann is a staunch Christian and has stated that the cost of monotheism was worth the benefits, his writings are helping me to determine what modern Paganism should be like. Are we truly engaged in a primary earth-based religion, or is our Paganism a protest against Christianity and monotheism in general? Can we go back to the simpler times and mindset of ancient Paganism, or do we have to come up with a completely different paradigm that takes 1,500 years of monotheistic religion into consideration? These are critical questions, and I am on the threshold of finally being able to answer some of them in a thorough and insightful manner.

One of the points that caught my attention when I was reading the book *Of God and Gods: Egypt, Israel and the Rise of Monotheism* written by Jan Assmann was quite startling. Dr. Assmann compared the Egyptian mythological concept of *Sep Tepy* or "First Time" to the first book in the Hebrew Bible, *Berasheth* or Genesis.[23] Seeing this comparison inspired me into thinking about the Bornless One all over again. Why would such a comparison bring that topic to mind? I had once written that I thought the famous ritual attributed to the Golden Dawn, whose origin is a spell found in the *Greek Magical Papyri in Translation* (*PGM V,* lines 96–172), was correctly and aptly named. The Godhead that is invoked in that spell is called *Akephalos*, or the "Headless One," and somehow it got renamed to "Bornless One."

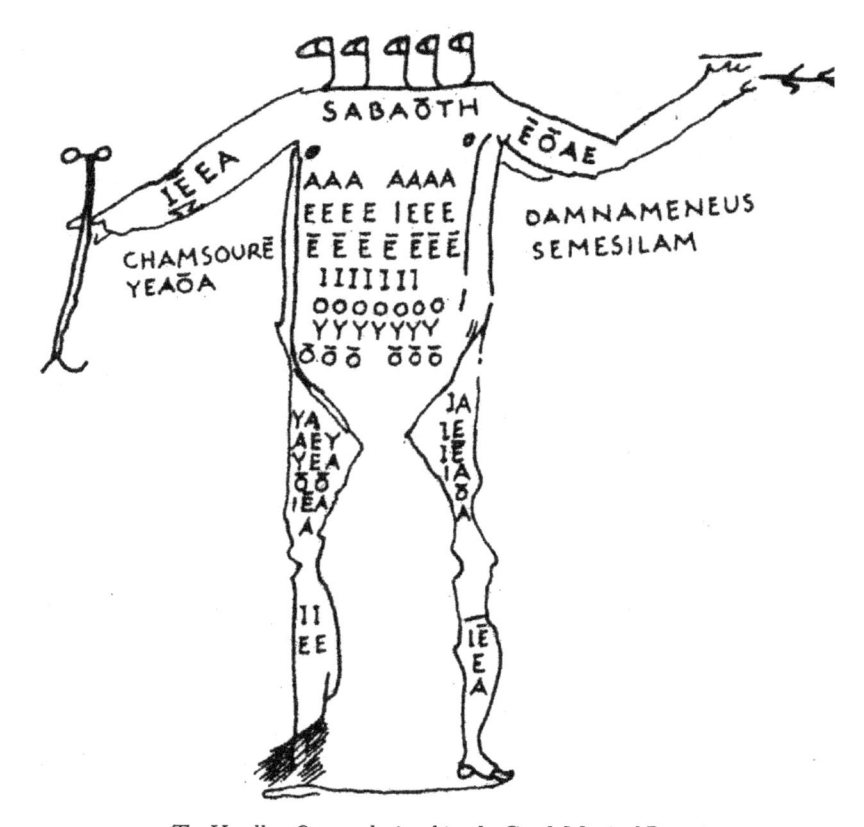

The Headless One as depicted in the Greek Magical Papyri

---

23   Assman, Jan, *Of God and Gods: Egypt, Israel and the Rise of Monotheism* (University of Wisconsin Press, 2008) p. 18.

The reason this happened was the simple fact that the word *headless* could also be considered a euphemism for a deity that had no origin—in other words, one that was without birth or *bornless*. Of course, that could only be the case if the ancient Egyptian language used the same idiom as Hebrew, where the term "without a head" could be considered the same as "without a beginning." The Hebrew word for head is *Rosh*, and the first book in the Hebrew Bible about the creation of the world is called by the first word in that book, *Berasheth*, or "in the beginning" (literally "in the head"). Coincidently, my thoughts about this term were similar to what Mathers and the Golden Dawn thought about the godhead named in this ritual, which is how it got to be called the "Invocation of the Bornless One." Others have pointed out the speciousness of this translation and its usage for this rite, since there are indeed images of this god without a head on a number of Gnostic magical coins from verifiably ancient sources.

However, the comparison that Dr. Assmann made between *Sep Tepy* and *berasheth* intrigued me quite a bit. I managed to look up the Egyptian words for *Sep Tepy* and found that *Tepy* does indeed mean "head." It also means "chief" or "first," but the hieroglyph is a man's head. To the ancient Egyptians, the term *Sep Tepy* represents the creation of the world from the watery abyss as performed by the creator god, who typically takes the form of Ra, Ptah, or Atum. The God that creates the world would have to exist before the world was created in order to perform that feat.

The Egyptian concept of the First Time (or First Day) is a very hallowed event, and the age that immediately followed it was one where the gods, humankind, and all of the flora and fauna lived together in peace. It was the golden age before the time of troubles, when humankind rebelled against the gods and caused the world to be permanently separated into the sphere of humanity and the domain of the gods. The pharaonic king was the intermediary for the gods, and his court was the mechanism through which the gods ruled the earth and maintained contact (through their cultic centers) with humanity. One could obliquely say that the creator god was in fact without a beginning, bornless, or headless.

The invisible and unknowable headless deity called Akephalos that is summoned in the *PGM* exorcism rite has qualities that make this being an unmistakable amalgamation, similar to the contemporary Gnostic god Abraxas (the solar godhead whose name adds up to 365).[24] He is said to be called *Osoronnophris* (*Ausar un-nepher*— "Osiris the Blessed"), but also compares him to *Iabes* and *Iapos* (probably corruptions of Bes and Apep). Only an amalgamation godhead would be able to reconcile opposed Egyptian deities such as Bes (the guardian) and the giant serpent Apep (personification of chaos and evil), not to mention also being associated with Osiris (fertility and resurrection) and the creative trinity of Ra, Ptah, and Atum. The analogy to Apep might be an allusion to the Greek daimon Agathodaimon, who was depicted as a giant serpent.

Akephalos is also associated with the primal creator godhead, and as such, represents the absolute spiritual master of everything in the material and spiritual worlds. This godhead would be the celebrated God who inaugurated the *Sep Tepy* or "First Time"

---

24 Betz, *op. cit.*, p. 106.

according to the Egyptians, and he would also be the ultimate source of all being, perfectly representing the One of the Platonists without name or features. It would make sense that the erstwhile sorcerer of antiquity would call on this being to assist them in performing a grand exorcism. If you wish to eject an evil spirit from some person, then summon the most powerful godhead available.

The odd epithet of this godhead, which states that he has eyes in his feet, seems to be a puzzle, but when you consider that the Headless God can be depicted as a serpent biting its tail, then the mystery is revealed as a symbolic analogue. A serpent biting its tail would then metaphorically have its eyes in its feet (tail). This symbol, called *Ouroboros* in Greek, represents the eternal cycle of self-creation and also primordial union, which would be a perfect emblem of the Headless or Bornless Godhead. This is also true of the phrase "my name is a heart encircled by a serpent" from the Bornless One rite, which could symbolize the sun in its eternal cycle, or that the core of one's being is forever regenerated.

While the original spell in the *PGM* was a basic operation of summoning the absolute deity to perform an extremely powerful exorcism, the layered symbology of this being has taken on other qualities since that time. Around the same time that Europe and the Middle East was in the midst of a profound collapse and the beginning of the Dark Ages (seventh century CE), India was fashioning a new philosophy, beginning with the Mahayana Buddhists (the two truths doctrine)[25] and continuing with the Hindu Vedantaists.[26] Both groups postulated that the ultimate reality was non-dual, and in order to rectify the obvious duality of God (absolute) and immortal human spirit (relative) without completely negating one or the other, they simply stated that there was no duality. The ultimate Cosmic One was synonymous with the inherent union within all human beings.

In Vedanta, this concept was stated succinctly as there is no difference between Brahman and Atman; in other words, there is no difference between the absolute Godhead and the individual Godhead—they were one and the same. This new philosophical perspective took the Neoplatonist creed to its highest and ultimate level and resolved the inherent dualism found within it. If we consider, then, that the highest aspect of deity is the same as the deity within each and every one of us, then the Headless or Bornless deity becomes an analogue for our own internal godhead. We therefore invoke the Bornless One (or Headless One) that is within us in order to realize the highest expression of our beings—the non-dual godhead within us.

Magicians throughout the ages have always taken the liturgies and magical rites of the past and crafted new rites and magical lore from them. It seems to be almost the

---

25 Thakchoe, Sonam, "The Theory of Two Truths in India," Stanford Encyclopedia of Philosophy (SEP), accessed December 24, 2023. plato.stanford.edu/entries/twotruths-india/

26 Menon, Sangeetha, "Advaita Vedanta," Internet Encyclopedia of Philosophy (IEP), accessed December 24, 2023. iep.utm.edu/advaita-vedanta

rule rather than the exception. We are shameless plagiarists and appropriators, and what we use as modern lore is often a mishmash of ancient and modern practices and beliefs. This also seems to be the case for the spells of the *PGM* that incorporated religious sources from a wide variety of religious cultures that were alive and accessible in late antiquity. We are no different today in regard to using all kinds of diverse sources for our magical rites and lore than the magicians and sorcerers in antiquity, and perhaps this is what unites us with them. Thus, the ancient exorcism rite of the Stele of Ieu the Hieroglyphist has become the epitome of one of the most powerful rituals in the arsenal of Western Magic used to realize and manifest the Bornless or Headless One, or Higher Self, within oneself.

BORNLESS OR HEADLESS ONE INVOCATION WORKING

The Bornless One invocation working has now been incorporated into the newly designed and structured Abramelin Lunar Ordeal, representing the rites performed in the second half of that working. The purpose of the Bornless One invocation rite, regardless of what larger ordeal or working it is deployed in, is that it is the one great ritual designed to invoke and manifest, to a lesser or greater extent, the Higher Self of the Celebrant and magician who performs it. In the Order, there are four different versions of the Bornless One rite, and the greater ordeal uses the more advanced version, which incorporates ritual structures and geometric prismatic powers associated with the Order's seventh degree. Therefore, this overall working is the primacy of the seventh degree, and initiates who are either already working at that level, having achieved their consecration to the Hierophant degree, or are working closely with someone who has achieved that degree of spiritual and magical development who can give them direction and guidance.

The Abramelin Lunar Ordeal has already been covered, and so, too, has the Bornless One rite been examined and explained to some degree in previous sections. So, what needs to be explained is the Bornless One Invocation working, which includes a total of four rituals. Previously, the Bornless One rite stood alone and had no other associated working in which to develop a context and utilize the powers and visions that may have been experienced. Now there are three ancillary rituals, and the complete working is performed as a major part of the Abramelin Lunar Ordeal.

The Bornless working consists of the following rituals in the order that they are to be performed. All of the new rituals have been distilled from the *Greek Magical Papyri*, identified in notation by the letters *PGM*. These new rituals were developed from source material analogous to the Bornless rite, which the Golden Dawn first promoted and Aleister Crowley lionized in Liber Samekh and Liber VIII. For a more detailed explanation, I would recommend consulting the rituals in question.

1. Bornless Ring Consecration Rite

This particular rite is from *PGM XII*, lines 201 through 350, and is distilled and adapted from that original Greek manuscript.[27] The original purpose of the Ring Consecration rite was to forge a powerful magical ring that would be able to act as a focus for the projection of magic power, much as a magic ring in legend and myth would be used. The ring was to be a particular kind: a band of gold with a semi-precious beveled stone, minutely carved with magical characters and words of power. The ring was then consecrated in a specific rite so it would be imbued with the powers of an absolute deity, a veritable god of gods. There are actually a pair of rites next to each other in this part of the manuscript, so I was able to distill material from both spells. These rites, like many others in the papyri, are written in isolation and there is little to indicate to the practitioner that these rites—or any others—are valuable if adapted and placed into a context, such as I have attempted to do.

The purpose for the Ring Consecration rite in the Bornless One rite series is to formulate a magical trigger or link to materialize the magical power of the Higher Self and project it into the world. The ring is therefore a linking device, not to be misconstrued as representing anything more than the symbolic and mythic quality that it represents. Once it is forged and formulated, it continues to live in the mind and soul of the magician. Stealing the ring or destroying it will in no way eliminate it, since it actually exists in the Inner Planes. The material ring is nothing more than a physical representation. If, by chance, the magician loses this ring or it is stolen, they may create a new one at any time. The old ring cannot be used to either attack or work black magic on the magician, since it symbolizes the bond between the magician and their Holy Guardian Angel or Higher Self, and nothing can disturb that connection except the foolish actions or impassioned pathos of the magician. So, because the ring is actually a symbolized tool, it can neither work for another nor can it benefit anyone else who might attempt to use it.

While one could spend a small fortune to produce an elaborate and expensive ring made of gold, and the gemstone cut and engraved with words of power (making it something of a magical artifact and worth something to someone besides the magician), it is my recommendation that the ring be made of either gold or silver and have a beveled semi-precious gemstone affixed to it. There should be no etched words of power, sigils, or characters—just a simple ring with little to no special qualities to it. It would also be smart for it to be rather quite common looking and inexpensive, since it is the symbol that's really important, not the ring. By charging and wearing a modest ring, the magician ensures that they will always know that the true ring exists in the Inner Planes and is merely represented in all its glory by a simple device.

The consecration ritual is easy enough since it is done immediately following a special Mass and Benediction. The sacraments are used to directly bless and empower the ring, and the powerful invocations distilled from the *Greek Magical Papyri* supply the verbiage. Little else is required for this simple rite, other than a careful and fixed concentration

---

27 Betz, *op. cit.*, pp. 161–165.

on the difficult but sonorous words of power. After charging the ring is done, a vigil is performed until just before the first dawning light, which should shine upon the ring and while the operator says further words of power over it. There is also an invocation of the godhead *Ouphōr*, which is used the first time that one wears the ring. From that moment onward, all one needs to do is just say the name when slipping the ring on the finger. I felt that this was a critical part that was missing from the Bornless One ritual, and it was well documented in the *Greek Magical Papyri*.

2. Bornless One Rite—also Bornless One Invocation Rite—Stellar Gnosis Version Four.

This is a greatly enhanced version of the Bornless One rite using the corrected and recovered words of power from the original *PGM* spell (specifically, *PGM V* lines 96 through 172), and deployed with five levels of concentric magical pyramid vortex structures.[28] These five steps or levels represent the power of ascendancy and the imbuement of a multi-tiered level of Godhead manifestation. The core of this rite is where the actual Bornless One rite is performed.

The Bornless One rite IV consists of three ritual levels. The first level is the Tetramorphic Archetypal Power Vortices for all four of the Qabalistic Worlds, resolving the combined forces in the fifth power, which is called the Jewel of the Gnostic Stellar Rays. My operating model is that the Higher Self (the Bornless One) resides in all four of the worlds, from Assiah to Atziluth. Within these unified vortices, the Celebrant invokes the Bornless One using the classical English translation as found in the rituals of the Golden Dawn (with corrections made from the original Greek Papyri). The final ritual action is where the Celebrant erects their own formula to establish the third level of this ritual, the Gate of Light (also called the Gate of Ascension), where they project outward the powers and profound insights found from summoning the Bornless One. This structure should represent the Celebrant's personal spiritual directive at that point in their life.

The Invocation of the Bornless One establishes a permanent manifested link to one's higher self. Therefore, it is necessary for the Celebrant to fast, say Mass, undergo rigorous purification, and other ascetic practices to facilitate the process. The Celebrant may also need to change the masculine pronouns in the ritual to feminine if her gender requires it. (Although that was the case, I have edited the ritual so that it has more neutral gendered attributes, except in some strategic instances.)

The Celebrant performs the consecration of the Temple of the Goddess, the Mass of the Goddess, and all four Elemental Worlds of the Tetrapatronis, completing the power vortices with the fifth power vortex in the order of Assiah through Atziluth. This progression is presented in the opposite order in the original ritual, so we have included them in the correct order in the following sections. However, the student is urged to read over the original ritual and become familiar with the structures of the power vortices

---

28 Betz, *op. cit.*, p. 103.

of the tetrapatrons.[29] In addition, there are invocations or calls from the *Ars Notoria of Solomon the King* (a thirteenth-century grimoire of great repute), seven of which are used to profoundly empower the four power vortices and unveil the mystery of the Eye in the Triangle, which is the new central mystery of the Bornless One rite.

3. Bornless One Assumption Rite

This particular rite is from *PGM IV*, lines 154 through 285, and is distilled and adapted from that original Greek manuscript.[30] It is used for the assumption of great powers and is performed immediately following the Bornless One rite. It is used to assume the powers and authorities, and thereby, to quicken the manifestation of the Bornless One as the Higher Self. This rite is based on a simulation of death and rebirth, and therefore invokes the dark god of the underworld, Typhon. The body of the subject is wrapped in three yards of gauze and lays upon the floor as if dead, crowned with ivy and blindfolded. Then a long incantation is said, and the subject arises, is vested in pure white robes of linen, and says an affirmation. Another incantation is read, this time before the rising sun. Later, in the temple, the subject performs divination to see the image or imago of the godhead assumption and speaks a final set of incantations. It would seem that the subject would have to perform a great deal of memorization in order to complete this rite, adorn oneself with the gauze wrapping, and so on.

Therefore, to aid the performance of this rite, there should be two individuals performing it: the candidate who is to undergo the process and assume the godhead of the Bornless One, and the initiator, who performs the incantations and guides and assists the candidate. If two people are performing this rite, they can take turns assuming the roles of the one going through the death and resurrection ordeal and the one who does the incantations and assists the other. If one is performing this rite alone, then I would recommend that they perform the incantation first, then wrap up in the gauze covering and perform a deep trance-based meditation to simulate the process of death and resurrection.

The papyrus spell advises that the assumption of great power is done at midnight, and then the candidate may properly greet the rising sun as the resurrected and empowered one. I would recommend performing the rite at a convenient time following the Bornless One rite. The period of being wrapped up in gauze can last only as long as one can assume the deepest trance state, followed by the resurrection. However, one should assume an evening vigil after, with light sleep and trance, and then arise and go outside to witness the rising sun, where additional incantations are said. Once that is accomplished, the candidate should immediately return to the temple to perform the mirror divination, and thereby perceive the nimbus and vision of the Bornless One surrounding one's person.

---

29 I discuss the Tetrapatrons in Part II, Chapter One, p. 54.
30 Betz, *op. cit.*, pp. 40–43.

The empowered magic ring should also be deployed for this rite, the candidate having assumed it and invoked the sacred god name during the Bornless One invocation before being wrapped in gauze, so that, on awakening, they shall be fully bonded with the power and glory of the Bornless One.

4. Bornless One Envisioning Rite

This particular rite is from *PGM IV* lines 850 through 1226 and is distilled and adapted from that original Greek manuscript.[31] This rite takes a total of three days and requires three Masses to be said, with an accompanying incantation to be read known as the Hidden Stele and Death Delivering Stele. The third evening is when the actual rite is to be performed, begun with another magical Mass and a Benediction rite. The preceding two days are a time of reflection, meditation, and purification, with special baths and the elimination of all worldly concerns, which might distract one from the work. The main operator should be crowned with a garland and have prepared a special phylactery that is to be worn around the waist. White robes are the preferred adornment, as is the controller crystal (to be worn around the neck). The Bornless One rite ordeal should have been performed just before or on the full moon, and this rite should be performed when the next full moon occurs.

The purpose of the Envisioning rite is to gather up the powerful visions that the Celebrant experienced while invoking their higher self into manifestation; these are used as subjects to project into a dark mirror as potent questions for the higher self, to be resolved as visions of confirmation as to the destiny and ultimate purpose of the Celebrant. Having this knowledge, the Celebrant can more unerringly live their life and proceed to accomplish the great work in a more clear and efficient manner than would be otherwise. Therefore, this rite is not only a divination rite, but it's an active and powerful one that literally generates the future for the Celebrant so they may revel in the glory of knowing and following one's spiritual and material destiny, however that is revealed.

The specific ritual begins with a circle consecration rite, Mass, and Benediction. After a suitable period of deep meditation, the Celebrant then proceeds to build up a powerful crossroads in the temple, using incantations from the *PGM* and the device of the inverted Rose Ankh. This is done in a widdershins manner, starting in the Southwest and completing in the Southeast, with an arc joining the Northeast with the Northwest. The center of the circle is set with a great inverted Rose Ankh in the Infrapoint, and all of the four angles are drawn together through it. There are five specialized incantations taken from the *PGM* to empower this crossroads vortex ritual structure.

At this point in the rite, the Celebrant puts on the magic ring, summons the associated godhead, and then performs the macro-rite for the Bornless One.[32] The Celebrant pauses to complete a full assumption of that entity before continuing.

---

31 Betz, *op. cit.*, pp. 55–61.

32 A "macro rite" is a part of ritual used to deploy a previously established ritual working. How this is done is explained in the Part II section where the rituals are explained, on page 48.

The lamp and black mirror are placed on a small altar in the center of the circle, the lamp is lit, and the phylactery is put on, along with the garland crown and controller crystal around the neck. At this point, the Celebrant intones four incantations: the light bringing charm, the light retaining spell, the summoning of the Godhead (to the Bornless One, said three times), and the envisioning spell, using the black mirror.

Once the envisioning with the black mirror is completed, the Celebrant performs the dismissal of the Godhead and the brightness, then performs an all-night vigil, greeting the sun's first light as it dawns in the morning.

These four rituals represent the complete suite of rites used in the Bornless One working, which has now fully enabled the Bornless rite with a complete array of functionality that was missing in the various and many previous iterations. The Abramelin Lunar Ordeal gives the Bornless working its complete context and will therefore ensure that a much more powerful effect will be realized when it is used by experienced practitioners.

CHAPTER FOUR

Winter 2009 Abramelin Lunar Ordeal Working

In order to perform a multiple day ordeal with sequestration, I had to construct a practical schedule for it. Since I needed some days free from my day job, I decided to schedule it during the Christmas holiday season. I would be taking a block of vacation time to accommodate this working, which will be quite easy to accomplish considering the generosity of my employer. My assumption going into developing this schedule was that the steps I had developed and determined were all that were needed to complete this ordeal. Of course, every plan made, whether in warfare, social interaction, or the works of magic, seldom matches expectations. This turned out to be quite true for me, since an important and critical step was omitted, and, in fact, I didn't even know that this step was missing until months later.

I will share the actual schedule of events as they occurred back in November 2009 and into May of 2011. However, I will also present a schedule the way it should be worked when including all of the actual steps. Developing a new ordeal and performing it for the first time can be a messy process, and this ordeal ended up being a bit messier than expected, since I was developing and revising it and then performing it during the same timeframe. Now that I have fully developed the structure of the ordeal, I am much more confident that all of the steps are now complete and in place for anyone who seeks to work this ordeal for themselves.

This is the schedule that I published in my blog to let my reading public at the time know what I was about to do. There were no comments, so I suspect that it likely went unnoticed or unremarked by my readers. It was to be one of the most momentous magical episodes of my life.

INTRODUCTION

I have written up the schedule of the Abramelin Ordeal that is based on three half lunar cycles: from new moon, to full, to new, and back again to full. The working takes around seven weeks to complete, although there may be variations due to the cycle of the moon. This particular one that I have planned for the weeks between now and the end of December will take less than seven weeks to conclude because of the cycle of the moon. It is likely that if anyone plans on doing this ordeal, they might encounter the same slight complexity for the final three days. During that time, I will be writing short articles based on my diaries to let you know about the results of these workings, although I will omit any really personal or intimate details, of course. (Since I will be placing the full diary entries later into this book, that editing will be far less extreme than it was for my blog.)

My purpose for letting people know that I am working this ordeal is to highlight that such a working can be accomplished, and that we don't necessarily need to follow the strictures laid down by the old grimoires—we can be selective regarding that material. I am certain that some will disqualify what I am doing because I am not performing the Scared Magic as it was written by Abraham the Jew. However, since there are now two versions of this book in print (French and German), and two different durations (six months and eighteen months), I believe that using yet another variation will not violate the spirit and intention of this ordeal.

However, I will never claim to have performed the ordeal as it was written and will clarify this by claiming to have completed the lunar version of the ordeal, which I have very loosely derived from the original.

THE ORDEAL

Since establishing the Abramelin Lunar Ordeal, which is a shortened version of the original ordeal, lasting six or seven weeks, I have decided to perform this working myself to verify that it does indeed work as I have speculated. This working combines the Abramelin working with the Invocation of the Bornless One, along with ancillary rites recently culled from the *Greek Magical Papyri in Translation* (*PGM*). Included in this chapter are the approximate dates and times of the working, which will officially begin on Monday, November 16, 2009, at 1:14 p.m. CST (all times are CST).

Special attention should be given to when the moon changes its phases; where possible, the magician should observe these occurrences with special periods of meditation and contemplation, especially during the actual advent of the working.

Daily meditations should be performed after waking and before retiring. Evening meditations will include one long session with a combination of breath-control, prayers, contemplation, and the use of sound to activate the energy chakras in the body. Additional meditations are to be performed when the moon changes phases and prior to a working. Ritual workings will be performed each weekend, except the weekend just before the Solstice. Special celebrations should be performed at that event, in addition to the consecration of the magical ring, an important preliminary working to the Bornless One rite series.

During this ordeal, you should perform a partial fast and avoid heavy foods such as meat, especially near the weekend workings. Keep a special journal and note anything of significance that occurs during meditation sessions, dreams, visions, insights, and the visual occurrences associated with the ritual workings. I will write up a final report and analyze the working as a whole to determine the efficacy of this ordeal. This is something that you might consider doing as well. Times for the various workings should incorporate the most auspicious planetary hours.

I began this ordeal after the new moon in November. The various phases of the moon are noted because this is a lunar ordeal, and as such, the lunar phases are critically important. Thus, I have included the dates and local time when these lunar events occurred.

Phase I: For Four Weekends— November 21 through December 13

- **New moon:** November 16, Monday—moon in Scorpio, 1:14 p.m.
- **First weekend working:** November 21 and 22. Invoke the Super-Archangels of Earth: Zahariel, Seraph of Earth, and Yofiel, Cherub of Earth.
- **First quarter:** November 24, Tuesday—moon enters Pisces (FQ), 3:39 p.m.
- **Second weekend working:** November 28 and 29. Invoke the Super-Archangels of Air: Yahoel, Seraph of Air, and Ofaniel, Cherub of Air.
- **Full moon:** December 2, Wednesday—moon is in Gemini, 1:30 a.m.
- **Third weekend working:** December 5 and 6. Invoke the Super-Archangels of Water: Metatron, Seraph of Water, and Kerubiel, Cherub of Water.
- **Last quarter:** December 8, Tuesday—moon is in Virgo, 6:13 p.m.
- **Fourth weekend working:** December 12 and 13. Invoke the Super-Archangels of Fire: Seraphiel, Seraph of Fire, and Rikbiel, Cherub of Fire.
- **New moon:** December 16, Wednesday—moon enters into Capricorn (NM), 6:02 a.m.

Phase II: Five Ancillary Workings Including Bornless One Invocation—December 20 through January 30, 2010

- **Lull weekend and Winter Solstice eve:** December 20, Sunday—Bornless One Ring Consecration.
- **Solstice:** December 21, Monday, 10:47 a.m. (Includes dawn working and observation.)
- **First quarter:** December 24, Thursday—moon enters Aries (FQ), 11:36 a.m.
- **Sixth weekend working:** December 25 and 26. Invoke Element Godhead of Water. Follow-up next day with Ogdoadic Godhead Vortex and Triple Tetrahedral Gate Ritual. (Special emphasis on Christmas for this working.)

- **Bornless One invocation rite with Assumption rite:** Begin with Triple Tetrahedral Gate Ritual on previous evening, December 29, Tuesday, and include all-night vigil. Perform Bornless One invocation rite on early evening of December 30, Wednesday.
- **Full moon:** December 31, Thursday—moon in Cancer, 1:13 p.m. Day of rest, meditation, and Feast of the New Year.
- **Bornless One Assumption of Great Powers rite:** January 9, 2010—moon in Scorpio and tenth day after Bornless One invocation rite. (This working was omitted. I felt that it was not required, although I do think that it should be part of the ordeal.)
- **Next full moon:** January 30, Saturday—moon in Leo, 12:18 a.m. Bornless One Envisioning rite performed during the following evening. (This working was omitted. There were a number of reasons why, but it was and still is an integral part of the ordeal, and in order to complete it, this ritual should be performed.)

Phase III: Remedial Work for Two Weekends— April 13 through May 14, 2011

The next set of rescheduled workings incorporated the Alchemical Hieromany rite that had been missing from the original schedule, and the Bornless Envisioning rite, which had not been performed as it should have been. These rites were performed in April and May of 2011, which was seventeen months from when the ritual ordeal started. Since these were ancillary workings, I did not feel the need to pay special attention to the cycle of the moon. I was working outside of the Lunar Ordeal to make up for the omitted ritual workings, so I gave only a cursory glance at the lunar cycle and astrological auspices.

- **First weekend working:** April 22 and April 23. moon in Capricorn, five days before full moon. On the first evening, perform the macro ritual to engage the preliminary steps of the Bornless One invocation rite. This includes the Ogdoad Godhead Vortex ritual and the Triple Tetrahedral Gate Ritual. Then, perform the Alchemical Hieromany rite. Second evening, perform the Bornless One invocation rite in full. This is to ensure that the process of unification occurs as it should. Performing this rite multiple times over a period of years, especially at the ordeal anniversaries, is not only acceptable but also required to keep the Higher Self steadfast in the conscious mind.
- **Second weekend working:** May 13 and May 14. Moon in Virgo into Libra, three days before the full moon. First evening, perform the Bornless One Envisioning rite. Consecrate the Liber Spiritus with included magic squares. Working performed within a solemn High Mass rite and with the Stele incantations from the *PGM*. (These are the Hidden Stele and Death Delivering Stele that are a part of the Envisioning rite.) Second evening, follow-up working with Mass rite, Stele incantations, and renewed envisioning scrying, if needed.

ACTUAL CORRECTED AND COMPLETE SCHEDULE

This is what the schedule would look like if it was performed with all of the elements in the seven to eight weekend period. Of course, the exact dates would depend on the phases of the moon as each step was executed. This is the idealized schedule:

- **First weekend:** Invocation of the Seraph and Cherub of Earth.
- **Second weekend:** Invocation of the Seraph and Cherub of Air.
- **Third weekend:** Invocation of the Seraph and Cherub of Water.
- **Fourth weekend:** Invocation of the Seraph and Cherub of Fire.
- **Fifth weekend:** Bornless One Ring Consecration rite.
- **Sixth weekend:** Invocation of Element Godhead. Follow-up with Ogdoadic Godhead Vortex and Triple Tetrahedral Gate Ritual.
- **Seventh weekend or three days before the full moon:** Three-day period, from Friday through Sunday. Sequestration, fasting, and intensive regimen of prayer and meditation. Triple Tetrahedral Gate Ritual performed the second evening. On the third evening, perform the Bornless One invocation rite, followed immediately by the Alchemical Hieromany rite. If there is time, perform the Bornless One Assumption of Great Powers; otherwise, it can be performed the following day.
- **Next full moon:** Perform the Bornless Envisioning rite. This may require two evenings, so a weekend would be necessary.

As you can see, the corrected schedule is certainly more concise and ordered than what I ended up having to do when I performed it. I was the test subject and, even with the extra ritual workings and times, the ordeal was not only successfully completed, but it also exceeded all of my expectations.

Now that we have the structure of the ordeal completely defined, it is important to examine the ritual technology that is used, the devices, formulations, and components that I extracted from the *PGM*. I will also need to explain how I came up with the list of Super-Archangels for the Seraphim and Cherubim, and this will be the first order of business as we begin the next part of this book.

PART II

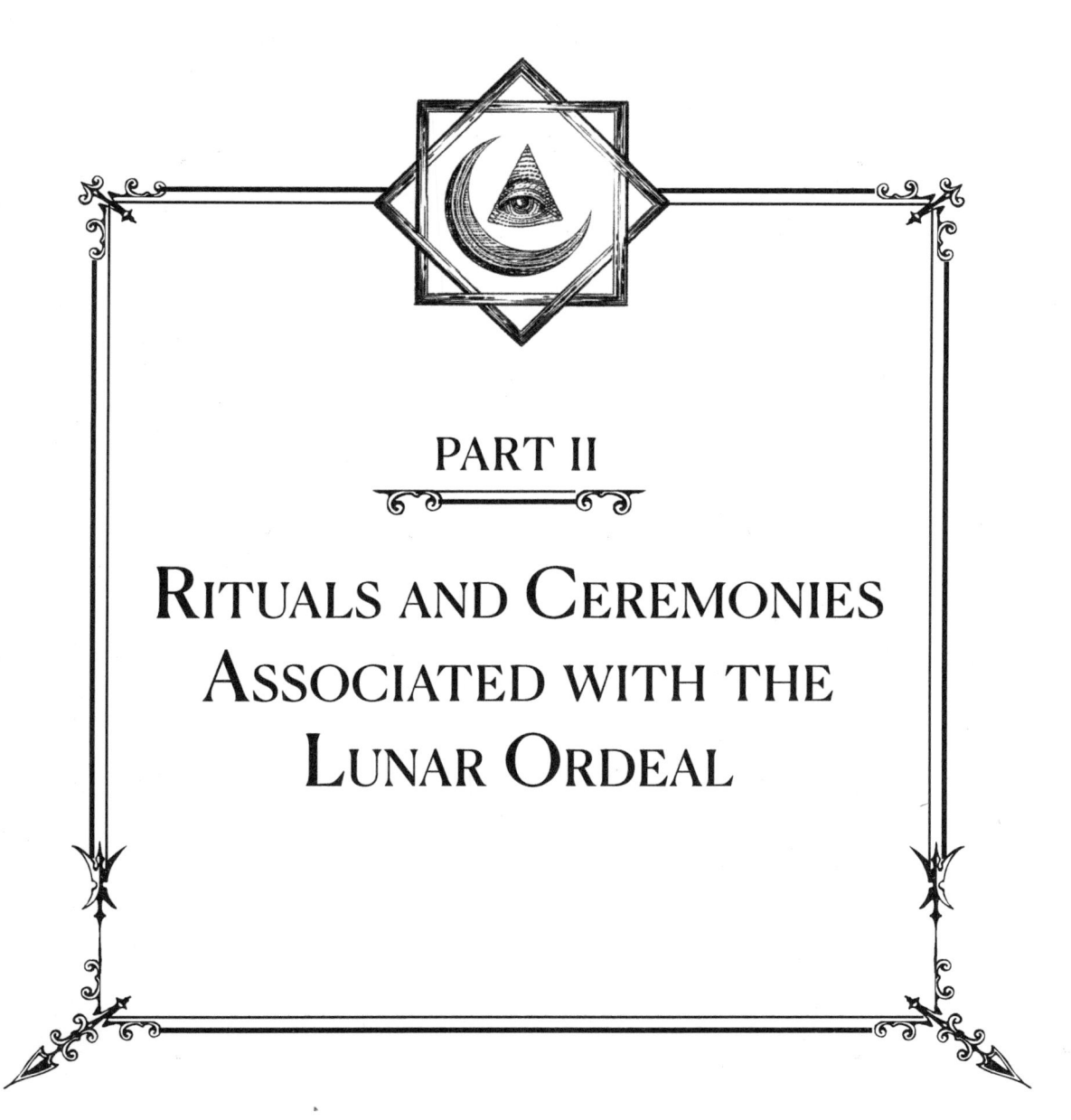

RITUALS AND CEREMONIES ASSOCIATED WITH THE LUNAR ORDEAL

CHAPTER ONE

Ordeals of Transfiguration, Super-Archangels, and Ritual Technology

The Abramelin Lunar Ordeal consists of a body of magical rituals that will, if performed properly within the correct magical and spiritual environment, produce a powerful transformation of consciousness similar to what one would expect to achieve using the traditional Abramelin working. Its intensity and the profound conscious impact of this overall body of ritual lore performed in a such short period of time represents what can be accomplished through the combined artifice of ritual workings and rigorous liturgical exercises. I have taken this as an important lesson, and after experiencing the results, I became a believer that a magician can achieve the fullness of enlightened consciousness through ritual and liturgy alone.

Yet this body of lore, without any kind of definition or background, might be daunting for someone to adopt in order to undergo this ordeal. This is why I have stated that only an experienced and advanced student can readily take and perform these rituals and practices within a seven-week period, then expect to achieve the full realization of the Higher Self as the Bornless One or HGA. However, anyone can study the rituals, writing them out and exploring their structures, images, energy, insightful verbal declarations, and sonorous intonations of mystical words of power to gain an insight into how they work and why. This is the plan I would promote to help anyone familiarize themselves with the lore in this book. I will not attempt to explain everything, of course, but through analysis and experimentation, a person with a moderate level of knowledge should be able to figure how to fully perform this ordeal.

This chapter is where I will discuss the various components of the suite of rituals in the Abramelin Ordeal. Despite the fact that these rituals are long and verbose, with complicated hybrid layered ritual structures, the actual devices and mechanisms used in them are simplistic and easy to catalogue. I will go over the magical tools, magical devices, and basic ritual structures, and talk about the mythic lore. I will also cover the specific components in this working that, when performed, can cause a deep and powerful permanent conscious transformation. What I am writing in this chapter is a necessary prelude to the actual rituals you will examine.

All the rituals use a combination of pyramidal pylons, vortices, octagons, and tetrahedral gateways to develop the energy and theme of the working. There are no complex planetary attributes, nor are there any complex tool constructs or symbolic mechanisms. The primary attributes are the combination of the four Elements and various fourfold Qabalistic qualities as found in the Tetragrammaton (YHVH). In fact, realizing this fact creates a simplicity to the ritual structures used in this working. What makes these rituals complex is the layering of structures found in the core rituals, such as the Archetypal Gate Ritual, the Ogdoadic Godhead Vortex Ritual, and the Bornless One invocation rite. Once you become familiar with how these layers function and interact, determining how they work will be elementary.

Additionally, these rituals contain the philosophical and metaphysical perspectives that I have gleaned over the decades. These are imbedded in the declarations that are verbalized at strategic points in the rituals. These declarations should be studied and even researched if one wants to understand what is being said as the ritual is performed. It is quite possible that some of my perspectives and beliefs may not correspond with yours, and so there is the inherent flexibility implied in modifying, reducing, or even omitting declarations that are contrary to your own basic practice or for making the execution of the ritual easier to manage. What is ultimately important are the ritual pattern and ritual actions, and these should not be changed or modified unless you truly understand what such changes will do to the effectiveness of the ritual.

One consideration is that, in order to perform a ritual heavily laden with declarations, the magician needs to have text to read while performing the ritual actions. I have readily adapted to this necessity by carrying ritual scripts with me while performing a ritual. This might be too awkward for some, so reducing or eliminating the declarations is an option to make the ritual easier to memorize, which would make the ritual actions flow without interruptions. This is purely a matter of esthetics, but I would recommend not eliminating the invocations, especially those that use the mystical language of the grimoires to empower ritual actions. So, retaining the barbarous words of evocation would still require using scripts, since memorizing such words of power would be beyond what most people could expect.

As a follow up, the devices and ritual structures used in the Lunar Ordeal follow the design of ritual lore in my recently published work, *Liber Nephilim*. I would recommend that you acquire that book and study the rituals that are contained in it. Additionally, my five-book *For Witches* series is also an excellent resource. Since this work uses a Mass rite and a Benediction rite, there is an excellent version of the Mass of the Goddess to be found in the book *Sacramental Theurgy for Witches*, published in 2024.[33]

Let us examine these various ritual components and cover the six categories of magical tools, magical devices, ritual structures, myth, lore, and the ordeals of transformation.

---

[33] See Barrabbas, Frater, *Sacramental Theurgy for Witches* (Crossed Crow Books, 2024) pp. 115–132 for the Mass of the Great Goddess, and pp. 133–142 for the Benediction rite.

MAGICAL TOOLS

The various ritual actions found in the working require only three tools. These are a transmutar wand, a sword, and a staff. The transmutar wand is a hybrid tool that is a wand with a heavy crystal tip. My version of this tool is all crystals—the rod, tip, and base. The transmutar wand replaces the wand and the dagger and can perform the operations of both. I use it throughout these rituals instead of having to exchange the wand and the dagger. I will let you, my readers, determine how this tool would work and its inherent utility, and understand that sometimes the requirement for using either a dagger or wand can be blurred.

When building the tetrahedral gateways, I like to use three talismanic gate keys, which are blocks of wood that are painted and decorated with a magic square and other devices, such as sigils or seals. I set them up at the watchtower and angles with specific Tarot Trump cards placed against them. This allows me to know the qualification of the gate node at a glance. The Tarot Trump card qualifies the gate node and has a Hebrew letter associated with it. You can also use standing photograph frames and place the cards against them instead of using elaborate gate keys.

There are also four iconographic tools that represent the five aspects of the Grail that I use as sacramental instruments in the Bornless One invocation rite. These are a crystal dagger-like sword, a small crystal lance or wand, a small golden chalice, a golden dish, and a crystal pyramid on a golden pedestal. These objects have been triple-consecrated as befit reliquary tools.[34] They are the physical representations of the four fathers or Tetrapatronis powers of the gnostic four-fold sacrament.

I also make use of a crystal necklace, a black scrying mirror with a holder, pure white cotton vestments, and three yards of a gauze material in off-white or powder blue hues. Other items are mainstays of the supplies and equipment that a magician might have on hand, including a blindfold, a plain black robe, strips of cloth to make phylacteries, and a wreath of ivy to wear on one's head.

MAGICAL DEVICES

There are a number of different devices used in the Lunar Ordeal, and perhaps a greater variety than I have previously written about in my books. Magical devices are symbolic forms or structures that are drawn in the air with the transmutar wand and imagined or perceived by the eyes of the magician. When I draw them, I can see them floating in the air, glowing with a barely perceptible luminescence. I use my vision coupled with my imagination to visualize devices and lines of force in the magic temple.

Lines of Force: A line connecting two objects, which can also be devices. I use the transmutar wand to draw lines of force.

---

[34] Barrabbas, Frater, *op. cit.*, pp. 149–151 includes instructions for sacramental consecration of relics.

Spirals: There are four types of spirals, where direction and vector determine their quality. There are spirals for invoking, banishing, sealing, and unsealing. Additionally, there are circumambulation spirals that the magician will perform in the ordeal to compress or exteriorize energy fields traversing the magic circle.

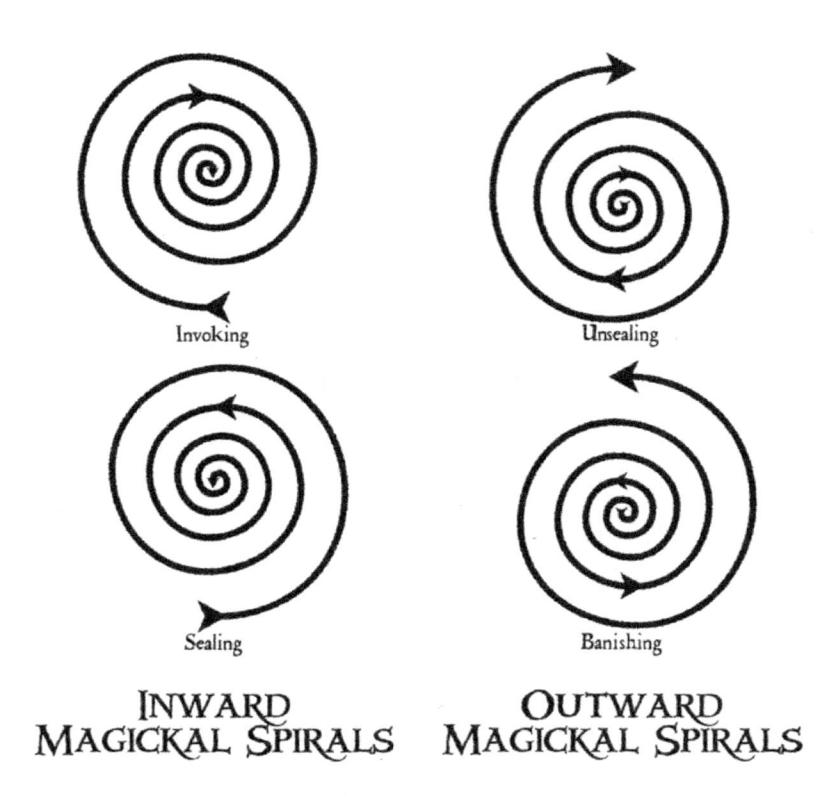

Invoking

Unsealing

Sealing

Banishing

INWARD MAGICKAL SPIRALS   OUTWARD MAGICKAL SPIRALS

Invoking Pentagrams of Fire, Air, Water, Earth, and Spirit: I use the full set of Element invoking pentagrams for the Lunar Ordeal. Invoking pentagrams for spirit has two options: creative (masculine) and receptive (feminine), depending on whether the right or left leg is used as the starting point. I also employ inverted invoking pentagrams, which are a bit more challenging to draw in the air. I don't use banishing pentagrams because the energy structures that I employ are vortices, which cannot be banished but only sealed. (You can get the proper way to draw invoking pentagrams from many sources; however, I would assume that an experienced magician would already know this information.)

Rose Cross and Rose Ankh: These are cross devices with an added invoking spiral in their center, which functions as the symbolic rose. A Rose Cross generates a very solar and archetypal masculine godhead energy, and a Rose Ankh generates a very lunar and archetypal feminine godhead energy. There is a power of Deity associated with either of these signs. Additionally, I employ an inverted Rose Ankh that symbolizes the orb of the world, an emblem of the orb that monarchs would possess as part of their monarchical regalia. It has the same connotation: that of a royal or magical materialized domain.

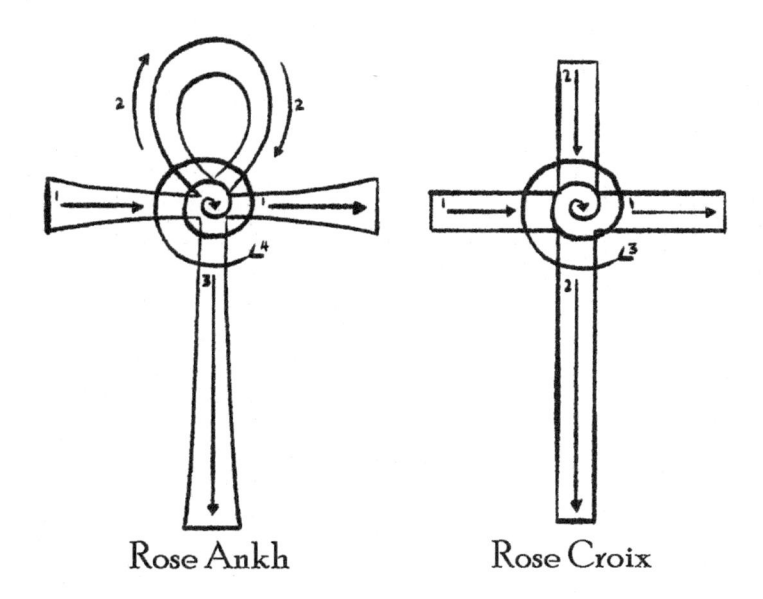

Rose Ankh   Rose Croix

Trapezoidal Cross: A cross device embedded in a diamond-shaped trapezoid. This device is a complex combination of a rose cross and a trapezoid, where the rose cross is distorted by the uneven lengths of the trapezoidal shape. When drawn in a circle node, it creates a non-Euclidean form that replicates the actual space-time continuum in a single drawn device. Drawing three or four of these devices in a ritual structure will generate a separate dimension of space-time that powerfully impacts the energies of the ritual working. The use of a trapezoid follows the occultic concept of the Law of the Trapezoid as followed by certain members of the Church of Satan and the Temple of Set. I have found it to be quite a fascinating device to use for empowering the points in the tetrahedral gateways. Here is an example of how it looks:

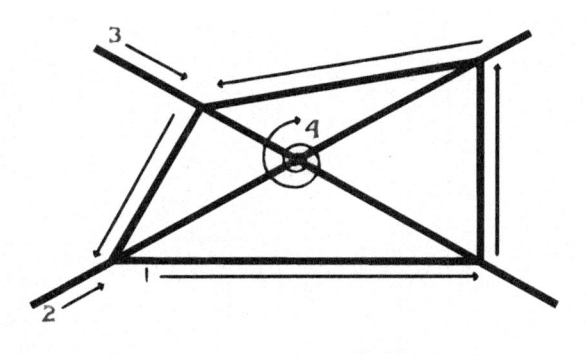

TRAPEZOIDAL CROSS

Deity Cross Indicators: In addition to the Rose Cross and Rose Ankh, I use an additional set of four crosses to denote attributes of Deity. These are the triangle cross, a cross with a triangle drawn at its center; the Pisces Cross, like the symbol for Pisces; the pentagram cross; and the hexagram cross, which are crosses with an invoking pentagram of spirit creative and a simple hexagram drawn in their centers.

The meaning of these crosses is determined by the context where they occur in the rituals, but, basically, they represent aspects of the Gnostic Tetrasacramentary, starting with the Pisces Cross for Thanatos, the pentagram and hexagram crosses for Thelema and Agape,[35] and the Rose Ankh representing Eros. The triangle cross is used to denote the Element Godhead, as in the Archetypal Gate Ritual. I also use a simple hexagram drawn as two triangles, one overlapping the other, as a symbol of unity or of entity demarcation (to indicate a spirit defined at a point or node in the magic temple).

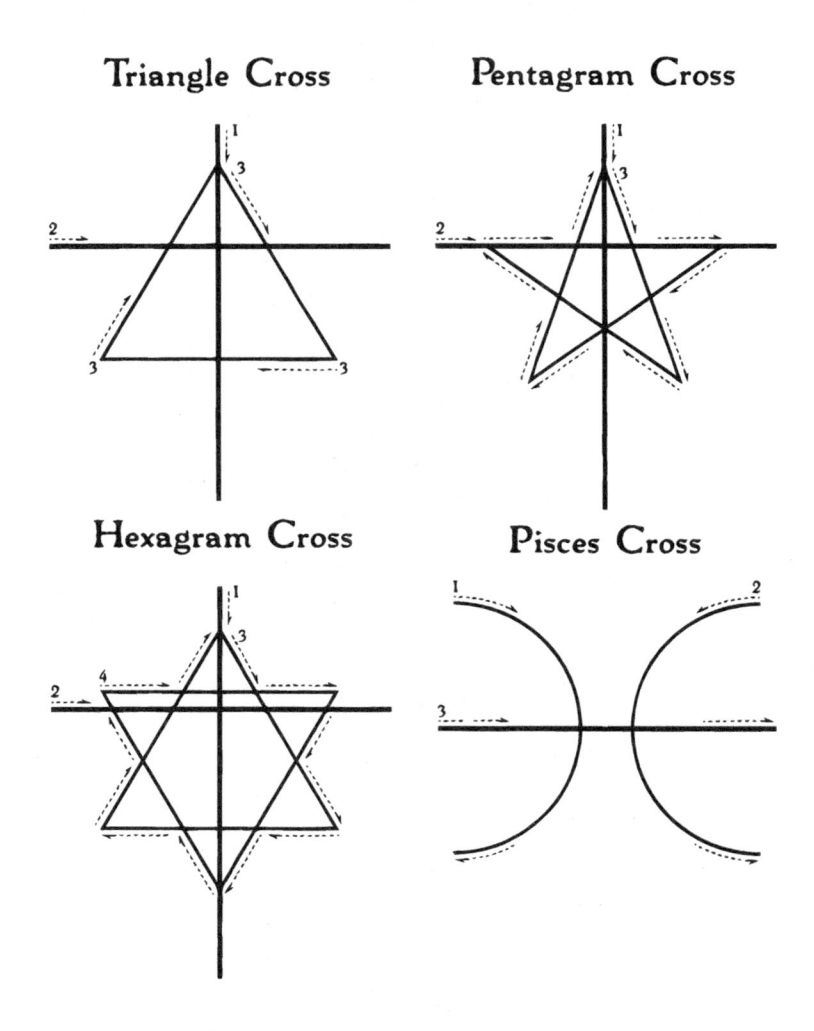

Triangle Cross

Pentagram Cross

Hexagram Cross

Pisces Cross

---

35 For the cross denoting the gnostic sacramentary of Thelema, I also use the Rose Cross in its Golden Dawn determinant.

Magic Pylon: A hybrid device consisting of two devices united by a line or an invoking spiral of force. A pylon device has many uses since it can join two different devices, like two invoking pentagrams, into a single fused device, where both devices function as one. I have found that a pylon can use the top and bottom of the line to join devices, but it can also use its midpoint as well, allowing for the joining of three devices together into a single force. The pylon can be used to define an Elemental or a zodiacal sign in more complex ritual workings. Here is an example of how it looks:

THE PYLON

Hebrew and Greek Letters and Magical Acronyms: The rituals of the Lunar Ordeal use letters and words in Hebrew, Greek, or other languages to denote points in a ritual structure, such as the watchtowers, angles, or gateway nodes. The letters and words are used to qualify points in ritual structures when they are defined as a magical formula or acronym at their resolution, thus pulling the structures together into a unified concept.

The use of formula words and acronyms was first shown in the Golden Dawn ritual of the Rose Cross, in the Analysis of the Keyword. I have found that using this approach causes a set of points or nodes in a ritual structure to be powerfully unified, becoming a unitary structure in the ritual. The combination of letters may form an acronym word, or they might just represent a formula that has no definition. The function of acronyms or formulas is to create unitary structures, and a set of unitary structures are layered one upon the other to formulate a ritual. That is the secret to how I write and perform rituals in my workings, especially in the Lunar Ordeal.

Colored Energy Projections: I use the projection of colored magical energies to qualify a device that is drawn in the air. Like the device itself, I can perceive these colors qualifying a device with my mind's eye using a combination of psychic perception and my imagination. The colors enhance the overall meaning of the device. To determine the meaning and quality for a given device set at the point of a ritual structure, you can examine the combination of letter, word, declaration, device qualification, and the color of the energy projected into it.

These qualifications work together to formulate the attributes of a specific point or node in a ritual structure. When these points are pulled together using a formula or acronym, then the combination of colors highlight the unitary ritual structure. Projecting colored energy into a device also helps to generate the various colored prismatic energy structures in a ritual working. When I observe a completed ritual structure, I can see the pattern of colors highlighting the points within it. While I have practiced for decades to gain this kind of perception, others that have shared these kinds of workings with me have seen them as well, lending a certain objectivity to their occurrence.

Invocations and Words of Power: I have generously borrowed specific incantations and invocations from various sources: the *PGM, Sworn Book of Honorius, Ars Notoria,* and even the poetry of Frater Achad. Additionally, I have translated a number of conjurations using my own version of the Enochian language to produce unique empowered expressions that are sonorous and meaningful to the angels and godheads that I am invoking. Where I have employed the *PGM* words of power, these have been taken from source rituals in that collection and modified to fit into a specific ritual. I have used these various mechanisms to give the rituals greater punch and emphasis, thereby empowering them in a traditional ritual magical manner. Most of the Enochian conjurations are accompanied with an English translation, but in most cases, the sounds and expressions that reciting the language produces is more important than the actual meaning expressed.

Macro Rituals: A macro ritual is a shortened version of a long ritual that can be employed once the longer version has been successfully completed. Since I work with vortices, an unsealing spiral will reveal the previous workings that reside in the temple. However, the control crystal necklace can also function in this manner. The Lunar Ordeal has three points associated with a macro ritual. The Ogdoadic Godhead Vortex rite combined with the Triple Tetrahedral Gate Ritual becomes the macro ritual for the entire six weeks of the Lunar Ordeal, encapsulating all that has been accomplished. This can be used to establish the base for the Bornless One invocation rite.

Additionally, there is the sacred name (bestowed by the HGA) and the consecrated ring of power that can be used to summon the magician's Higher Self whenever required. The act of setting consecrated space, saying a Mass and Benediction, and then putting on the ring, holding it up to the Ultrapoint, and uttering the sacred name, then performing a centering downward projection, should suffice entirely as a surrogate for the entire Lunar Ordeal.

TEMPLE ARCHITECTURE

As stated in my book *Liber Nephilim,* the magical rituals that I employ in a temple use a magic circle that has externally defined around its circumference eight points of reference. These include the four cardinal directions and an additional four in-between points that reside on the plane of the magic circle. The cardinal directions are called watchtowers, and the four in-between points are called angles. Having eight points in a magic circle allows me to build geometric shapes that generate prismatic energy structures when I work magic, and I define them using different devices drawn at these points within a ritual working. The eight points of the magic circle make it easy to define and generate an Elemental power field, since the watchtowers assume the base attribute and the angles assume the qualifying attribute.

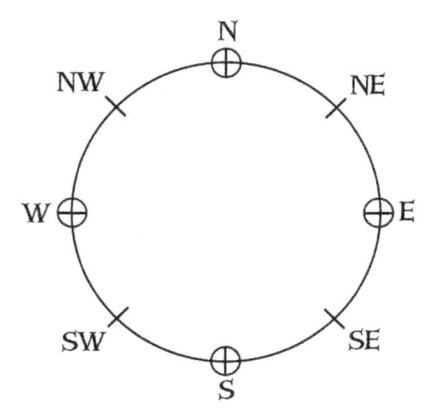

EIGHT POINT MAGIC CIRCLE

In the center of the magic circle, there are three additional points that can be added to the eight outer points. These three points in the center of the circle represent the zenith, the nadir, and the mid-point. When standing in the center of the circle, these three points are below one's feet, above one's head, and at the point where one's heart resides. They take on these qualities when we work with them using various ritual structures. I call these three points the Infrapoint (nadir), the Ultrapoint (zenith) and the Mesopoint (mid-point).

Temple furniture occupies various locations in the temple based on practical considerations. The magic circle encloses the space of the entire temple since it is projected beyond the walls when it is drawn during the circle consecration rite. I typically employ a main altar and, opposite it, a shrine. Then, I place small altars to the unallocated watchtowers and angles so that there can be some kind of light and placement of artifacts at those nodes. There is also a chair set against the wall and a cushion used for meditation; set these aside when not needed.

The main altar is used for saying a magical Mass, generating sacraments, holding ritual scripts and grimoires in a book holder, and placing the magical tools, except the sword and staff. I will place two lamps on either side of the watchtower lamp. The shrine is used to hold icons, ancestor artifacts, sacramental offerings, talismans, amulets, and other sacralized objects. Other decorations, such as pictures, artwork, tapestries, flags, or banners, can be used as one sees the need, or the temple can be kept sparsely with just the tools needed to work magic.

A couple of the rituals call for the use of a small, portable center altar, which is used to elevate and centralize certain tools, sigils, and sacramental objects. This piece of equipment is very useful, and because it is small and portable, it would be less intrusive if not needed.

RITUAL STRUCTURES

As I stated previously, the primary ritual structures consist of the pylon pyramids, positive (deosil) and negative (widdershins) vortices, tetrahedral gateways, and layered ritual structures that produce powerful prismatic energy fields suffused with occult symbols and metaphysical declarations. It is the layering of these simple ritual structures that make the rituals complex and not easy to translate at first glance.

While I have an aversion to overusing the Qabalah for ritual workings and I have avoided using it in my Witchcraft magic, in the Lunar Ordeal I have found that using the Qabalah allows for a greater accuracy, particularly in defining attributes of the Godhead and its relationship to the magician's Higher Self. Therefore, to create the theme of ascension to the unity of the Godhead in search of one's own inner Deity, I have employed the four Qabalistic Worlds of Assiah, Yetzirah, Briah, and Atziluth, representing the elements of the formula of the Tetragrammaton YHVH.

If you add the letter *Shin* to this divine tetrad, then you have an extension of the manifestation of the Holy Spirit and the Avatar God as Humankind. It is a mechanism of making the Deity both immanent and transcendental, which is also the method of uniting the Macrocosm with the Microcosm. At the crossroads of the confluence of divine personages is the ritual magician who seeks to know their own godhead as the Bornless or Headless One, the Higher Self, or the HGA. This represents the array of symbolic and metaphysical elements that are found in Lunar Ordeal, thereby making it possible for a ritual magician to achieve union with their Higher Self.

Octagram or Octagon: If the four watchtowers and angles are used together, the combined form will generate an elemental energy field.

The magician will draw the devices of an invoking pentagram to each point, where the watchtowers possess the qualities of the base Element and the angles possess the qualities of the qualifier element. The four watchtowers are joined to the Infrapoint with lines of force made with a sword, each joined with themselves to form a square in the circle. The four angles are joined to the Ultrapoint and to themselves to form another square in the circle. We have, then, one element energy field occupying the watchtowers and Infrapoint, and another energy field occupying the angles and the Ultrapoint, and when the magician stands in the center of the circle armed with a staff, then the two energy fields are immediately fused together to generate the Elemental power. The body of the magician absorbs that power, but it can also produce a foundation for another set of rituals. There are, of course, many uses for an octagon ritual structure—generating an elemental energy field is just one of them, and it is the simplest one to deploy.

The octagon also employs a simpler structure: the crossroads or confluence of two vectors that join the East with the West, and the North with the South. These structures are the basic elements of a vortex, and whether it is negative or positive is based on the direction of the circumambulation spiral performed upon it. Some of the rituals employ the crossroads in a unique manner and outside of an octagon ritual structure.

The crossroads themselves, when employed in a ritual, represent the locus or point where the magician may achieve a transference of spiritual influences either from above or below the plane of the magic circle. This also fits with the traditional perspective of a crossroads representing a lintel or gateway between worlds.

Western and Eastern Gateways: A basic premise that I use to define the shape of a ritual structure is that a triangle is always some kind of gateway or doorway. It is also the philosophical manner of resolving any kind of problem through the artifice of thesis, antithesis, and synthesis. I also use it to define the mechanism of psychic transformation as the roles of the guide, guardian, and the ordeal, as representing both the inner outer cycle of the Hero's Journey. When standing in the opposite quarter and facing the gateway that one is to enter, the ordeal is always in front of you, the guide is to your left, and the guardian is to your right.

An eight-point magic circle allows for the definition of four such gateway structures, although I typically use only two. If we elect the western watchtower as the point of departure into the underworld and the eastern watchtower as the point of return into the waking world, then the corresponding angles of northeast and southeast would be part of the triangle gateway of the west, and the angles of northwest and southwest would be part of the triangle gateway of the east. These are the two gateways that I use in my workings to represent the western gate of mysteries or entrance into the underworld, and the eastern gate of ascension or exit into the waking world. In the Lunar Ordeal, I also employ a gateway that uses the northern and southern points and the Ultrapoint to form a crossroads gateway when overlaid on the western and eastern gateways. I call this special gateway the Gate of Ascension.

Unlike the triangle of evocation used in ceremonial magic, I use the gateways that are inside of the temple circle architecture. This means that I enter the gateway of mysteries and exit it all within the confines of my temple. There is no protection from any spirits invoked or evoked. I ensure my full empowerment and immunity from potential spiritual harm through the use of a godhead assumption enacted at the beginning of any working that I might perform. Functioning as a deity in my magic circle makes certain that no spirit nor any other kind of entity, whether deity or demigod, can cause me harm. I do make certain that I am properly aligned to the Deities that I humbly serve and worship, so there is little chance for arrogance or hubris to affect me.

While the simple version of the gateway is defined by three points, the tetrahedral gateway uses the Ultrapoint to shape the gateway into a tetrahedron, where the apex is locked into an ultimate point in the circle, thereby giving it a greater spiritual context than it would otherwise possess. The Lunar Ordeal uses the tetrahedral gateway exclusively to define the place in the ritual where a unified and higher spiritual expression is sought.

Archetypal Gate Ritual: This ritual is used to invoke the four Super-Archangels of Seraphim and Cherubim, and the Element Godhead. It has a purely Elemental foundation based on the absolute Qabalistic World of Atziluth, and the tetrahedral

Element gateway used to distinguish them by Element association and overall role. The purpose of this ritual is to invoke the pair of Seraph and Cherub on two separate days of a weekend for each of the four elements. The final use of this ritual is to invoke one specific Element Godhead that represents the ritual magician's particular spiritual alignment and metaphysical perspective. I chose the Element of Water for my working, to emphasize my alignment with my personal Goddess, and the fact that I am a Witch following a pathway that is feminine and also sinister (left-handed, denoting my crooked path). You will, of course, pick the Element Godhead most suitable for your own version of this working.

Ogdoadic Godhead Vortex Ritual: Once all eight of the Super-Archangels have been invoked, as well as the Element Godhead, then these entities can be brought into fusion within an octagon vortex pattern. The Seraphim and Cherubim are placed in the four watchtowers using a pylon to integrate them, and the Element Godhead components are set to the four angles using pylon structures to represent the combination of Element and gender, where Fire and Air are considered archetypally masculine and Water and Earth are archetypally feminine. The pylon points for the Seraphim and Cherubim employ simple hexagrams to denote their position within that structure, and the pylon points for the Element Godhead are set with a base invoking pentagram of the Element and an apex set with the invoking pentagram of spirit creative or receptive. In the center of the circle is a pylon consisting of the Seraphim and Cherubim joined to the Infrapoint and the Element Godhead attributes joined to the Ultrapoint. Fusing these center points together produces what I call the tabernacle of the Holy Ogdoad, symbolizing the temple domain where the mystery of the Bornless One will be revealed.

Triple Tetrahedral and Ascension Gateways: When the Ogdoadic Godhead vortex is established, then it can only be superseded through the use of gateway structures. The purpose of these gateways is to open up the threshold of the Absolute Godhead, or, as I call it, the Union of All Being to expose the ritual magician to the highest spiritual authority and intelligence possible. This opening is the beginning of a powerful transformation of consciousness visited upon the magician prior to performing the invocation of the Bornless One. It is an important and strategic opening that makes the operator's profound transfiguration almost impossible to avoid.

The triple gateway consists of the tetrahedral western and eastern gateways that form the double gateway structure of descent and ascent, which is the basic thematic pattern of transformative initiation. The northern and southern points, typically neglected in this pattern, become the anchor points of an equilateral triangle gate whose apex is the Ultrapoint; this is the structure of the gateway of spiritual ascension. The Ultrapoint, which holds the apex of the double gateway of west and east, also holds the apex of the Ascension Gate, thus fusing them together into a single crossroads gateway structure. The fourth point is the Mesopoint to the Ascension Gate, where is positioned the heart of the magician.

Triple Tetrahedral Gateway

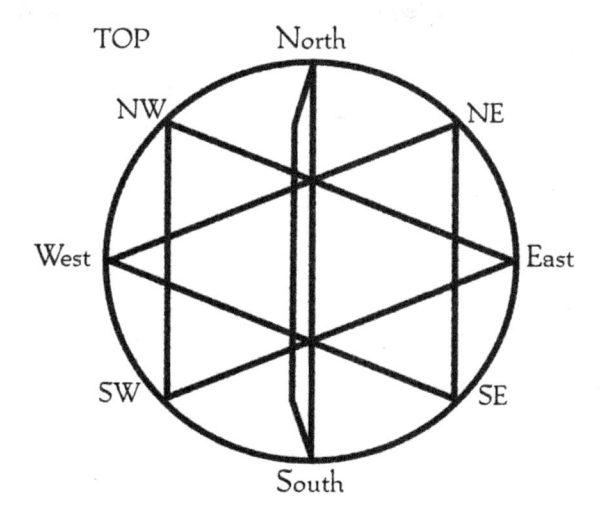

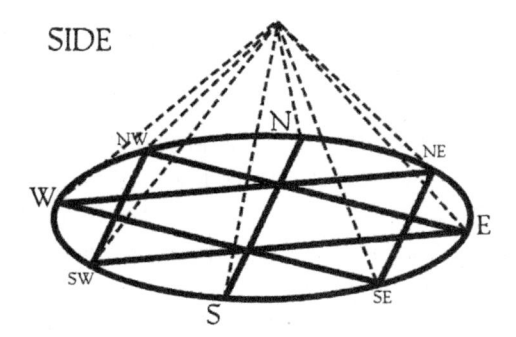

(Diagram: TOP view — circle with hexagram, labeled North, NE, East, SE, South, SW, West, NW. SIDE view — ellipse with cone/tetrahedral lines rising to apex, labeled N, NE, E, SE, S, SW, W, NW.)

This gateway crosses the double gateways of initiation and draws the pathway between them into the Absolute Plane, where the unitary Godhead can descend and the magician ascends to the highest level of consciousness to briefly join with it, which then becomes the transcendental plane where Deity and humanity are one. This Triple Tetrahedral Gateway is therefore the chief ritual mechanism that forms a bridge between the Absolute Godhead and the magician, where the base is the Ogdoadic tabernacle of the Holy Godhead.

Bornless One Invocation Rite of Stellar Gnosis: I have been working and developing this ritual for decades, and this version, added to the Order's Seven-Rayed Gnostic system, is the final stage of that development. The basic premise of this ritual is that it is an ascent through the four Qabalistic Worlds, from Assiah to Atziluth, entering a fifth level representing the sacred portal temple between the exalted conscious state of the magician and blinding reality of the Absolute Godhead. In that fifth and exalted level, which could be likened to the Qabalistic Negative Veils of Light, the magician performs a variation of the traditional Bornless One rite as defined by Crowley and the Golden Dawn, with rectifications gleaned from the *PGM*. This ritual uses a construct named the Tetrapatronis Powers of Sacramentation to further define and sacralize the Qabalistic World, making it more tangible and focusing a materialization of that world into the body and conscious mind of the magician. While this ritual is long, verbose, complex, and intensely powerful, it does make the Bornless One invocation more capable of producing the results that modern occultists and magicians have sought from it. This ritual can be used to not only pass through the lesser abyss but could also assist the magician in crossing the Greater Abyss, if other elements defined in the Gnostic Seven-Rayed system are incorporated.

Tetrapatronis Powers of Sacramentation: The Bornless One invocation uses the Tetrapatronis powers to qualify the ascension of the four Qabalistic Worlds. These four powers are the formulations for the Tetrapatronis patterns that are used in the Bornless One invocation rite of Stellar Gnosis. The four fathers (patrons) are the four sacramental power bases through which the septa-stellar (seven) mothers, or seven virtues of the Goddess, are expressed in the Order's ritual system of the Seven Rays. The entire systems of four (Tetrapatronis) and seven (Heptamatronis) join to create the Hendecade or Undecigram pattern that is the preliminary pattern for the gate of the abysmal crossing. The Undecigram pattern is the fulfillment of the seven stellar rays, and the beginning of a greater mystery involving the hidden ogdoad of the greater abyss, the culmination of which establishes the initiatory grade of the Magister Templi (Eighth Degree). When used in the context of the Bornless One invocation rite and the Lunar Ordeal, it represents the crossing of the lesser abyss, or parting the veil of Paroketh.

Each of the four powers of the Tetrapatronis are specific, unique patterns of force overlaid with the formula and invocation of the Elemental Qabalistic World and associated Godhead. In addition, there is an elementary exposition of one of the four Gnostic Masters (Basilides, Simon Magus, Valentinus, and Honorius), representing the basic magical wisdom or philosophical underpinnings of the Elemental sacraments.

Each Elemental sacrament has, as its source, one of the four philosophical masses, and the sacrament generated from these masses are used to power the vortex of the Tetrapatron. These four powers are represented by complex vortex structures: Atziluth (Fire) is empowered by the Yod-lode or Double-wand; Briah (Water) is empowered by the Grail Womb-matrix or double-concentric vortices; Yetzirah (Air) is empowered by the Septagonic Sword (Gladius Veritus); and Assiah (Earth) is empowered by the Octagon Shield (Aegis of the Masters). The greater mystery is established through the serial generation of these four power-vortices in order from lower to higher worlds, with an enneagram set at its core, representing the fifth power structure (the fifth Grail is the Stone or Gem-crystal—the Eye of Lucifer). Each power-vortex has its own specific ritual pattern and structure based on the basic pattern and structure of the Qabalistic Pyramid of Power Ritual. Therefore, before each ritual will be a brief explanation of the ritual pattern and formula structure.

The four vortices of the Tetrapatronis use the base pattern as found in the Qabalistic Pyramid of Power Ritual—additional formulas are used to fill out the number of nodes required for each unique ritual pattern, including a formula concept and letter that allows all four of the tetra-vortices to be fused into a single power structure. The following list illustrates the combination of Elements, Qabalistic Worlds, spiritual qualities, and godhead formulas. (Note: the formulas are not to be confused with the actual God-names normally associated with the four Elemental worlds.)

Element	Qabalistic World	Quality	Godhead Formula
Fire	Atziluth	Masculine Spirit	AHYH (Ehieh)
Water	Briah	Feminine Spirit	ShDAY (Shadai El Chai)
Air	Yetzirah	Masculine Spirit	ALHM (Elohim)
Earth	Assiah	Feminine Spirit	YShVH (Yashua)

Alchemy Hierogamy Rite of Union: This ritual is performed immediately after the Bornless One invocation rite. It follows, in a ritualized format, the Alchemical Wedding of Christian Rosenkreutz. The function of this ritual in the context of the Lunar Ordeal is that it causes the newly realized and manifested Higher Self to be brought into conscious union with the mind of the magician, thus fulfilling the overall tasks that the Lunar Ordeal seeks to achieve. I have already written a very thorough analysis of this ritual in the actual chapter attributed to it (see page 135), so I will only copy a paragraph from that writing here for my readers to apprise as part of the presentation of the ritual lore for this ordeal.

This ritual working consists of a four-part layer of ritual structures that represent the Magic Castle of Mysteries, the Descending Tetrahedral Gateway or Underworld Tower of Transformation, the Inner Domain of the Crossroads and inner circle, which denotes where the core of the mystery is revealed, and then, finally, the Ascending Tetrahedral Gateway or Tower of Resurrection. The central or core mystery is a simple three-way handfasting between the three elements revealed in the Abramelin Ordeal—the archetypal feminine, the archetypical masculine, and the magician, fused together in space and time. The elements of the ring, magic mirror, and the vestments of glory are blessed, empowered, and sacralized so that they may be used by the high adept to represent the union of Spirit, Mind, and Body—the Three-fold Initiation.

Ancillary Bornless One Rites: Because I was not content with incorporating the Headless One invocation from the PGM as the principal rite in this Lunar Ordeal, I decided to examine the PGM closely to find other rituals that function as a suite of rituals from the PGM. I needed to perform at least two objectives in the working that were omitted. I wanted to incorporate a magic ring that would function as a kind of wedding ring between the Higher Self and the ritual magician who had completed this ordeal. It would function as a link between the HGA as Higher Self and the magician, who could call upon the HGA whenever necessary. I also needed a ritual that would bundle up the accumulated powers and intelligences associated with the completed Bornless

One invocation rite and use them to determine and project one's fate or assumed destiny into the world as a magical adept. So, what I was looking for was a ring consecration rite and an envisioning rite, and I found perfect examples of both in the PGM. I also found a rite that represented the rebirth of the operator, wrapped up like a mummy and brought back to life through the agency of Typhon. I collected these rites and used them in my Lunar Ordeal, and they were quite effective. I used the text found in the original ritual introductions for each rite since they describe the ritual actions quite succinctly.

Bornless One Ring Consecration Rite: The purpose for the Ring Consecration rite in the Bornless One series is to formulate a magical trigger or link to materialize the magical power of the Higher Self and project it into the world. The ring is therefore a linking device, not to be misconstrued as representing anything more than the symbolic and mythic quality that it represents. Sacraments are used to consecrate the ring, and the words of power assist in greatly charging the ring. A night-long vigil is employed, and the ring is exposed to the first rays of the dawning light of the sun.

Bornless One Assumption of Great Powers: This rite is used for the assumption of great powers and is performed a day or two following the Bornless One invocation rite. It is used to assume the powers and authorities, and to quicken the manifestation of the Bornless One as the Higher Self. This rite is based on a simulation of death and rebirth, and therefore invokes the dark god of the underworld, Typhon. The operator is wrapped up in a gauze covering and wears a wreath and blindfold, and, reclining on the temple floor, assumes a deep trance. After a lengthy but powerful incantation, the operator is assisted in rising and assumes the state of a resurrected initiate. A black mirror is used to visualize the nimbus of the Higher Self shrouding the operator, and a nightlong vigil meeting the dawning light of the sun is a feature of this rite.

Bornless One Envisioning Rite: The Bornless Envisioning rite takes a total of three days and requires saying three masses and reading an accompanying incantation, known as the Hidden Stele and Death Delivering Stele. The third evening is when the actual rite is to be performed, beginning with another magical Mass and a Benediction rite. The preceding two days are a time of reflection, meditation, and purification, with special baths and the elimination of all worldly concerns that might distract one from the work. The main operator should be crowned with a garland and have prepared a special phylactery that is to be worn around the waist. White robes are the preferred adornment, as is the optional controller crystal (to be worn around the neck). The Bornless One invocation rite ordeal should have been performed just before or on the full moon, and this rite should be performed for the next full moon that occurs.

Of these three ancillary rites, the Ring Consecration and Envisioning rites are the most important, and the assumption of great powers, although useful, is less important. When I performed this working, I skipped performing the assumption because the Bornless One invocation rite had so overwhelmed me that performing any additional rites, at least for the scheduled period of the ordeal, seemed superfluous. I had originally scheduled the assumption of great powers rite to be performed immediately after the Bornless One invocation rite, but I now know that there is a follow up ritual—the Alchemy Hierogamy rite of Union. The assumption of great power, if one desires to perform it, can be performed a day or three after the Bornless One invocation rite and rite of union are performed.

SUPER-ARCHANGELIC LORE

When I had envisioned the invocation of the Seraphim and Cherubim, I did some detailed research to help me to build up a structure where these angels could be worked into the pattern that I had developed for a revised version of the Archetypal Gate Ritual. In different religious systems through the ages, most authorities agreed that the Seraphim and Cherubim were the two highest rankings of angels and the closest to the Deity. The Cherubim were throne angels who warded and empowered the throne or chariot of God, and the Seraphim were the protectors of the heavenly abode, warding the four gateways leading into paradise. These angels had peculiar forms, since they had multiple wings and were girded for war. I felt that these two rankings of angels would be perfect for the ritual working in which I planned to employ them. I called them Super-Archangels because they were located on the plane of Atziluth and were in close proximity to God, unlike the other angels.

Archaic images of a Cherub (left) and a Seraph (right).

I set out to put together a definitive list of Seraphim and Cherubim angels to use in my ritual. The only problem was that the authorities in the different disciplines and through the ages did not agree on the names of these angels nor their number. Because I was working through a four-fold Qabalistic attribute of God based on the Tetragrammaton, I decided that there should only be four of each. So, what I had to do was go through the various lists of angel names and choose those that best fit my requirements. If an angel was listed as one of the Archangels or were in some other list, then I decided to omit them to eliminate duplicates. Satan had been a Seraph before his supposed fall, but I wanted to avoid having his name on the list. After a bit of careful research, I came up with my list of four Seraphim, four Cherubim, and their Elemental configurations.

Four Seraphim

Seraphiel (Fire): Chief of the Seraphim and Prince of the Merkabah, the Chariot of God. He is a great inspirer who shed illumination on the elect.

Metatron (Water): Lord of the Archangels and Prince of the Divine Face. He is the Chancellor of Heaven and Scribe of the Lord. He is also the Archangel of Kether and was once the mortal Patriarch named Enoch.

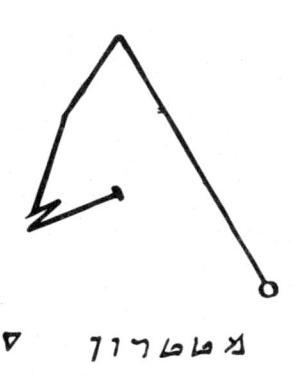

Yahoel (Air): Divine emissary of the Godhead, heavenly guide, protector, and agent of revelation.

▲ יהואל

Zahariel (Earth): The spiritual beauty of all creation, echoing the perfection and beauty of the One in All.

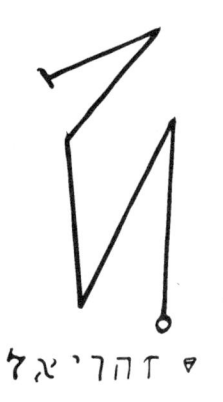

▽ זהריאל

Four Cherubim

Rikbiel (Fire): The Crown Prince of Heavenly Judgement, and Ruler of the Divine Chariot or Wheels of Fire.

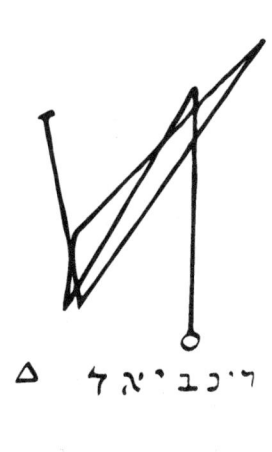

△ רכביאל

Kerubiel (Water): The angel of divine love, messenger, and protector of the holy beloved of the Godhead.

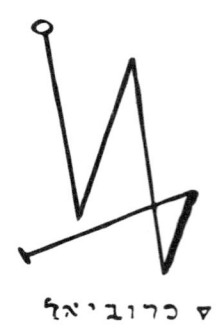

כרוביאל

Ofaniel (Air): The Chief of the Order of Thrones or Celestial Wheels, and ruler of the celestial wheel of the moon.

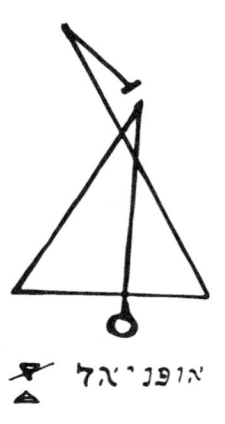

אופניאל

Yofiel (Earth): The Angel of divine beauty and the angelic prince of the Torah, the guardian and guide of written scriptures and the mysteries of the word.

יופיאל

The images—or *imago,* as I call it—which further characterize these Super-Archangels, can be found in the Archetypal Gate Ritual and do not need to be further clarified here.

ORDEALS OF TRANSFIGURATION

If you carefully read over the sections of the ritual patterns, you will see that the combination of rituals in the Lunar Ordeal will cause a profound transformation to occur in the operator who faithfully performs it.

The foundation of this working consists of the tabernacle of the Holy Ogdoad, consisting of the fused invocations of the eight Super-Archangels and the Element Godhead. That by itself is a powerfully sacralized temple environment, but it is only the base of the working. That base is overlaid with the Triple Tetrahedral Gate and the Gate of Ascension, opening the temple to the direct impact and influence of the Absolute Godhead. Within that gateway structure, the operator ascends the four Qabalistic Worlds to a fifth level above it, and in that sacred portal temple, performs the Bornless One invocation rite. With the inclusion of the Hierogamy rite of Union and armed with the consecrated wedding ring of the Higher Self, the Bornless Envisioning rite completes the overall ordeal.

These rituals alone would cause a profound transfiguration in anyone performing them as a combined working. To this collection, we also add the liturgical devotions, meditations, prayers, fasting, purification, and sequestration. While I have covered the rituals in detail, I need to discuss the liturgical obligations of this working.

Underlying all of these rituals and their consecutive performance are the liturgical practices that are also an important requirement. How the magician approaches this working, their attitude, and how they comport themselves during the working is critically important to the success of the operation. A successful outcome requires a strong spiritual alignment to a specific Deity or set of Deities. Realizing that all Deities ultimately merge into a single unnamed Unity that has no definition nor characteristics make this working intelligible to Pagans, Witches, or those of a monotheistic persuasion. Piety, devotion, love of God, and purity of intent are the spiritual foundation for this working.

To keep the spiritual intensity as high as it can be, the operator is required to perform daily sessions of meditation, votive offerings, prayers, and the purification of body and mind, fasting and foregoing sleep on occasion. The operator needs to develop a single-minded approach to the objective, where all else fades into the background. This leads to the three-day sequestration, where the complete omission of any interaction (except with those of one's household) and blocking out all distractions will greatly assist the operator in obtaining the correct mind state to successfully conclude the ordeal. There are other liturgical practices required, such as the Mass and Benediction rites that are performed to empower and sacralize the environment and spiritual fortify the operator.

When these liturgical practices are joined with the scheduled ritual performances, I am certain that most people will experience some degree of transfiguration. Also, it should be noted that transfigurations are not a one-time event in the life of the operator. There are levels to this kind of experience, and those who perform it can experience either crossing the lesser abyss or the Greater Abyss. Full enlightenment is possible, and even achieving a kind of God-mind, either briefly or even permanently, can be achieved. While the traditional Abramelin working is thought to be performed just once in a lifetime, the Lunar Ordeal can be performed repeatedly over a magician's lifetime to gain ever greater transfigurations and a more permanent possession of full enlightenment.

As you can see, the potential for this Lunar Ordeal is considerable. Therefore, it is a worthy challenge to anyone who seeks to gain a higher conscious state or achieve the vista of a higher state of permanent being.

An Important Note: When I performed the Lunar Ordeal many years ago, I did not do it alone and without any help or participation. I had my beloved wife to assist me, and as it turned out, if she would not have been there to help, I would likely have failed to complete the ordeal as planned. She was instrumental in helping me to complete this series of intense workings, providing me with help and assistance, witnessing the rites, providing me with food and drink, and keeping a watchful eye on me. Without her help, I would have found this ordeal to be too difficult to complete. What I am saying is that you shouldn't attempt this working unless you have at least one person to help you, and, in fact, a few more wouldn't be a bad idea to consider. While this is a very private and intimate working, it is beneficial for someone else to witness it as it is happening and help objectify it for the one undergoing it.

CHAPTER TWO

Circle Consecration Rites

In the style of magic that I use, there is always a ritual to consecrate the magical temple to start any working with a sacralized environment. This is particularly true if the magical working is strategic or part of an ordeal. For the Abramelin Lunar Ordeal, I employ two custom rituals to consecrate and empower the temple prior to performing the main of body of rituals for that evening's working. These two rituals are the Consecration of the Enochian Star Temple and the Consecration of the Temple of the Magna Dea, or Great Goddess. These rituals are taken from the arsenal of rituals written for use by the Order of the Gnostic Star, and the authors are Frater Arjuna and me for the two rituals, respectively.

The baseline or common circle consecration rite used in most of the rituals for the Ordeal is the Enochian Star Temple. The Bornless One invocation rite uses the Temple of the Magna Dea and is, therefore, considered a more specialized ritual. The first five weekends consist of performing the rituals that invoke the Seraph and Cherub pairs and the Element Godhead, so these will employ the Enochian Star Temple. The Bornless suite of rituals uses the Temple of the Magna Dea, which is the difference between their use. It should be noted that the Temple of the Magna Dea has the Celebrant as a priestess due to the respect paid to the Goddess, but anyone might perform this ritual for the Ordeal.

Of course, you can employ, modify, or replace any ritual that you feel will prepare the magical temple for these workings. However, I felt that it was important to provide the rituals that I used in this Ordeal for you to examine and consider.

Consecrating a temple is an elaborate ritual based on the simple circle consecration rite that most modern Pagans and Witches use to sacralize their environment and make it fit for the Gods to reveal themselves at that place between worlds. Since I am a Witch and a ritual magician, I have sought to expand the basic lore that I was given so that it has a greater utility. Since these rituals are based on the simple rite of the circle consecration, I don't feel the need to examine them in any detail, although I will do that for other, more complex rituals used in the Ordeal.

CONSECRATION OF THE ENOCHIAN STAR TEMPLE

Introit

The magician stands before the altar, rings the bell five times, and then intones the following:

In ancient times, long before the rise of humankind's civilization, unity became duality and war was waged throughout the Inner Planes between the powers of light and darkness. Thus, duality and its eternal conflict came into being. The forces of light and darkness each included four hundred stellar beings, called angels by the ancients. Separate from these beings, a third force existed of four hundred angels who remembered the state of unity and who chose to transcend the duality of light and darkness. They became the Stellar Guardians of the Graal, the Keepers of the Divine Gnosis—that towards which we aspire.

Generation of the Aqua Sancta

The magician first charges the water contained in the chalice which rests upon the altar. They then state:

In the name of the Stellar Guardians of the divine wisdom, I bless the water contained in this chalice. May it become sacred as the flowing waters of the infinite cosmic sea.

The magician next charges the salt which rests upon the pentacle, saying:

I bless the salt upon this pentacle with the divine force of Gnosis that transcends all polarities. May it embody the strength of formation.

The magician then mixes the consecrated salt and water, charges it, and intones:

The divine magic of Chenok is the perfect union of opposites. The mixing of the sacred salt and water is the first act of uniting the polarities, as the creation of a Holy Elixir, which shall consecrate this Stellar Temple.

Purification by the Elements

The magician or, if present, those assisting consecrate the perimeter and center of the circle, proceeding deosil starting in the East, with the symbols of the Elements: holy water, incense, and candlelight. The magician then states:

The aeons passed and humanity proceeded to evolve. As we increased our capabilities, the conflicting forces of light and darkness utilized us as pawns in their struggle. The Stellar Guardians of the Graal, who wished to assist the process of human evolution and free us from ignorance, sent two hundred of their number to the earth. Bringing with them the fire of Divine Wisdom, the Nephilim descended upon the earth and taught humankind the sacred art of magic, the secrets of the stellar realms, and the blessings of the Elements.

The Ring of Fire

Taking the sword, the magician draws an arc around the perimeter of the circle, proceeding deosil starting in the East, projecting a fiery energy from the point of the sword. The magician intones:

Humanity was not prepared to receive the ancient stellar wisdom of the Nephilim. We abused the powers, using the highest magic for petty purposes and to gain control over others. Great magical battles were fought, and a contagion of evil covered the earth. The Stellar Lords, seeing mankind's folly, dispatched four mighty Archangels who sealed the Nephilim and their magical arts in the dimensions between worlds—where they silently wait for our coming. To once again acquire the ancient Star Lore of the Nephilim, we must prove ourselves worthy. Having done so, we will be given the keys to unlock the stellar gates and commune with the Keepers of the Divine Wisdom.

Establishing the Watchtowers

The magician proceeds and stands before the eastern altar, makes the sign of Air, and intones the word *Lehusanu* (sky). The magician then draws an invoking pentagram of Air and charges it with an invoking spiral while intoning the name of the Elemental King *Tahaoeloji*. The magician then says:

I summon the whole of the Tablet of Air, who is envisioned as a Great Circle on whose hands rest the twelve vast Celestial Kingdoms. Teach us the mysteries of Air, which are equanimity and balance, healing, and compassion for others. Deem us worthy to receive the first key so we may attain the secrets of the high star magic.

The magician proceeds and stands before the southern altar, makes the sign of Fire, and intones the word *Malperegi* (Fire). The magician then draws an invoking pentagram of Fire and charges it with an invoking spiral while intoning the name of the Elemental King *Ohooohaatan*. The magician then says:

I summon the whole of the Tablet of Fire, who is envisioned as the Spirits of the Fourth Angle, who are mighty in the firmament of waters and are a torment to the wicked and a garland to the righteous. Teach us the mysteries of Fire, which are openness to divine wisdom and illumination. Purify us with your flames and grant that we are worthy to receive the second key so we may unlock the stellar gates and pass into the realms of the star lords.

The magician proceeds and stands before the western altar, makes the sign of Water, and intones the word *Zodinu* (Water). The magician then draws an invoking pentagram of

Water and charges it with an invoking spiral while intoning the name of the Elemental King *Thahebyobeeatan*. The magician then says:

I summon the whole of the Tablet of Water, who is envisioned as thirty-three Thunderers of Increase who reign in the Second Angle. Teach us the mysteries of Water, which are love, devotion, and selfless service. Aid us in our deepest meditations so we may become connected with the source of all consciousness. Help us attain the ecstatic states of being that reveal to us the third key to the gates of stellar awareness.

The magician proceeds and stands before the northern altar, makes the sign of Earth, and intones the holy word *Faregite* (Domain or Land). The magician then draws an invoking pentagram of Earth and charges it with an invoking spiral while intoning the name of the Elemental King *Thahaaotahe*. The magician then says:

I summon the whole of the Tablet of Earth, who is envisioned as a Mount of Olives looking with gladness upon the third angle. Teach us the mysteries of Earth, which are centeredness and inner contemplation, so we can hear the silent voice of the inner self. Make manifest the fourth key which shall allow us to enter the in-between spaces, the inner dimensions of our being.

Unity of the Center

The magician approaches the center of the circle, facing East, makes the sign Osiris Risen, and intones *Eheieh* (holy name of Kether). The magician then draws a pentagram of spirit receptive to the Infrapoint and a pentagram of spirit creative to the Ultrapoint, drawing an invoking spiral around each while intoning *Enubeha*. The magician then unites the Infrapoint and Ultrapoint into a central pylon and says:

Through learning the virtues of the Mysteries of the Four Enochian Tablets, we are given the keys to understanding the self. It is the underlying unity of the four Elemental Tablets that bestows upon us the fifth key to the stellar reaches. When we unite the four Elements within ourselves, we truly become human. And in becoming human, we can attain the stars.

The magician then faces the West and makes the Opening Portal Gesture and intones:

The expanse of stars reveals itself! We rush towards the stellar threshold! Come to us, O Star Lords of the Nephilim! We call upon you, Shemichaz and Azael, Lords of the Aralim! Teach us your secrets, reveal to us our inner selves, help us attain the celestial spiritual heights!

Ol Vinu Il-micalazoda De A-el Das Trian-odo A-aiyon De Oresa Antar A-comiselahot Azonezoda. Odo Cicale-qaa Ta Lorasalaq Pamabit-ol-i Noromi Aoiveae-ot Goholor-te Od Cahirlan-te! Do A-omaos De Yadnah! A-lanash-i ca Ol-mononas Ol-balam Do Ol-owanoanim Od Do-ol-gahe!

(I invoke the Powers of the First, which shall open the Gate of Darkness beyond the Spirals of the Azonei. Open thy Mystery like a flower. Unto me is the Star Child Reborn and Resurrected! In the Name of the Unity of Being, the Power is on my heart, my lips, in my eyes, and in my soul!)

The rite is completed.

CONSECRATION OF THE TEMPLE OF THE MAGNA DEA

Introit

The priestess stands before the altar, rings the bell seven times, and then intones the following:

Strange curves; and every Curve a Number woven into a Musical and Harmonious Pattern.

Such was the design showed me by my friend when first we met.

It was like an exchange of greetings by means of an inward recognition.

Oh! Could I but grasp the Ever-changing Design of Thy Star Body, Mother of Heaven!

Yet it is written: "Every man and every woman is a star. Every number is infinite; there is no difference."

Such then is Life, for those who love Thee: Strange Curves, and every Curve a Number woven into a Musical and Harmonious Design.[36]

Generation of the Aqua Sancta

The priestess first charges the water contained in the chalice which rests upon the altar. She then states:

I bless the water held in this blessed Chalice of the Holy Goddess, so that it is transformed into the water of life, bringing renewal to all.

The priestess next charges the salt which rests upon the pentacle, saying:

I bless the salt that lies upon this sacred Pentacle of the Holy Goddess, so that it is imbued with power and charged with the fortification of all life.

---

36 Achad, Frater, *XXXI Hymns to the Star Goddess Who is Not* (W. Ransom, 1923) p. 15.

The priestess then mixes the consecrated salt and water, charges it, and intones:

> *Thus is the water of life joined with the salt of continued existence, and therein is made the Holy Brine from which all life on this world arose—and therein is the divine joining of the marriage of feminine with masculine, the source of eternal renewal and sacramentation.*

Purification by the Elements

The priestess, or if present, those assisting, consecrate the perimeter and center of the circle, proceeding deosil starting in the East, with the symbols of the Elements: holy water, incense, and candlelight. The priestess then states:

> *I bless this sacred space with the essence of the sacraments of creation—the lustral water, the perfumed essence of the flower of life, and the light of knowing, that which embraces them and makes them one.*

The Ring of Sacred Light

Taking the sword, the priestess draws an arc around the perimeter of the circle, projecting a fiery energy from with her transmutar wand, proceeding deosil starting in the East. The priestess intones:

> *O Circle of Sacred light that I send out from my heart, the source of all love and the seat of the soul, I make this place of purity and light, the shrine of my spirit, and the place of repose of my mind, so that all work accomplished herein shall be released in both heaven and Earth, and cause the Grace of the Great Goddess to bless us and make us wise and full of wondrous life—the mystery of the Love of the Spirit, and the One Mind that encompasses and protects us. So mote it be.*

Establishing the Pylons of Light

The priestess proceeds and faces the Eastern altar, makes the sign of Air, and intones the holy Name *On* (Strength). The priestess then draws an invoking pentagram of Air and charges it with an invoking spiral while intoning *Exarepe*. The priestess then draws an inverted invoking pentagram of spirit receptive above the invoking Elemental pentagram and draws both devices together with an invoking spiral. The priestess then says:

> *O Airy Virtue of the Great Goddess—Sthenathea, the strength of the will and the seat of manifested power is thy goodness to bestow. We open our hearts to your gifts and presents.*

Heihazay Heihazar Samy Zamyn Helihel Samahelihel Siloth Silereht Gezemathal Iecroronay.[37]

The Power of the Yod is joined with the Tetrahedral Gate of Fire to forge the Great Sword of Power—or Veritis Gladius (Sword of Truth), a true weapon of the Holy and Sacred Gnostic Magician. The Gate of Fire has purified my Will, and all spurious and deceitful works are herein cast aside, and the True Will of the Holy Guardian Angel is herein empowered and projected into the world!

The priestess proceeds and faces the southern altar, makes the sign of Fire, and intones the holy name *Bachirot* (Chosen). The priestess then draws an invoking pentagram of Fire and charges it with an invoking spiral while intoning *Biatome*. Then, the priestess draws an inverted invoking pentagram of spirit receptive above the invoking Elemental pentagram and draws both devices together with an invoking spiral. The priestess then says:

O Fiery Virtue of the Great Goddess—Elekta, the Chosen and Consecrated Women of the Grace of the Goddess, those who create life, give ecstasy, and also death. We open our hearts to your gifts and presents.

Messamarathon Gezomothon Ezomathon Haihatha Hagibar Hagihar Hagiathar Haihatha, Lethasiel Lechisihel Gethiduhal.[38]

The Power of the Double Wand of Power is thus activated. I draw the double powers of the Brilliant Vortex and the Dark Cone of Power, and therefore, in this wand that I hold are the forces of Light and Darkness tightly bound so that they are one. The Yod-lode is the thunderbolt of the Great God, the Power of the Father of Fire, and the Primal Emanation of Creation!

The priestess proceeds and faces the western altar, makes the sign of Water, and intones the holy name *Ahavah* (Love). The priestess then draws an invoking pentagram of Water and charges it with an invoking spiral while intoning *Hecomea*. The priestess then draws an inverted invoking pentagram of spirit receptive above the invoking Elemental pentagram and draws both devices together with an invoking spiral. The priestess then says:

O Watery Virtue of the Great Goddess—Philathea, the Power and Grace of Spiritual Love, the Love of God, and the Love of the Union of God—these two paths spring from a common source—one emanates from the Heart of the Spirit, and the other emanates from the Soul of Humanity. We open our hearts to your gifts and presents.

---

37 Peterson, Joseph, *The Sworn Book of Honorius*, p. 153, starting at the twenty-first word.
38 Peterson, *op. cit.*, p. 153, starting at the first word.

Geguhay Iethonay Samazaraht Samazarel Zamazthel Sergomazar Hazomathan Hazothynathon Iesomathon Iezochor.[39]

I invoke and reveal the Double-Vortices of the Womb Matrix—the Grail of Power, the inner and outer vortices of the mysteries of Sophia, that conjoined shall act as my most Holy Vault of the Adepts. This chalice of the Grail that resides upon the altar trigon of the Greater Mysteries, contains the elixir of the Feminine Spirit—may it become for all who partake of it the salvation of inequality, and the redemption of all erroneous presumptions. Through it we are all profoundly inspired by the hidden truth!

The priestess proceeds and faces the northern altar, makes the sign of Earth, and intones the holy name *Shoftot* (Judges). The priestess then draws an invoking pentagram of Earth and charges it with an invoking spiral while intoning *Nanutea*. The priestess then draws an inverted invoking pentagram of spirit receptive above the invoking Elemental pentagram and draws both devices together with an invoking spiral. The priestess then says:

O Earthy Virtue of the Great Goddess—Dikasthea—the Divine Wisdom that knows the difference between the path of goodness and the path of dissolution. Thus all are judged by the shrewd eye of She who is the Judge of Fate, and the knower of the One Way to Spiritual Union. We open our hearts to your gifts and presents.

Iecomenay Samyhahel Hesemyhel Secozomay Secozomay Sedomasay Sethothamay Samna Rabihathos Hamnos Hamnas—Amen.[40]

Thus is the Aegis of the Masters, Crown of Glory, Holy Octagon Shield of Power; I set forth and establish the base of all powers, wherein the magus has defined their domain and (planted therein his seed into the Egg of the World/received into her egg the Seed of the Holy Spirit/rejoiced in their union of life). And the Dragon of the World Tree shall encircle this place, and the Great Goddess shall bless it with life and eternal renewal. In this sacred place are formulated the Dawn Creation of all Kings, in this place is Eden and Paradise, the Blood and Host of the True Graal, the Cornucopia and Cauldron of Rebirth. The Wisdom of the Structure of the Emanation of Spirit is herein given as a Gnosis of Spirit and Mind conjoined—the Universal Intelligence.

This power wards, protects and guides the seeker on the path to realization and awards them the mastery of life—the Keys to Heaven, Earth and Hell are herein given to the wise mage who knows the Mystery of the Grail—the three Questions and their Answers.

---

39 Peterson, *op. cit.*, p. 153, starting at the tenth word.
40 Peterson, *op. cit.*, p. 153, starting at the thirtieth word.

Unity of the Center

The priestess approaches the center of the circle, makes the sign Osiris Risen, and intones *Eheieh* (holy name of Kether). The priestess then draws an invoking pentagram of spirit creative to the Infrapoint and an invoking pentagram of spirit receptive to the Ultrapoint, drawing an invoking spiral around each, while intoning *Enubeha*. The priestess then unites the Infrapoint and Ultrapoint into a central pylon through her body, and says:

Sthenathia, Elekta, Philathea and Dikasthea—The Virtues of Strength, Consecration, Spiritual Love, and Judgement are given through the Priestesses of Light, the Soul of Magna Dea. We weave this pattern for the Love of the Spirit, and that which draws us into Union!

The Emerald Eye of Lucifer, Jewel Star of Gnosis, Crystal Stone of Sion is the Fifth Graal, which is the amalgamation of the Vortex Power Fields of the Tetrapatron: the Four Powers of Tetra-sacramentary of Gnosis. Through this Eye are all mysteries revealed; through this Jewel are all awards, honors, and accolades given, the highest rank of the master adept; through this Stone are all other symbols of the Graal derived—their virtues and powers. The Sacred Seven Stellar Gnostic Rays shine through the abyss of all time and space, radiating upon us all their glories and wisdom. Thus is the sacrament of the Stars, the One True Vision of all that was and shall ever be—and that which is Nought. We seek the Power and Vision of the Spirit of God, through the aegis of the Bornless One, who is known and never known, understood, and inexplicable, the mystery and the manifestation of the single individual sentient being—the Sorcerer of Time and Space—and the myriad infinite beings that have been and always shall ever be—the One that is eternal and unfathomable.

The priestess then makes the Opening Portal Gesture and intones:

Long have I lain and waited for Thee in the Rose Garden of Life; yet ever Thou withholdest Thyself from mine understanding. As I laid, I contemplated Thy nature as that of an Infinite Rose. Petals, petals, petals…but where, O Beauteous One, is Thy Heart? Hast Thou no heart? Are Thy petals Infinite so that I may never reach the Core of Thy Being? Yet, Thou hast said: "I love you! I yearn to you! Pale or purple, veiled or voluptuous, I who am all pleasure and purple, and drunkenness of the innermost sense, desire you: come unto me!" Yea! Mine innermost sense is drunken; it is intoxicated upon the Dew of the Rose. Thy Heart is my Heart; there is no difference, O Beloved. When I shall have penetrated to the Heart of Thine Infinite Rose, there shall I find Myself. But I shall never come to myself—only to Thee.[41]

---

41 Achad, *op. cit.*, p. 11.

Ol Vinu Il-micalazoda De A-el Das Trian-odo A-aiyon De Oresa Antar A-comiselahot Azonezoda. Odo Cicale-qaa Ta Lorasalaq Pamabit-ol-i Noromi Aoiveae-ot Goholor-te Od Cahirlan-te! Do A-omaos De Yadnah! A-lanash-i ca Ol-mononas Ol-balam Do Ol-owanoanim Od Do-ol-gahe!

(I invoke the Powers of the First, which shall open the Gate of Darkness beyond the Spirals of the Azonei. Open thy Mystery like a flower. Unto me is the Star Child Reborn and Resurrected! In the Name of the Unity of Being, the Power is on my heart, my lips, in my eyes, and in my soul!)

The rite is completed.

CHAPTER THREE

ARCHETYPAL GATE RITUAL FOR INVOKING THE CHERUBIM, SERAPHIM, AND ELEMENT GODHEADS

THIS RITUAL IS USED TO INVOKE one of the Element Godheads, the Seraphim, or the Cherubim. The act of invoking any one of these spiritual entities is a very serious endeavor. The magician is advised to prepare for this working by performing, at the very least, a light fast, a period of atonement, and mental purification not less than twenty-four hours before the rite is to begin. The magician's intention should be very lofty, selfless, and deeply pious, so as not to offend the invoked Godhead entities.

The rite consists of two consecutive rituals: the Qabalistic Pyramid of Power Ritual set to the Qabalistic World of Atziluth, and the Archetypal Gate Ritual, which is used to perform the invocation of the Element Godhead or the Super-Archangelic entries.

INTRODUCTION

The shortened Qabalistic Pyramid of Power Ritual is used to create a base for the Archetypal Gate. This is accomplished through invoking the world of Atziluth, which is the domain of the Godhead and Super-Archangels: the Seraphim and Cherubim. Because the Archetypal Gate invokes one of the four Element Godheads or the eight Super-Archangels, the establishment of Atziluth as a Qabalistic World foundation assists the process of establishing the Element gateway for the invocation. It joins the Qabalistic World with the Elemental Gate. The differentiation between the Godhead and the Super-Archangels is defined through the subtle use of the invocation pentagram of spirit, whether receptive (feminine) or creative (masculine), set to the pylon established at each watchtower.

The pattern of this ritual consists of the creation of pylons in each watchtower and the center of the circle. The pylon structure consists of an Element base (invoking pentagram of Fire for Atziluth) and a spiritual qualifier (invoking pentagram of spirit), which is either creative or receptive depending upon whether the Godhead or the Super-Archangel is being invoked. The center of the invoking staff established in the center of the circle is qualified with either a hexagrammic cross (Seraphim), pentagrammic cross (Cherubim), or trigon cross (Godhead).

The Archetypal Gate uses an inverted pentagram qualified pylon ritual structure set to the Infrapoint to direct and concentrate the energy of the Qabalistic World, which it covers so that the gateway can be resolved through the manifestation of the Super-Archangelic Intelligence or the Element Godhead, which is based on the four-fold Tetragrammaton.

The basic structure of this ritual is where the center of the circle is set with an inverted invoking pentagram of spirit receptive (representing the descending Holy Spirit bestowing its blessings) and surrounded by a vortex consisting of the four circle angles arrayed in the pattern of a crossroads, and each point is set with a simple hexagram device. Then, a specific gateway is erected that manifests the Godhead and ultimate Super-Archangelic levels within it. There is a total of four Gates that the magician may utilize, one for each of the Four Elements of the Godhead or Super-Archangelic Intelligence, yet all four Element gateways are eastern gateways, with the qualifying Element established through an invoking pentagram set to the Mesopoint.

ARCHETYPAL GATE RITUAL FOR THE QABALISTIC WORLD ATZILUTH

The Celebrant performs the Consecration of the Enochian Star Temple, then begins with the working.

QABALISTIC ELEMENT PYRAMID OF ATZILUTH

The Celebrant proceeds to the eastern watchtower and therein bows and gives salute. The Celebrant draws the invoking pentagram of Fire and intones the letter *Aleph*, projecting a golden energy into the pentagram. The Celebrant then draws the invoking pentagram of spirit creative or receptive above the Element pentagram and fuses it to the element pentagram with an invoking spiral. The Celebrant says:

> *Aleph— the beginning of all creation was the Light which illuminated the darkness and caused self-realization! The First Thought of consciousness was the primal "I am," and this thought, when uttered within the Mind of All, became the cause of all subsequent manifestation! Thus, we seek the primordial cause in order to understand the mystery of our own creation.*

The Celebrant proceeds to the southern watchtower and therein bows and gives salute. The Celebrant draws the invoking pentagram of Fire and intones the letter *Heh*, projecting a scarlet energy into the pentagram. The Celebrant then draws above the Element pentagram the invoking pentagram of spirit creative/receptive and fuses it to the Element pentagram with an invoking spiral. The Celebrant says:

Heh—the symbolic image within the thought has given birth to the concept of "I am," for to utter "I am" is to make a distinction between that which one is and is not. The separation between subject and object is embodied within the image of the Self. For the image presages the form and thus establishes the transformation of unity into multiplicity.

The Celebrant proceeds to the western watchtower and therein bows and gives salute. The Celebrant draws the invoking pentagram of Fire and intones the letter *Yod*, projecting an azure energy into the pentagram. The Celebrant then draws the invoking pentagram of spirit creative/receptive above the Element pentagram and fuses it to the Element pentagram with an invoking spiral. The Celebrant says:

Yod—the Will of the Primary Cause seeks union within itself, fusing the "I am" within the "I am not." The subject and object have joined as the primordial state, but within this union are engendered new creations and the multiplicity of objects surrounding the "I am." This is the beginning of the process of emanations, wherein the symbolic structure of the consciousness of God is given expression—Fiat Lux!

The Celebrant proceeds to the northern watchtower and therein bows and gives salute. The Celebrant draws the invoking pentagram of Fire and intones the letter *Heh*, projecting a green energy into the pentagram. Above the Element pentagram, the Celebrant then draws the invoking pentagram of spirit creative/receptive and fuses it to the Element pentagram with an invoking spiral. The Celebrant says:

Heh—the Body of the Absolute consists of the emanations and their symbolic contents. For although the absolute consists of distinct emanations, they are part of a unity which expresses the Infinite Body of God. For each emanation contains its own identity ("I am"), yet is locked in the eternal state of union wherein the "I am" is coincidental. Thus is the mystery of the form of the Absolute—each unique individual is expressed as the embodiment of the whole without division!

The Celebrant proceeds to the center of the circle and therein bows and gives salute. The Celebrant draws the invoking pentagram of Fire to the Infrapoint and intones the letter *Lamed*, projecting a violet energy into the pentagram. The Celebrant then draws, in the Ultrapoint, the invoking pentagram of spirit creative/receptive and intones the letter *Aleph*, projecting a brilliant energy into it. They fuse the two pentagrams with an invoking spiral, thus creating the central pylon. The Celebrant says:

The source and origin of all manifestation exists in the center, the core of the confluence of all realities. The magician as God stands in the center of the universe, contemplating all creation. For the name of the center is the primordial name of all names which in its essence knows no distinctions nor any differences—it is the name of unity itself! Thus, the magician invokes through the ineffable name, EL, and all manifestation follows.

The Celebrant then proceeds to draw the four watchtowers to the Ultrapoint in the order North, West, South, and East, using the sword. They proceed to the center of the circle and face South, saying the following:

Aleph, Heh, Yod, Heh—Ehieh!—I shall be! Behold, the image of Atziluth, a World of the Holy Qabalah! Therein shall you find the individual awareness of selfhood which precipitated all creation—the primordial "I am!" For the core of all being consists of the knowledge of the self, which distinguishes itself from all that is subject to it. Everything that exists in consciousness is based upon the precepts of the definition of the individual self! The "I am" which promises to become is the identity of potential from which all future creation occurs. Yet, the individual Self is never static, but ever-changing and transforming. However, the individuality of God represents the source of all spiritual change, but is itself unchanged and undisturbed by the continuous emanation of its Being!

Archetypal Gate: Setting the Crossroads Pylon Vortex

The Celebrant, standing in the center of the circle, salutes the eastern and western watchtowers and draws an inverted pentagram of spirit receptive in the center of the circle in the Infrapoint, intoning the letter *Aleph* and charging it with a white energy, saying:

The internalization of consciousness reveals the hidden Spiritual Domain that lies deep within the Self. To be a magician, it's necessary for the spiritual Self to awaken so that one becomes aware of the powers of the archetypal mind and is able to harness them as an instrument of transformation.

The Celebrant proceeds deosil to the southeastern angle and draws a simple hexagram and charges it with a violet energy, intoning the letter *A'ain* and saying:

The Spiritual Domain is the Secret House of the Mysteries. The Mind of All shall possess it and fill it with wisdom, life, and power. The wise mage is open to its influences and walks humbly within its hallways; the fool sees their reflection and thinks it a god.

The Celebrant proceeds directly across the center of the circle to the northwestern angle, drawing a simple hexagram, charging it with a violet energy, intoning the letter *Nun*, and saying:

The continuous process of conscious transformation is realized through the progress of spiritual growth. But the greatest rite is where the false self is sacrificed upon the snow-white marble altar in the House of the Mysteries. Only then is the true self revealed as the Eternal and Immortal Light that existed in the beginning—the Bornless One.

The Celebrant proceeds deosil to the northeastern angle and draws a simple hexagram, charging it with a violet energy, intoning the letter *Daleth*, and saying:

Archetypal Gate Ritual for Invoking the Cherubim, Seraphim, and Element Godheads

The Spirit of Life manifests throughout all time and space and shines forth with a golden light for those who have learned to see the world without bias or self-deceit. All of nature is but a manifestation of the pure and the whole Union of Being, and that the realization of this fact begins the process of the grand illumination.

The Celebrant proceeds directly to the southwestern angle, drawing a simple hexagram, charging it with a violet energy, intoning the letter *Gimmel*, and saying:

The guiding powers of our Godhead lead us to the sacred place of union beyond all suffering or pain. Yet the Source of Life and Death transcends individual and mortal self-consciousness. We as magi seek to know this source, and it in turn reaches out to us and assists us to see the truth in all matters.

The Celebrant circumambulates the circle once widdershins, beginning and ending in the southwestern angle. They then proceed directly to the center of the circle and draw in the Ultrapoint a simple hexagram and charge it with a violet fluid. Then, the Celebrant draws a line of force from the Infrapoint up to the Ultrapoint, joining both nodes together. They then draw each of the angles together through the Ultrapoint with the transmutar wand, starting in the southwestern angle and proceeding widdershins. In this manner, the Celebrant expands the hexagrammic vortex into an ascending wave. They say:

Nun, Aleph, Gimmel, Daleth, A'ain—Na Gada'a! (Pray! He is broken!)

The power of manifestation shines through the Gate of the Inverted Star. It is the Holy Spirit shedding forth its grace and bounty upon the seekers who wait below. Thus is the formula for the powers which move and transform us, which cause us to see and to know. Thus, we are shown the spiritual path and in what manner we should walk upon it.

Then the Celebrant intones the appropriate Enochian Invocation for the first time, chanting the Name of the Godhead or Super-Archangel repeatedly.

Establishing the Elemental Gateway

The Celebrant then chooses the Elemental gateway, which represents the further qualification of the Archetype, and performs the respective Gate Formula for it. Notice that the gateways all face the East and represent an ascent out of darkness.

Elemental Gate of Fire

The Celebrant sets the three talismanic gate keys along with a Tarot Trump: one in the southwest angle (The Sun XIX), one in the eastern watchtower (Strength XI), and one in the northwest angle (Art XIV). The Celebrant then meditates on the Tarot cards, building up the energies and noting the significance of the Gate Tarot Trumps. The Celebrant then stands in the West, facing the East.

The Celebrant draws a trapezoidal cross and seals it with an invoking spiral in the southwestern angle, charging the gate key therein, and says:

[Atu XIX] The sleeper must awaken! The dead must become resurrected! The blind must see! For when the light has illuminated the sky of one's aspirations and established the new dawn of potentiality, the initiate can't ignore what is revealed and must act upon it.

The Celebrant draws a trapezoidal cross and seals it with an invoking spiral in the eastern watchtower, charging the gate key therein, and says:

[Atu XI] When the eyes are opened and perceive the truth, the compassion of the Bornless One sunders the false self and possesses the soul of the seeker. This is the task that is achieved by being passive and steadfast in one's spiritual alignment. The power of this vision passes through the adept and reveals the light of truth, but it sweeps the unworthy aside into the well of madness.

The Celebrant draws a trapezoidal cross and seals it with an invoking spiral in the northwestern angle, charging the gate key therein, and says:

[Atu XIV] The vision has come and gone, leaving the seeker filled with its power and beauty. Yet the seeker shall always recall and remember what has transpired. The task is to translate this visionary experience so that its essence may be captured and used to build a symbol that will transform the world.

The Celebrant then draws an invoking pentagram of Fire and projects it into the Mesopoint in the center of the circle.

The Celebrant then takes the transmutar wand and draws the three nodes of the gate structure together through the center of the circle in the Ultrapoint. They then draw an exterior circle, unifying the three nodes of the gate within its arc.

The Celebrant makes the sign of the parting of the threshold while standing in the West and facing the East; then, they advance through the gate to the center of the circle. The Celebrant says:

Shin—The Vision is the Light Which Reveals!
Tet—The Vision is the Power Which Inspires!
Samekh—The Seeker Translates the Vision into Knowledge!
Shin—Tet—Samekh—Shatas!

The Spirit of Enlightenment is the Gate of Fire which illuminates and reveals the hidden inner truth of life. The seeker must invoke the vision, realizing all that which

Archetypal Gate Ritual for Invoking the Cherubim, Seraphim, and Element Godheads

is revealed. Then the seeker must translate this vision using the symbols and myths that are at hand and weave them together to form a ritual matrix. This tool, forged in the Temple of the Mysteries, shall allow that vision to become realized by all those who are initiated into its mystery.

Elemental Gate of Water

The Celebrant sets the three talismanic gate keys along with a Tarot Trump: one in the southwest angle (Death XIII), one in the eastern watchtower (The High Priestess II), and one in the northwest angle (The Lovers VI), with the appropriate Tarot Trumps placed on each. The Celebrant then meditates on the Tarot cards, building up the energies and noting the significance of the Gate Tarot Trumps. The Celebrant then stands in the West, facing the East.

The Celebrant draws a trapezoidal cross and seals it with an invoking spiral in the southwestern angle, charging the gate key therein, and says:

[Atu XIII] The end of delusion has come, and with it is change and the beginning of renewal! The ignorant fear death but the wise perceive it merely as another sustainable change. Through death is unleashed the forces of Light and Liberation, which confers to the mage aware of the Bornless One eternal life in Spirit.

The Celebrant draws a trapezoidal cross and seals it with an invoking spiral in the eastern watchtower, charging the gate key therein and says:

[Atu II] The passion and power of the Holy Feminine Spirit stands at the threshold of worlds and is the guardian of the cauldron of all rebirths. Yet she is the womb and the tomb! She is the one who establishes all fate, apportioning out the thread of life's destiny and cutting it after it has reached its full measure. The potency of our fate can't be thwarted, but only understood and accepted. This knowledge is indeed power!

The Celebrant draws a trapezoidal cross and seals it with an invoking spiral in the northwestern angle, charging the gate key therein, and says:

[Atu VI] The task of the spiritual seeker is to integrate the Light and Darkness of the self into a fusion of wholeness. The higher spiritual self is thus realized, and it becomes the beginning of a true spiritual process of awakening and joining with the Godhead! Yet beware; if one is not whole, then the apprehension of Deity is futile.

The Celebrant then draws an invoking pentagram of Water and projects it into the Mesopoint in the center of the circle.

The Celebrant then takes the transmutar wand and draws the three nodes of the gate structure together through the center of the circle in the Ultrapoint. They then draw an exterior circle, unifying the three nodes of the gate within its arc.

The Celebrant makes the sign of the parting of the threshold, standing in the West and facing the East, then they advance through the gate to the center of the circle. The Celebrant says:

Nun—The Transformation of Life is Through Death.
Gimmel—The Feminine Spirit is the Author of Life.
Zain—The Seeker Becomes Whole and Regenerated!
Nun—Gimmel—Zain—Nagaz!

The Power of Death is revealed as the Spirit of Love and Ecstasy that liberates the spirit from the cares of the body. Thus is the state of cosmic fusion that unites the dark and light within the Microcosm of the self and the Macrocosm of the Universal Mind, which is the fusion of all conscious sentience. This exalted state begins as the simple selfless love of one individual for another and ends in the infinite embrace of the totality of All Being.

Elemental Gate of Air

The Celebrant sets the three talismanic gate keys along with a Tarot Trump: one in the southwest angle (The Magician I), one in the eastern watchtower (The Wheel X), and one in the northwest angle (Adjustment VIII), with the appropriate Tarot Trumps placed on each. The Celebrant then meditates on the Tarot cards, building up the energies and noting the significance of the Gate Tarot Trumps. The Celebrant then stands in the West, facing the East.

The Celebrant draws a trapezoidal cross and seals it with an invoking spiral in the southwestern angle, charging the gate key therein, and says:

[Atu I] The True Will is the ally of the magician and assists the process of becoming single-minded in purpose and pursuit. The mind is thereby finely honed to become a weapon of great power and exacting preciseness. Thus, the magician must always be able to shape and transform the world according to their will.

The Celebrant draws a trapezoidal cross and seals it with an invoking spiral in the eastern watchtower, charging the gate key therein, and says:

[Atu X] The challenge of life is found in its diversity and multiplicity. The simple fact of terrestrial existence is that it is changeable and ephemeral. For every ebb and flow, there is a zenith and a nadir. One must learn to adapt to the highs as well as the lows, knowing that gains made are but fleeting and lost all too soon.

The Celebrant draws a trapezoidal cross and seals it with an invoking spiral in the northwestern angle, charging the gate key therein, and says:

[Atu VIII] The path toward eternity is found in balance. It is the way of nature that excess is leveled by the forces of necessity. Thus, balance is the one true law of nature. To

be balanced, one must be devoid of desire, steadfast but also yielding. In this manner, the mage follows the path of purity and reduction: the Golden Path. The constant waxing and waning of life can't affect the spiritual mind that is aware of everything while holding onto nothing.

The Celebrant then draws an invoking pentagram of Air and projects it into the Mesopoint in the center of the circle.

The Celebrant then takes the transmutar wand and draws the three nodes of the gate structure together through the center of the circle in the Ultrapoint. Then, they draw an exterior circle, unifying the three nodes of the gate within its arc.

The Celebrant makes the sign of the parting of the threshold while standing in the West and facing the East. They then advance through the gate to the center of the circle. The Celebrant says:

Beith—The Power of Magic is the Singular Pursuit!
Kaph—Diversity and Multiplicity is the Challenge of Life!
Lammed—Eternal Balance in the Skill of Masters!
Beith—Kaph—Lammed—Bekal!

The beauty of the perfected True Will is a mirror of the balanced Spirit. The mind is poised but does not dominate the soul, the body, or the mind. In this fashion is revealed the Spirit of Inspiration and Ideas. The Universal Mind is exalted through the glorified power of the True Will that is released and manifested in the Higher Self. The world changes, and empires shall ascend and then crumble into dust, but the spiritual Will of the Godhead is infinite and eternal within the Light of the Thought of All.

Elemental Gate of Earth

The Celebrant sets the three talismanic gate keys along with a Tarot Trump: one in the southwest angle (The Empress III), one in the eastern watchtower (The Chariot VII), and one in the northwest angle (The Universe XXI), with the appropriate Tarot Trumps placed on each. The Celebrant then meditates on the Tarot cards, building up the energies and noting the significance of the Gate Tarot Trumps. The Celebrant then stands in the West, facing the East.

The Celebrant draws a trapezoidal cross and seals it with an invoking spiral in the southwestern angle, charging the gate key therein, and says:

[Atu III] When Spirit merges with the forces of the earth, then shall the sacramentation of matter become realized. The Holy Sacrament is the medium through which one finds the solace of spiritual union, the state where the flesh and blood of the Dying and Resurrecting God fuses with the soul of humanity.

The Celebrant draws a trapezoidal cross and seals it with an invoking spiral in the eastern watchtower, charging the gate key therein, and says:

> [Atu VII] *The Eternal Soul of Life is the arbiter of the secret of immortality. Life is never-ending and forever transforming, but individuals are born and die. We must grasp the thread of life which leads us beyond this existence to others in the infinite chain of transmigrating consciousness. The true self extends through many beings in space and in time, yet all are coexistent and one at the highest level.*

The Celebrant draws a trapezoidal cross and seals it with an invoking spiral in the northwestern angle, charging the gate key therein, and says:

> [Atu XXI] *The Source of Being is never-ending, infinite in magnitude and eternal in duration. It existed before creation, and it shall survive at the end of dissolution. From the Eternal Source is derived all manifestation that has ever been and ever shall be. It's the Well Spring that all seekers must draw from to drink and integrate it into their bodies, thus harnessing the means to fulfill their destiny and that of the whole universe.*

The Celebrant then draws an invoking pentagram of Earth and projects it into the Mesopoint in the center of the circle.

The Celebrant then takes the transmutar wand and draws the three nodes of the gate structure together through the center of the circle in the Ultrapoint. They then draw an exterior circle, unifying the three nodes of the gate within its arc.

The Celebrant makes the sign of the parting of the threshold while standing in the West and facing the East, then advance through the gate to the center of the circle. The Celebrant says:

> *Daleth—The Sacramentation of Matter is Made Manifest.*
> *Chet—The Eternal Soul of Life is Revealed!*
> *Thav—The Source of Being is the Wellspring of the Spirit!*
> *Daleth—Chet—Thav—Dacheth!*

> *The Source of Life is inexhaustible and can become a resource to the seeker who is able to grasp the eternal process of transcendental illumination. Life is eternal yet always mutable. The Spirit of Passion and Life exists as the doorway of materialized being. It represents the effects of ecstasy that manifest the transcendent consciousness of all life—the matrix of living beings and disembodied awareness. The spiritual life is one that is lived in the heightened awareness of the One within the All.*

Establishing the Qabalistic Charge

The Celebrant emerges from the Gate in the center of the circle and bows facing the East, drawing an invoking spiral around the center of the circle. The Celebrant then takes the staff and re-enters the center of the circle, facing the East, holding the staff parallel to the ground. They begin to slowly spin in a counterclockwise direction, ever-increasing the velocity of the spinning until the power is strongly felt. Then the Celebrant stops spinning and places the staff into the center node of the circle. They draw the Infrapoint up through it to the Ultrapoint with their right hand, while the left is holding the staff. Then the Celebrant intones the appropriate Enochian Invocation for the second time, chanting the name of the Godhead or Super-Archangel repeatedly afterwards.

Invocation of the Archetypal Spirit

The Celebrant, still holding the staff in the center of the circle, draws an invoking spiral at the base of the staff and summons the Archetypal Intelligence in the following manner:

I summon the Spirit of the Gate of (Fire, Water, Air, Earth) who shall qualify and quicken the potency of the archetype (name of Godhead or Super-Archangel) and cause it to become manifest! In the names of Iao Sabaoth, Adonai, Abrasax, Ablanathanalba! So mote it be.

The Celebrant then draws an invoking spiral at the top of the staff and summons the Unified Intelligence of the Archetype in the following manner:

I summon the Unified Spirit of Atziluth, which is the origin and creation of the spiritual emanation of the Archetype (name of Godhead or Super-Archangel) and cause it to become manifest! In the names of Iao Sabaoth, Adonai, Abrasax, Ablanathanalba! So mote it be.

The Celebrant then draws either a hexagrammic cross device (Seraph), a pentagrammic cross device (Cherub), or a trigon cross (Godhead) in the center or core of staff.
They then draw the Infrapoint to the Ultrapoint through the staff and thus establishes the Pylon of Sentient Energies. They say:

I invoke the potencies and intelligences of (Super-Archangel or God Name) herein, within this Sacred Gate between the worlds of spirit and matter! I seek to commune with the powers that create and preserve! Come forth and show thyself to me! In the names of Iao Sabaoth, Adonai, Abrasax, Ablanathanalba! So mote it be.

The Celebrant then intones the Invocation of the Super-Archangel or Godhead and describes the nature and characteristics of its being, thereby creating an imago of its spirit to use for contacting and communicating with it.

The Celebrant then intones the Enochian Invocation for the third and final time, then begins to chants the name of the Super-Archangel or Godhead while visualizing its imago and then slowly, with ever-increasing intensity, draws the power of the Super-Archangel or Godhead from the top of the staff down to its base, condensing the Archetypal charge and manifesting it according to the further qualification of the Qabalistic World of Atziluth.

Once the Spirit of the Super-Archangel or Godhead is present, the Celebrant communes with it until it has finally faded away. Then the Celebrant proceeds to the East and makes the closing portal gesture, departing the Gate and sealing the three gate nodes and the eight points of the circle while holding the staff in the left hand. The Archetypal Vortex is now closed, but the Celebrant should remain in the circle and meditate for a period of time until all contact has ended.

The rite is completed.

APPENDIX I

THE CALL OF INVOCATION OF THE TETRAMORPHIC GODHEAD

Ol i-tustinusado a- (Bietome, Hecomea, Exarepe, Nanutea, Enubeha) de a-Gohed-Ancheonas-Gah-de-Iabes, ol-i-umide al a-(Yod, Heh, Vau, Heh) a-Eregohe-Embahzoda-Gah das i-antar tol balcathu od lehuslach! i-Solpeth pamabet ol, il-zarexa od Qishifen; Dapia i-niiso adar ol-butemona od ol-mononas i-olanu-imathazoda od i-eac ca-etharezi. Niisate da-ol, Ic Micalazodim de a-Eregohe-Gohed! Niisate da-ol od i-zamran a-cicale de gi-olna! Do a-dooanim de IAO SABAOTH, ABRASAX, ADONAI, Ol-i-yolacame gi pamabit gi-olna od gi-odoefe!

I summon forth the (Fire, Water, Air, Earth, Spirit) of the One Eternal Spirit of God, I call upon the (Yod, Heh, Vau, Heh) of the Infinite Unified Being who is beyond all Light and Darkness, Good and Evil! Hear me, the Priest and Magician; honey flows from my tongue and my heart is pure and calm. Come to me, O Powers of the Infinite One, come forth and show the Mysteries of thy Manifestation! In the Names of IAO SABAOTH, ABRASAX ADONAI, I bring you to manifestation and revelation.

(Fifty-eight words in this Enochian Call. This call summons the Godhead of the Tetramorph.)

THE CALL OF INVOCATION OF THE TETRAMORPHIC SUPER-ARCHANGEL

Do-a-dooain de (Yod, Heh, Vau, Heh) das i-olna ado a-vohim de ol-soyga od das i-embahzoda ca-ol pamabit a-Eregohe-i-Ovof de a-Lanushim-de-a-Eregohe-Gohed-Anceonas-Gah-de-Iabes; Ol-vinu gi, Ic (Name of Super-Archangel) de Seraphim/ Kerubim, i-zamrante od i-odoefete a-cicale de gi-olna. Ic ilasa das i-a-Iaida-al-gi niisa! Olnate pamabit-ol, lape ol-i-lonushi de Oboleh-de-a-Iabes de Qadah od Ol-i-bahal a-Vanaz—Aran i-trian! Ol-i-umada-gi. Do a-dooanim de IAO SABAOTH, ABRASAX, ADONAI, Niisate!

In the Name of (Yod, Heh, Vau, Heh, Shin) who is manifest through the might of my will and who has joined with unto the Infinite Multiplication of the Powers of the One Eternal Spirit; I summon thee, O (Super-Archangel Name) of the (Seraph/Cherub), to appear and to show the Mysteries of thy Manifestation. O thou who are the Highest Spirit of God, the Mind of the Powers of the One Eternal Being, I call upon thee to appear! Reveal thyself unto me, for I have become empowered by the Mantle of the Spirit of thy Maker and have uttered the Word—thus it shall be! I summon and call thee to appear! In the Names of IAO SABAOTH, ABRASAX ADONAI, come to me!

(Forty-nine words in this Enochian Call. This call summons the Super-Archangel of the Tetramorph.)

APPENDIX II

IMAGO OF THE EIGHT SUPER-ARCHANGELS AND FOUR ELEMENT GODHEADS

FOUR SERAPHIM

SERAPHIEL: FIRE

The Celebrant says the following to build the imago of Seraphiel, the angel of the Seraph.

I summon and call thee, O Seraphiel (God is a Flaming Serpent), Chief of the Seraphim and High Prince of the Merkabah! Thou art clothed in flames and brilliant light, and thou hast six wings and four faces that face the four directions. Thou art an author of divine inspiration and brilliant illumination, casting away all darkness and gloom, all falsehoods and deception. Only truth and purity can withstand your fiery scrutiny. Thou shalt raise up the fallen, make just what was is unjust, and aid those who have no resources. In thine eyes, all feel the rapture of the Spirit of the One and sing praises to the eternal and everlasting presence. All hail and praise the infinite and immortal light!

METATRON: WATER

The Celebrant says the following to build the imago of Metatron, the angel of the Seraph.

I summon and call thee, O Metatron (Mana from God), lofty Lord of the Archangels, Prince of the Divine Face, Chancellor of Heaven, Scribe of the Lord, and great Seraphim! Thou art clothed in mist and smoke, and thou art tall, vast, and inscrutable. Thou art the author of divine love, the grand arbiter of the covenant between heaven and mankind, and the revealer of the mysteries of spiritual union—the One that is All. Thou art a poet and singer of psalms, praising the glories of the great Godhead. Thou dost inspire spiritual love between humanity and God, and thou art the great reconciler and redeemer of humankind. Thou art the dispenser of God's grace and the instrument through which the Godhead manifests its glory.

YAHOEL: AIR

The Celebrant says the following to build the imago of Yahoel, the angel of the Seraph.

I summon and call thee, O Yahoel (Yah is my God), perfect divine emissary of the Godhead, heavenly guide, protector, and agent of revelation. Thou art dressed in sapphire robes and a turban, like the priests of old. The look of thy countenance is like chrysolite, and the hair on thy head is the color of snow. Thou art the great intellect, master of all knowledge, the Eyes and the Mouthpiece of the Godhead. Thou art the wisdom of ages, and no one can contain even a tiny fraction of thy knowledge. All questions are answered, and all answers are questioned! Nothing is beyond thy scrutiny, but the telling of this wisdom requires great insight indeed, since it is told in parables, riddles, and often is inexplicable. Such is the way of the inspiring mind of the Godhead. Thou art the artificer of the Universal Mind and container of the thoughts of the Deity.

ZAHARIEL: EARTH

The Celebrant says the following to build the imago of Zahariel, the angel of the Seraph.

I summon and call thee, O Zahariel (God is Brilliant). Thou art the spiritual beauty of all creation, echoing the perfection and beauty of the One in All. Thou illuminate the dullness of life and eliminate despair, give hope where there is hopelessness, and ensure victory in all of one's achievements, but only if they are just and participate in the master plan of the Deity. Thou knowest this secret, since thou art its chief architect. For thou art the designer of the perfection of spiritual manifestation and thou art the grace and beauty that inspires everyone to discover the Spirit in their beings. Thou art like the tall mountains of majesty that are always snowcapped, and thou art like great forests that cover the verdant earth. Thou art the ecstasy of the love of God realized in the vitality of all life.

FOUR CHERUBIM

RIKBIEL: FIRE

The Celebrant says the following to build the imago of Rikbiel, the angel of the Cherub.

I summon and call thee, O Rikbiel (Chariot of God). Thou art the Crown Prince of Heavenly Judgement, Ruler of the Divine Chariot or Wheels of Fire. Thou art one of the fierce and powerful Cherubim, an angel with two faces and four wings; thou dost represent the judgment of truth over falsehood and the protection of the illumination of the Deity (Light). Thou art a teacher of divine wisdom and insight, and thou art a stern judge of deception, falsehood, and delusion. Thy sword is fiery and mighty, used to protect the inspiration of the Godhead. Thy wings are of crimson fire, thy armor, helm, and robes are scarlet and orange, and thou dost ward the eastern gate of the fields of paradise from the ignorant and profane.

KERUBIEL: WATER

The Celebrant says the following to build the imago of Kerubiel, the angel of the Cherub.

I summon and call thee, O Kerubiel (God's Guardian). Thou art the angel of divine love, messenger, and protector of the holy beloved of the Godhead. Thou art Chief of the Cherubim and principal source and wellspring of the spiritual ecstasy. Thou art the weigher of the heart and conscience of humanity, and thou dost punish the betrayer, the unfaithful, and traitor to all causes of love and allegiance to the Deity. Thou art the warden of the love that emanates from the Deity. Thou art a teacher of faith and devotion. Thy sword is frozen fire, icy and vast, used to protect the compassion of the Godhead. Thy wings are of blue fire; thy armor, helm, and robes are purple and indigo; and thou dost ward the western gate of the field of paradise from the ignorant and profane.

OFANIEL: AIR

The Celebrant says the following to build the imago of Ofaniel, the angel of the Cherub.

I summon and call thee, O Ofaniel (God's Celestial Wheel). Thou art the Chief of the Order of Thrones or Celestial Wheels, and thou dost rule the celestial wheel of the Moon. Thou art the guide and guardian of hidden or forbidden knowledge, and an initiator of the (lunar) Mysteries of light and darkness. Thou art the angel of divination, especially astrology, able to reveal any celestial portend to one who is worthy of thy wisdom. Thou art the principal judge of all actions and intentions, even ones purporting to be good. Nothing can hide from thy gaze or thy limitless scrutiny. Thy sword is like a great thunderbolt of sky fire, used to ensure the purity of the Will of God. Thy wings are pale azure and gold; thy helm, robes, and armor are the color of the sky at sunset; and thou dost ward the northern gate of the field of paradise from the ignorant and profane.

YOFIEL: EARTH

The Celebrant says the following to build the imago of Yofiel, the angel of the Cherub.

I summon and call thee, O Yofiel (God is Beautiful). Thou art the Angel of divine beauty and the angelic prince of the Torah, the guardian and guide of written scriptures and the mysteries of the word. Thou art known as the angelic teacher of the Qabalah and the dispenser of alms and various forms of dispensation. Thou dost assist in the writing of beautiful psalms and words of praise for the Deity, and thou bestow elegance and grace on those who are worthy to receive it. Thou art the ward of the life force and well of souls, from which all living things arise and have their source. Thy sword is like a great massive sequoia, used to ward the Life Force of God. Thy wings are bright green and russet; thy helm, robes, and armor are the color of moss—green, black, brown, and amber; and thou dost ward the southern gate of the field of paradise from the ignorant and profane.

IMAGO OF THE FOUR GODHEADS

The imago of the four Godheads is associated with the four Qabalistic Worlds. The usual God name for Assiah is Adonai Ha-Aretz (Lord of the Earth), but we have substituted that with the mystical name of the deliverer, a formula variation of Joshua (YHShVH).

Godhead Image of Fire—Atziluth—Ha-Shem

Heh, Shin, Mim—Ha-Shem—The Name! Behold, the image of Atziluth, a World of the Holy Qabalah! Therein shall you find the individual awareness of selfhood which precipitated all creation—the primordial "I am!" For the core of all being consists of the knowledge of Selfhood, which distinguishes that self from all that is subjective to it. Everything that exists in consciousness is based upon the precepts of the definition of the individual self! The "I am" that promises to "become" is the identity of potential from which all future creation occurs, for the individual self is never static, but ever-changing and transforming. However, the individuality of God represents the source of all spiritual change, but is itself unchanged and undisturbed by the continuous emanation of its Being!

Godhead Image of Water—Briah—Shadai

Shin, Daleth, Aleph, Yod—Shadai—the Almighty! Behold, the image of Briah, a World of the Holy Qabalah! Therein shall you find the potency of the forces of creation. For creation began with the fusion of polarities, and as such, it shall also terminate when the polarities once again merge in their full potency. Yet at this time, the violence of that joining has been superseded by the gentle mind of the Absolute working through the Primal Will upon the body or Throne of the creative matrix. From that union issues forth a stream of pure consciousness differentiated in awareness of self but unified in its formlessness. This is a model of the ideal method of magic, which is the ever-creative impulse establishing new formulations through its eternal transformations. This process of creation perfectly balances the intellect with the manifested spirit, and therefore represents the goal of the true theurgist.

Godhead Image of Air—Yetzirah—Elohim

Aleph, Lamed, Heh, Mim—Elohim—the Beloved Spirit! Behold, the image of Yetzirah, a world of the Holy Qabalah! Therein shall you find the formulation of spirit into the consciousness of form, for thus is the generation of meaning and the awareness of spiritual values. The spirit has become a body both beauteous and filled with love. Therein is beheld the compassion of judgement and execution of divine retribution. This is the Deity of the creation of individual consciousness and that to whom the masses pray and give sacrifice. Yet the spirit of consciousness is aware of a higher source and translates the inspiration which it receives from that great transcendence into a powerful creed which leads the individual to true self-knowledge. Yet herein are also the limitations which contain the world of individual consciousness. The process of self-identification stratifies the entity of awareness and holds it in the body of spiritual formation.

Godhead Image of Earth—Assiah—Yeshua

Yod, Shin, Vav, Heh—Yeshuah—the Deliverer. Behold, the image of Assiah, a world of the Holy Qabalah! Therein shall you find the expression of spirit as the powers of procreation and transformation. Between these opposing powers is poised the soul of humanity, which strives to find a point of balance and resolution. There is desire and lust which causes the eternal continuation of material existence. There is death and transformation which continually alters and destroys existence. The Self navigates upon the path of life, feeling the pleasures of the fulfillment of gain and the pain of loss. The laws and structures of the physical reality bind the spirit to the individual body, yet this pattern, however complete, has the means of release from the endless cycle of procreation and dissolution within itself. The process of release is unlike death because it leads the self-aware spirit back through all the worlds of expression, formation, and creation to the source.

CHAPTER FOUR

OGDOADIC GODHEAD VORTEX RITUAL

The Ogdoadic Godhead Vortex Ritual is used as part of the Abramelin Lunar Ordeal. The eight Super-Archangelic spirits are bonded to the Element Godhead, creating an octagon vortex structure powered by the fusion of all nine entities. It is expected that the operator will perform these nine invocations over a five-week period, with the Ogdoad Vortex performed immediately following the Archetypal Gate Ritual for the Element Godhead.

This ritual employs an octagon vortex structure, yet there are some interesting variations on the overall ritual formulation. The four Seraphim and the four Cherubim, previously invoked during the first four weeks of the seven-week ordeal, are set to the four watchtowers, where there are erected four charged pylons. What this does is join the Seraphim and Cherubim for each of the four Elements. The charged sigils that were used to invoke the Super-Archangels are set to each watchtower altar, where the Cherubim is the base and the Seraphim is the apex, so the sigils are placed with the Seraph above the Cherub in that sequence. A simple hexagram is set to the base of each watchtower and one to the apex, and a pylon is formed when they are joined together in an invoking spiral. As each hexagram is drawn, representing the spirit of the Super-Archangel, the operator will also perform an invocation and activate the sigil by drawing an invocation spiral over it and intoning the first letter of their name. There will be two formula letters per pylon—a total of eight to draw them together into union.

The four circle angles are set with a combination of the cross device of the tetra-sacramentary (Rose Cross, Rose Ankh, Pisces cross, and hexagrammic cross), drawn to the base, and the invoking pentagram of the Godhead Element to the apex, joined with an invoking spiral and intoned with the formula letter of the Godhead name. This will establish the already invoked Element Godhead, and its charged sigil is placed on the central altar previously set there prior to beginning the ritual.

The center of the circle is set with a pylon consisting of the cross-triangle device drawn over the sigil of the Element Godhead on the central altar acting as the base, and a great inverted invoking pentagram of the Element associated with the Godhead Element acting as the apex. The two points are drawn together with an invoking spiral, and the Celebrant then summons the Godhead and speaks the invocation of its specific imago. Then the four watchtowers are drawn to the Ultrapoint, the four angels are drawn to the Infrapoint, and the double formula is revealed and intoned.

A square is drawn, connecting the four watchtowers together in a widdershins arc with the sword. The four angles are drawn to the Infrapoint and the formula of the Godhead is revealed and intoned. A second square is drawn with a sword, connecting the four angles together in a deosil arc and thereby forming the octagon. Then the Celebrant takes the staff, sets it up in the center of the circle, and draws the Infrapoint up to the Ultrapoint through it, producing the empowered Ogdoadic Godhead through the agency of the octagon vortex.

In this manner, all of the spiritual entities of the past nine workings are fused into union. The Celebrant should then sit in the center of the circle and commune with the resounding Godhead manifestation, acting through its eight emissaries.

Once this is accomplished, then the operator should perform the Triple Tetrahedral Gate Ritual to forge a gateway of ascension and transformation with these nine superlative entities.

OGDOADIC GODHEAD VORTEX RITUAL

The Celebrant performs the Consecration of the Enochian Star Temple and the Mass of the Great Goddess and the associated Benediction rituals before performing this working. The temple environment must be super charged and thoroughly sacralized in order for it to be ready for the performance of this ritual.

Super-Archangelic Pyramid Pylon Base

The Celebrant begins this working by placing the sigils for each of the eight Super-Archangels to the four watchtowers, arranging them by Element and placing the Seraphim above the Cherubim. They should be arranged as:

Cardinal Direction	Element	Seraph/Cherub Pair
East	Fire	Seraphiel/Rikbiel
South	Earth	Zahariel/Yofiel
West	Water	Metatron/Kerubiel
North	Air	Yahoel/Ofaniel

In addition, the Celebrant should place a small portable altar in the center of the circle, and upon it the sigil for the already invoked Element Godhead. The Celebrant uses the transmutar wand to formulate the pyramid pylon base.

Eastern Watchtower

Celebrant proceeds to the eastern watchtower, bows before it and therein charges the sigil of the associated Cherub of Fire, drawing an invoking spiral to the base of the watchtower, intones the letter *Resh*, and draws a simple hexagram of union therein, saying the truncated Enochian call:

> *Do-a-dooain de Yod das i-olna ado a-vohim de ol-soyga od das i-embahzoda ca-ol pamabit a-Eregohe-i-Ovof de a-Lanushim-de- a-Eregohe-Gohed-Anceonas-Gah-de-Iabes; Ol-vinu gi, Ic Rikbiel de Kerubim, i-zamrante od i-odoefete a-cicale de gi-olna.*

The Celebrant draws a final invoking spiral around the parchment sigil of the Cherub of Fire, and says the following truncated imago:

> *I summon and call thee, O Rikbiel (Chariot of God). Thou art the Crown Prince of Heavenly Judgement, Ruler of the Divine Chariot or Wheels of Fire.*

Then the Celebrant charges the sigil of the associated Seraph of Fire, drawing an invoking spiral to the apex of the watchtower, intones the letter *Samek*, and draws a simple hexagram of union therein, saying the truncated Enochian call:

> *Do-a-dooain de Yod das i-olna ado a-vohim de ol-soyga od das i-embahzoda ca-ol pamabit a-Eregohe-i-Ovof de a-Lanushim-de- a-Eregohe-Gohed-Anceonas-Gah-de-Iabes; Ol-vinu gi, Ic Seraphiel de Seraphim, i-zamrante od i-odoefete a-cicale de gi-olna.*

The Celebrant draws a final invoking spiral around the parchment sigil of the Seraph of Fire and says the following truncated imago:

> *I summon and call thee, O Seraphiel (God is a Flaming Serpent), Chief of the Seraphim and High Prince of the Merkabah!*

The Celebrant then bows before the two summoned entities in the East, and, with the wand, draws an invoking spiral so as to join them into a single empowered entity. The Celebrant bows for the third time and proceeds to the next watchtower, tracing a line with the wand.

Southern Watchtower

Celebrant proceeds to the southern watchtower, bows before it, and therein charges the sigil of the associated Cherub of Earth. They draw an invoking spiral to the base of the watchtower, intone the letter *Yod*, and draw a simple hexagram of union therein, saying the truncated Enochian call:

Do-a-dooain de Heh das i-olna ado a-vohim de ol-soyga od das i-embahzoda ca-ol pamabit a-Eregohe-i-Ovof de a-Lanushim-de-a-Eregohe-Gohed-Anceonas-Gah-de-Iabes; Ol-vinu gi, Ic Yofiel de Kerubim, i-zamrante od i-odoefete a-cicale de gi-olna.

The Celebrant draws a final invoking spiral around the parchment sigil of the Cherub of Earth and says the following truncated imago:

I summon and call thee, O Yofiel (God is Beautiful). Thou art the Angel of divine beauty and the angelic prince of the Torah, the guardian and guide of written scriptures and the mysteries of the word.

Then the Celebrant charges the sigil of the associated Seraph of Earth and, drawing an invoking spiral to the apex of the watchtower, intones the letter *Zain* and draws a simple hexagram of union therein, saying the truncated Enochian call:

Do-a-dooain de Heh das i-olna ado a-vohim de ol-soyga od das i-embahzoda ca-ol pamabit a-Eregohe-i-Ovof de a-Lanushim-de-a-Eregohe-Gohed-Anceonas-Gah-de-Iabes; Ol-vinu gi, Ic Zahariel de Seraphim, i-zamrante od i-odoefete a-cicale de gi-olna.

The Celebrant draws a final invoking spiral around the parchment sigil of the Seraph of Earth and says the following truncated imago:

I summon and call thee, O Zahariel (God is Brilliant). Thou art the spiritual beauty of all creation, echoing the perfection and beauty of the One in All. Thou dost illuminate the dullness of life and eliminate despair.

The Celebrant then bows before the two summoned entities in the South and, with the wand, draws an invoking spiral so as to join them into a single empowered entity. The Celebrant bows for the third time and proceeds to the next watchtower, tracing a line with the wand.

Western Watchtower

Celebrant proceeds to the western watchtower, bows before it, and therein charges the sigil of the associated Cherub of Water. They draw an invoking spiral to the base of the watchtower, intone the letter *Kaph,* and draw a simple hexagram of union therein, saying the truncated Enochian call:

Do-a-dooain de Heh das i-olna ado a-vohim de ol-soyga od das i-embahzoda ca-ol pamabit a-Eregohe-i-Ovof de a-Lanushim-de-a-Eregohe-Gohed-Anceonas-Gah-de-Iabes; Ol-vinu gi, Ic Kerubiel de Kerubim, i-zamrante od i-odoefete a-cicale de gi-olna.

The Celebrant draws a final invoking spiral around the parchment sigil of the Cherub of Water and says the following truncated imago:

I summon and call thee, O Kerubiel (God's Guardian). Thou art the angel of divine love, messenger, and protector of the holy beloved of the Godhead. Thou art Chief of the Cherubim, and principal source and well spring of the spiritual ecstasy.

Then the Celebrant charges the sigil of the associated Seraph of Water, drawing an invoking spiral to the apex of the watchtower, intones the letter *Mim*, and draws a simple hexagram of union therein, saying the truncated Enochian call:

Do-a-dooain de Heh das i-olna ado a-vohim de ol-soyga od das i-embahzoda ca-ol pamabit a-Eregohe-i-Ovof de a-Lanushim-de-a-Eregohe-Gohed-Anceonas-Gah-de-Iabes; Ol-vinu gi, Ic Metatron de Seraphim, i-zamrante od i-odoefete a-cicale de gi-olna.

The Celebrant draws a final invoking spiral around the parchment sigil of the Seraph of Water and says the following truncated imago:

I summon and call thee, O Metatron (Mana from God), lofty Lord of the Archangels, Prince of the Divine Face, Chancellor of Heaven, Scribe of the Lord, and great Seraphim!

The Celebrant then bows before the two summoned entities in the West and, with the wand, draws an invoking spiral so as to join them into a single empowered entity. The Celebrant bows for the third time and proceeds to the next watchtower, tracing a line with the wand.

Northern Watchtower

Celebrant proceeds to the northern watchtower, bows before it, and therein charges the sigil of the associated Cherub of Air. They draw an invoking spiral to the base of the watchtower, intone the letter *Ain*, and draw a simple hexagram of union therein, saying the truncated Enochian call:

Do-a-dooain de Vav das i-olna ado a-vohim de ol-soyga od das i-embahzoda ca-ol pamabit a-Eregohe-i-Ovof de a-Lanushim-de-a-Eregohe-Gohed-Anceonas-Gah-de-Iabes; Ol-vinu gi, Ic Ofaniel de Kerubim, i-zamrante od i-odoefete a-cicale de gi-olna.

The Celebrant draws a final invoking spiral around the parchment sigil of the Cherub of Air and says the following truncated imago:

I summon and call thee, O Ophaniel (God's Celestial Wheel). Thou art the Chief of the Order of Thrones or Celestial Wheels, and thou dost rule the celestial wheel of the moon.

Then the Celebrant charges the sigil of the associated Seraph of Air, drawing an invoking spiral to the apex of the watchtower, intones the letter *Yod*, and draws a simple hexagram of union therein, saying the truncated Enochian call:

Do-a-dooain de Vav das i-olna ado a-vohim de ol-soyga od das i-embahzoda ca-ol pamabit a-Eregohe-i-Ovof de a-Lanushim-de-a-Eregohe-Gohed-Anceonas-Gah-de-Iabes; Ol-vinu gi, Ic Yahoel de Seraphim, i-zamrante od i-odoefete a-cicale de gi-olna.

The Celebrant draws a final invoking spiral around the parchment sigil of the Seraph of Air, and says the following truncated imago:

I summon and call thee, O Yahoel (Yah is my God), perfect divine emissary of the Godhead, heavenly guide, protector, and agent of revelation.

The Celebrant then bows before the two summoned entities in the North, and, with the wand, draws an invoking spiral so as to join them into a single empowered entity. The Celebrant bows for the third time and proceeds to the starting watchtower (east), tracing a line with the wand.

TETRA-SACRAMENTARY CROSSROADS

The Celebrant proceeds to the northeast angle and draws therein a hexagrammic cross at the base of the angle, and, at the apex, draws an invoking pentagram of the specific Element of the Godhead Element already invoked. The Celebrant intones the first letter of the Godhead name, and then draws the base and apex together with an invoking spiral.

I reveal the sacred sacramental path of Agape. O Agape, thou art the fusion of social unity that represents the evolution of humanity into the Novahomine, the "New Humanity," they that touch in mind and body and are one—a linking of love.

Thy sacrament is mediation, contemplation, and inner stillness, and thy children are the Pedoipsyche, Guardians of the Light of Truth, Beauty, Justice, and Peace. For the uncertain future holds a double path: of Golden Wisdom or total destruction. Peace! Peace! Peace! The bells toll as unseen reminders in a dark world of ignorance and prejudice—all of the unenlightened evils that threaten to undo us all. Yet the wise ones who hold the new secret truths (in trust) shall light the darkness with many candles as beacons of enlightenment, shining out amidst the thickening gloom of a new dark age. Carry us through our trials on Earth and guide us to the light, of which our greater souls are very much a part.

Then the Celebrant draws a line with the wand and proceeds directly to the southwest angle and draws therein a Pisces cross at the base of the angle, and, at the apex, draws an invoking pentagram of the specific Element of the Godhead Element already invoked.

The Celebrant intones the second letter of the Godhead name, and then draws the base and apex together with an invoking spiral.

> *I reveal the sacred sacramental path of Thanatos. O Thanatos, the Light of Liberation is revealed unto the select, those who have mastered death and life. Thy sacrament is dreams and visions from drugs, sleep, and death, and thy children are the Nosferatu, who obey the Law of Limitations. For Death is the guide and the instrument of freedom and unity: life within light.*
>
> *Know thy limitations and the bonds of the world of darkness, for the flesh is doomed from its inception, and thereby is all existence cursed with futile mortality. Yet, through the mystery of the hidden light, which is the source of all Being, consciousness is restored by those who have established communion with it in life. Awake! Awake! Awake! All ye dead and rejoice, for the light cometh and all lost spirits are joined to it in eternal life.*

The Celebrant then circumambulates widdershins to the northwest angle, drawing a line to that point, and then draws therein a Rose Cross at the base of the angle, and, at the apex, draws an invoking pentagram of the specific Element of the Godhead Element already invoked. The Celebrant intones the third letter of the Godhead name, and then draws the base and apex together with an invoking spiral.

> *I reveal the sacred sacramental path of Thelema. O Thelema, thou art the Joy of the Will executed and sent forth into the multiverse, lighting the myriad facets of reality. Thy sacrament is obsession, which is the trance of power, and thy children are magicians who obey the Law of Control. For the Will is the tool of the Magi—and they must discipline themselves so the Will is one-pointed and irresolute.*
>
> *Seek thy true vocation and know thy hidden value and worth, for there are no barriers and infinity is possible to conquer. There are no limits, only the self-creation directed by the Will. There are no gods who will deny thy Will or who will send thee to thy destruction because of thy sin of self-direction. For behold! Thou art bright; thou art great amongst all gods. For thou art humanity, and thou hast fashioned gods in thy image. Thou art the crown of creation, and thy will shall be the bride of thy kingdom.*

Then the Celebrant draws a line with the wand and proceeds directly to the southeast angle and draws therein a Rose Ankh at the base of the angle, and, at the apex, draws an invoking pentagram of the specific Element of the Godhead Element already invoked. The Celebrant intones the fourth letter of the Godhead name, and then draws the base and apex together with an invoking spiral.

> *I reveal the sacred sacramental path of Eros. O Eros, the Life Pattern is revealed as the joining of polarities, the mixing of genetic information, the core of love and lust. The expanding cellular life-pattern forever regenerating!*

Thy sacrament is the seed and the egg conjoined, the sexual wine of lust and love, the creative matrix—and thy children are All-Living Creation! For the individual is not important, only the genetic memories that encode spiritual evolution: the somatic god-mutation. Fuck! Fuse! Fructify! Thus is the essence of love—the intense potency of procreation. All bodies are one body, Human, God, and Beast, and the genetic computer knows the path for the evolution of the species. Let us understand the Serpent and the Gate of Heaven and reveal their manifestations!

The Celebrant then starts at the Southeast, and circumambulates widdershins from that point, tracing with the wand a line force that connects the four angles into a square. The octagon is now fully established.

PYLON OF SUMMONING AND SACRAMENTATION

Celebrant proceeds to the center of the circle and draws an invoking spiral on the charged sigil of the Element Godhead that is lying upon the central altar. Then, above the altar, the Celebrant draws a great inverted invoking pentagram of the Element associated with the Element Godhead. They draw, with lines of power, the sigil on the trigon up to the great inverted pentagram above with an invoking spiral. The Celebrant then draws the four angles together into the Infrapoint, beginning in the Northeast and proceeding widdershins. Then, the Celebrant performs the summoning of the Element Godhead.

First, intone the truncated Enochian Call of the Godhead:

Ol i-tustinusado a-(Bietome, Hecomea, Exarepe, Nanutea, Enubeha) de a-Gohed-An-cheonas-Gah-de-Iabes, ol-i-umide al a-(Yod, Heh, Vau, Heh) a-Eregohe-Embahzoda-Gah das i-antar tol balcathu od lehuslach!

Fire:

Aleph, Heh, Yod, Heh—Ehieh—I Shall Be! Behold, the image of Atziluth, a World of the Holy Qabalah! Therein shall you find the individual awareness of selfhood which precipitated all creation—the primordial "I am!" For the core of all being consists of the knowledge of the self, which distinguishes that self from all that is subjective to it. Everything that exists in consciousness is based upon the precepts of the definition of the individual self! The "I am" which promises to "become" is the identity of potential from which all future creation occurs. The individual self is never static, but ever changing and transforming. However, the individuality of God represents the source of all spiritual change but is itself unchanged and undisturbed by the continuous emanation of its Being!

Water:

Shin, Daleth, Aleph, Yod—Shadai—the Almighty! Behold, the image of Briah, a World of the Holy Qabalah! Therein shall you find the potency of the forces of creation. For creation began with the fusion of polarities and, as such, it shall also terminate when the polarities once again merge in their full potency. Yet, at this time, the violence of that joining has been superseded by the gentle mind of the Absolute working through the Primal Will upon the body or Throne of the creative matrix, and therein issues forth the stream of pure consciousness differentiated in awareness but unified in its formlessness. This is a model of the ideal method of magic, the ever-creative impulse establishing new formulations through its eternal transformations. This process of creation perfectly balances the intellect with the manifested spirit and therefore represents the goal of the true theurgist.

Air:

Aleph, Lamed, Heh, Mim—Elohim—the Beloved Spirit! Behold, the image of Yetzirah, a world of the Holy Qabalah! Therein shall you find the formulation of spirit into the consciousness of form. For thus is the generation of meaning and the awareness of spiritual values. The spirit has become a body both beauteous and filled with love. Therein is beheld the compassion of judgement and execution of divine retribution. This is the god of the creation of individual consciousness and that to whom the masses pray and give sacrifice. Yet the spirit of consciousness is aware of a higher source and translates the inspiration, which it receives from that great transcendence, into a powerful creed which leads the individual to true self-knowledge. Herein are also the limitations which contain the world of individual consciousness. The process of self-identification stratifies the entity of awareness and holds it in the body of spiritual formation.

Earth:

Yod, Shin, Vav, Heh—Yeshuah—the Deliverer! Behold, the image of Assiah, a world of the Holy Qabalah! Therein shall you find the expression of spirit as the powers of procreation and transformation. Between these opposing powers is poised the soul of humanity which strives ever to find a point of balance and resolution. There is desire and lust, which causes the eternal continuation of material existence. There is death and transformation, which continually alters and destroys existence. And the self navigates upon the path of life, feeling the pleasures of the fulfillment of gain and the pain of loss. The laws and structures of physical reality bind the spirit to the individual soul, yet this pattern, however complete, has within itself the means of release from the endless cycle of procreation and dissolution. The process of release is unlike death because it leads the self-aware spirit back through all the worlds of expression, formation, and creation to the source.

Then the Celebrant bows before the central altar and says the following:

I summon the Holy Ogdoad, the Emissaries of the Highest Absolute Godhead. The four are squared against each other, thereby producing the greatest generation of mystical and magical power. For such powers as these were used in the creation and ensouling of the universe—the embodiment of the Pleroma and the sacral distribution of spirits throughout the multiverse. Their purpose is to come into the Union of Being and become again the pristine and unbegotten Bornless One that existed before all time and space.

Points to the East:

I summon the Super-Archangels of Fire, Seraphiel, and Rikbiel—may they join and fuse in the body of the Light of the Sacral Godhead.

Points to the South:

I summon the Super-Archangels of Earth, Zahariel, and Yofiel—may they join and fuse in the body of the Light of the Sacral Godhead.

Points to the West:

I summon the Super-Archangels of Water, Metatron, and Kerubiel—may they join and fuse in the body of the Light of the Sacral Godhead.

Points to the North:

I summon the Super-Archangels of Air, Yahoel, and Ofaniel—may they join and fuse in the body of the Light of the Sacral Godhead.

Thus, I have joined the Ogdoad of the Divine Emissaries to the Godhead of (Element). I evoke the power and wisdom of this Enneagramic Godhead to bless and grace me with the pure ambition and insight of enlightenment. For I seek the union of the Godhead, and all else is as nought!

Using the wand, the Celebrant draws the four watchtowers together into the Ultrapoint, beginning with the East and proceeding deosil. Once this is completed, the Celebrant takes up the staff, places it before the central altar, and draws the power from the sigil up through the staff into the Ultrapoint, where the inverted invoking pentagram discharges its power down through the staff. The Celebrant absorbs the power flowing through the staff, and then, after fully absorbing it, takes the staff and sets it down before the central altar so that its ends are directed East and West. The Celebrant bows and prostrates themselves profoundly before the trigon and remains in this state for some time, absorbing the blessing and combined powers and wisdom of the Element Godhead and the eight Emissaries as a single empowered being.

When the rite is completed, the Celebrant performs the Triple Tetrahedral Gate of Ascension rite.

CHAPTER FIVE

TRIPLE TETRAHEDRAL GATE RITUAL

THE RITUAL OF THE TRIPLE TETRAHEDRAL GATE, also known as the Double Gateway with Ascension Gate, is a ritual structure which specifically unlocks the power of the Abramelin Lunar Ordeal. Through the passage of the gate of darkness, the seeker enters the super-symbolic world of spiritual consciousness, and therein undergoes extreme transformation as symbolized by the Ascension Gate. This gateway-inspired transformation resounds within the individual, affecting their inner and outer perceptions, which in turn causes changes to resonate in the material world (here portrayed as the gate of light). What fuels these changes is represented as the psychological process of radical changing and evolving awareness, symbolized mythically as the transmutation of the previously invoked Godhead as derived from the Archetypal Gate Ritual and the Ogdoadic Godhead Vortex.

The tetradic pattern of this cyclic process (the cycle of darkness and light) is controlled by the double gates, which are symbolized as the gateways of light and darkness (dawn and dusk), conjoined in the mystery of the ascending and descending emanations of the Godhead (the east to west pathway of the sun). Thus, the Double Tetrahedral Gate Ritual pattern is the ritualized representation of this mystery, where the Gate of Ascension pulls the rest of the ordeal working into a single profound expression. What follows is the complete realization of the Godhead, completing and fulfilling the Ogdoadic process.

The structure of this ritual consists of the joining of the western gate (the Gate of Night) with the eastern gate (the Gate of the Coming Forth by Day), and, between them, performing the Ascension Gateway, which crosses them. This invocation accompanies the assumption of an invoking trance wherein the visionary experience of the Godhead is obtained. Both Gate structures use a five-fold formula and a five-point circle structure, thus establishing the double tetrahedral gate in each point. The Ascension Gateway is a simple three-point structure, using the undefined northern and southern nodes and the Ultrapoint, producing an equilateral triangle that crosses the concourse of the dual gateways.

TRIPLE TETRAHEDRAL GATE RITUAL

The Celebrant performs the Consecration of the Enochian Star Temple, the Mass of the Great Goddess and the associated Benediction rituals, and the Ogdoadic Godhead Vortex Ritual before performing this working.

THE DESCENT THROUGH THE GATE OF NIGHT.

The Celebrant sets the three talismanic gate keys along with a Tarot Trump: one in the southeast angle (Justice VIII), one in the western watchtower (The Fool 0), and one in the northeast angle (The World XXI), with the appropriate Tarot Trumps placed on each. The Celebrant then meditates on the cards placed therein, building up the energies and noting the significance of the gate Tarot Trumps. The Celebrant then stands in the East, facing the West.

The Celebrant draws a trapezoidal cross and seals it with an invoking spiral in the southeastern angle, charging the Gate Key therein, intoning the letter *Lamed,* and then saying:

> *[Atu VIII] The initiate begins the path with many difficulties and issues that dim the reflected light of the Absolute Spirit and make the knowledge of its wisdom silent and obscure. Found herein is the mystery of the self, and by the use and manipulation of mythic symbols and images, the initiate may unlock this inner mystery and come to know and conquer these issues, thus allowing the divine light of the Spirit to shine through the veil.*

The Celebrant draws a trapezoidal cross and seals it with an invoking spiral in the western watchtower, charging the Gate Key therein, intoning the letter *Aleph,* and then saying:

> *[Atu 0] The inner mystery is enacted upon the stage of the soul in the theater of the mind. The symbolic experiences become filled with psychic intensity which rivals material reality. Herein, the soul undergoes the willed transformation of the Self, which, when exposed to the symbols of myth, is dramatically affected. The mask is ripped away from the Self, and one is invited to discover the truth thus revealed. (Yet another mask is behind it.)*

The Celebrant draws a trapezoidal cross and seals it with an invoking spiral in the northeastern angle, charging the Gate Key therein, intoning the letter *Thav,* and then saying:

> *[Atu XXI] Deep within the unconscious, where the mystery play of the Self unfolds, is the treasure house of images and psychic patterns which make up the soul and define the structure of one's spirit. The symbols which deeply reflect the soul are taken from this source of psychic holistic patterns, and thus give knowledge in the form of visions and revelations. Yet because this process is one that is selected with care and willed through the core of the self, a fabric of symbols like a harmonious symphony profoundly unfolds.*

The Celebrant proceeds to the center of the circle and stands in the East facing the West. The three gate nodes are drawn to the Ultrapoint in the center of the circle, in the sequence of northeast, west, and southeast. The Celebrant then draws the three nodes together in an arc, generating a triangle in a ring. The Celebrant makes the sign of the parting of the threshold and, as the Enterer, crosses into the gate of the western watchtower, then turns to face the East and proceeds subsequently to the center of the circle.

The Celebrant draws in the Ultrapoint an invoking hexagram (union of Fire and Water), sealing it with an invoking spiral and intoning the letter *Mim*. They say:

> *[Atu XII] The stillness of the inner soul is established through the deeper grounding of the self, and the images which clothe it are stripped away. When the final layer is removed, therein is revealed the ending of all emotional tensions and clinging illusions, thus stilling the mind and making it a perfect mirror for the Absolute Spirit. The interplay of mythic symbols awakens one's deeper spiritual connections, which begin to resonate with a primal music that is the song of the soul, harmonized by the greater and purer intonations of the Absolute Spirit.*

The Celebrant draws down the energies from the Ultrapoint to their crown chakra and performs the self-crossing mantle of glory. They then intone the letter *Kaph*, and say:

> *[Atu X] The Absolute Spirit reveals the larger issues which confront our conscious aspiration to join with our higher selves. Those issues are the archetypes of the process of social and spiritual evolution and represent the trials of life and death which face all individuals who are on their spiritual path at this time and in this place. To know the cultural issues that affect the social egregore is to become an agent in the process of spiritual evolution. The task of growth for the individual mirrors the task of growth for the whole of society.*

Then the Celebrant says the following, while pointing to each of the five nodes in sequence:

> *Lamed—The Initiate Seeks Inner Peace.*
> *Aleph—Therein Begins the Inward Journey.*
> *Thav—The Source of the Spirit is Encountered.*
> *Mim—Through Self-reduction, One is Purified.*
> *Kaph—Thus Are Revealed the Trials of the Soul!*
> *Lamed, Aleph, Thav, Mim, Kaph—Lathamika.*

> *Thus is the process of the inner journey: the quest to discover the answers to the issues of the soul is in conflict with the seemingly chaotic process of the mundane world. We must persevere and win our release from the cares of the world so that the inner spiritual process may be activated.*

Vortex Domain of Envisioning

A pillow or chair is prepared next to the central altar, upon which is the parchment sigil of the Element God. Also placed within the operator's reach is a shew-stone or magic mirror, having been removed from its covering of black silk. It is sealed therein with a violet energy and fumigated with a special trance-inducing herbal incense.

The Celebrant proceeds to the northern watchtower and draws the invoking pentagram of spirit receptive, fills it with a violet energy, vibrates the letter *Yodh*, and says:

> *The traveler has retreated from their senses and focuses inward unto the beckoning world which lieth beyond. Behold me, for I am the walker of the Inner Planes, and all distractions from that path have been nullified.*

The Celebrant then draws an invoking spiral into the pentagram and intones the Enochian formula word *Enubeha*.

The Celebrant proceeds to the western watchtower and draws the invoking pentagram of spirit receptive, fills it with a violet energy, and vibrates the letter *Chet* and says:

> *The inner self is revealed through ascetic self-denial. For the flesh is but a transitional state and the joy of liberation from that flesh is found in union with the Absolute, producing an eternal bliss of spiritual ecstasy within that enlightened state.*

The Celebrant draws an invoking spiral into the pentagram and intones the Enochian formula word *Enubeha*.

The Celebrant proceeds to the southern watchtower and draws the invoking pentagram of spirit receptive, fills it with a violet energy, vibrates the letter *Lamed*, and says:

> *The balance between the spirit and the mind is established, for the inner self contains the knowledge to gain spiritual purpose and direction for oneself and for all humanity.*

The Celebrant draws an invoking spiral into the pentagram and intones the Enochian formula word *Enubeha*.

The Celebrant proceeds to the eastern watchtower and draws the invoking pentagram of spirit receptive, fills it with a violet energy, vibrates the letter *Resh*, and says:

> *The revelation of the Inner Planes frees the spirit from the fetters of mundane existence and opens the spirit to the awe and mystery of the Dance of the Archetypes — the continual spiraling manifestation of spiritual evolution.*

The Celebrant draws an invoking spiral into the pentagram and intones the Enochian formula word *Enubeha*.

The Celebrant then draws the northern, western, southern, and eastern watchtowers together to the center of the circle (focusing upon the Sigil of the Godhead sitting upon the central altar) using the transmutar wand. They say:

Yod—The Hermetic Path.
Chet—The Spiritual Image of the Self.
Lamed—The Art of Being Centered.
Resh—The Liberation of the Soul.
Yechelar! The revelation of the spiritual self as the body of light!

Then the Celebrant draws an inner circle that will contain the focus of the gateway structures. They make the parting of the threshold sign before the gate and step into it, projecting its energy to the outer periphery of the magic circle.

The Celebrant performs a deep trance exercise. At this point, the Celebrant should attempt to gain a complete connection with the Godhead that has been previously invoked.

An envisioning is then acquired and fully experienced before the Celebrant proceeds to the next stage of the ritual.

Erecting the Ascension Gate

The Ascension Gate structure requires three nodes: the northern and southern watchtowers (not used for any points throughout the ritual), and the Ultrapoint. The Ascension Gate is thus an equilateral triangle and represents a greater threshold wherein the powers and emanations from the supernal triad may be observed, interacted with, or entered through by the magician. The northern and southern points are the orbital nodes of winter and summer, representing death and life.

The Celebrant faces the East and draws an equal arm cross in the northern watchtower, then an equal arm cross in the Ultrapoint, and finally an equal arm cross in the southern watchtower.

The Celebrant then stands in the West, facing the East, and draws all of the gate nodes (northern, Ultrapoint, and southern) together to form an equilateral triangle. The Celebrant advances from the West toward the East to the center of the circle, making the sign of the enterer, and makes the sign of silence as they slowly approach the threshold of the Ascendent Gate.

Then, as the Celebrant stands before the gateway, they make the sign of the rending of the veil and the opening portal gesture, opening their arms to receive the blessing of power and insight from the Ultrapoint, and then circles around the central altar to sit before it on the opposite side of the circle. The Celebrant begins to deeply meditate on the Ascension Gate, and then after a pause, performs the following incantation.

The Celebrant then intones the incantation: the *Invocation of the Grand Threshold*.

Triple Tetrahedral Gate Ritual

Enochian	English Translation
Ado-ioadaf i-as Mahorela a-Taotegaraz de tofarach a-Ovoares comselah de agoas a-Ooge de Zylna	In the beginning was the Void the Wormhole of between-ness the spiral pattern of non-being the container of itself.
Aran gedothoi-zizop i-as gedothbar darilpa oresa-zodinu de olpiret das i-embahate do diu-ethamaz Cacaregi At-agaon-adgat-fifazoda tarasaf de Zylna od oi At-nafali nafalate ado-zylna oi Otlarazodu-At	Thus from this construct was the generation of a great negative liquid of dark-energy, which collected in fields until it could no longer support its own mass and then it collapsed, causing a great catastrophic implosion which rebounded.
Aran owanoanim de toltan a-Albanas-garaz de ialpor busadir At-tustinusa a-lanashim de qaa ado-tol-cocasabe de olpiret od de Nanutea Ste-osahia!	Thus, the Eyes of Eternity, the Quasars of pulsating energy, emitted the powers of manifestation throughout all ages of light and matter— so mote it be!
a-Layad de-a-Adotoforach At-maasi tofarach a-es orop-es Sagaot do-embahzoda a-es-orop-es de cocasabe a-Qabal-od-Thazua Ado a-Qabal-od-Noraz.	The secret of the in between— it (doth) lie(th) between the four-fold multiverse, in conjunction with the four-fold-four dimensions, The Seventeenth among the sixteen.

The Celebrant then intones the final Gnostic reading and invocation.

I am the invisible One within the All. It is I who counsel those who are hidden, since I know the All that exists in it. I am numberless beyond everyone. I am immeasurable and ineffable, yet whenever I wish, I shall reveal myself. I am the movement of the All. I exist before the All, and I am the All, since I exist before everyone.

I am a Voice speaking softly. I exist from the first. I dwell within the Silence that surrounds every one of them. And it is the hidden Voice that dwells within me, with the intangible, immeasurable Thought, within the immeasurable Silence.[42]

IAŌ IAŌ IAŌ—(name of Element Godhead)—I call upon you, Phtha Ra Phtha Iē Phtha Dun Emēcha Erōchth Barōch Thorchtha Thōm Chaieouch Archandabar Ōeaeō Ynēōch Ēra Ōn Ēlōph Bom Phtha Athabrasia Abriasōth Barbarbelōcha Barbaiaōch; let there be depth, breadth, length, brightness, Ablanathanalba Abrasiaoua Akramma Chamarei Thōth Hōr Athōōpō. Come in, lord, and reveal.[43]

The Celebrant may then perform a deep meditation session, an interactive trance state or astral projection, or simply just exist in the lower causal eternal moment, experiencing all that is revealed.

The Crossing of the Gate of Light

The Celebrant resets the three talismanic gate keys along with a Tarot Trump: one in the southwest angle (The World XXI), one in the eastern watchtower (Death XIII), and one in the northwest angle (The Wheel of Fortune X), with the appropriate Tarot Trumps placed on each. The Celebrant then meditates on the cards, building up the energies and noting the significance of the Gate Tarot Trumps. The Celebrant then stands in the West, facing the East.

The Celebrant draws a trapezoidal cross and seals it with an invoking spiral in the northwestern angle, charging the Gate Key therein, intoning the letter *Kaph*, and saying:

> [Atu X] *The Absolute Spirit reveals the larger issues which confront our conscious aspiration to join with our higher selves. Those issues are the archetypes of the process of social and spiritual evolution and represent the trials of life and death which face all individuals who are on their spiritual path at this time and in this place. To know the cultural issues that affect the social egregore is to become an agent in the process of spiritual evolution. The task of growth for the individual mirrors the task of growth for the whole of society.*

The Celebrant draws a trapezoidal cross and seals it with an invoking spiral in the eastern watchtower, charging the Gate Key therein, intoning the letter *Mim*, and saying:

> [Atu XII] *From death is given life, and so from stillness comes forth movement. The Gates of Light and Darkness open to reveal the seeker naked and purified of all*

---

[42] Robinson, James M., ed., *The Nag Hammadi Library* (Harper & Row, 1977) p. 462. Trimorphic Protennoia, NH 35 v. 25.
[43] Betz, *op. cit.*, p. 159.

extraneous thoughts and feelings. They are awakened to the inner knowledge of the spirit, yet this needs to be applied to the world at large. The realization of death and mortality, and the revelation of the nature of the human spirit, cause the follies of mundane existence to fall away and become irrelevant. Thus, the light of the spirit shines upon the life of the seeker, making it simple and pure so that it shall be ultimately prepared for the final dissolution.

The Celebrant draws a trapezoidal cross and seals it with an invoking spiral in the southwestern angle, charging the Gate Key therein, intoning the letter *Thav*, and saying:

[Atu XXI] Deep within the unconscious, wherein the mystery play of the Self unfolds, is the Treasure House of images and psychic patterns which make up the soul and define the structure of one's spirit. The symbols which darkly reflect the soul are taken from this source of psychic contents, and thus give knowledge in the form of visions and revelations. Yet because this process is one that is selected with care and willed through the core of the self, a fabric of symbols like a harmonious symphony profoundly unfolds.

The Celebrant proceeds to the center of the circle and stands in the West facing the East. The three gate nodes are drawn to the Ultrapoint in the center of the circle, in the sequence of southwest, east, and northwest. The Celebrant then draws the three nodes together in an arc, generating a triangle in a ring. The Celebrant makes the sign of the parting of the threshold, and, as the Enterer, crosses into the gate of the eastern watchtower, then turns to face the West and proceeds to the center of the circle. The Celebrant draws therein an invoking hexagram (union of Fire and Water) in the Ultrapoint, sealing it with an invoking spiral and intoning the letter *Aleph*. They say:

[Atu 0] The inner mystery is enacted upon the stage of the soul in the theater of the mind. The symbolic experiences become filled with the psychic intensity which rivals the material reality, for herein, the soul undergoes the willed transformation of the self, which, when exposed to the symbols of myth, is dramatically affected. The old mask was ripped away from the self, and a new one is fashioned from the visage of the Deity itself. Thus, clothed in myth, the seeker has become a spiritual agent.

The Celebrant draws down the energies from the Ultrapoint to their crown chakra, and then performs a centering exercise (descending wave). They then intone the letter *Lamed* and say:

[Atu VIII] The initiate begins the path with many difficulties and issues, which dims the reflected light of the absolute spirit and makes the knowledge of its wisdom silent and obscure. Herein was found the mystery of the self, and by the use and manipulation of mythic symbols and images, the initiate has unlocked this inner mystery and come to know and conquer these issues, thus becoming the divine light of the spirit which shines through the veil.

Then the Celebrant says the following, while pointing to each of the five nodes in sequence.

Kaph—Thus Are Revealed the Trials of the Soul!
Mim—Through Self-creation, One is Reborn!
Thav—The Source of the Spirit is Emulated.
Aleph—Therein Concludes the Inward Journey.
Lamed—The Initiate Becomes the Agent of Spirituality.
Kaph, Mim, Thav, Aleph, Lamed—Kamitheal.

Thus is the process of the inner journey, the quest to discover the answers to the issues of the soul; finding resolution within the eternal still-point of the spiritual source. We seek the means of reintegrating with the world after gaining this holy knowledge, and so to translate and communicate our inner wisdom.

The rite is completed.

CHAPTER SIX

BORNLESS ONE INVOCATION RITE OF STELLAR GNOSIS

The Bornless One rite (version four) consists of three ritual levels. The first level is the Tetramorphic Archetypal Power Vortices for all four of the Qabalistic Worlds, resolving the combined forces in the fifth power, which is called the Jewel of the Gnostic Stellar Rays. The assumption is that the Higher Self (the Bornless One) resides in all four worlds, from Assiah to Atziluth. Within these unified vortices, the Celebrant invokes the Bornless One, using the classical English translation as found in the rituals of the Golden Dawn (with corrections made from the original Greek Papyri). In the final ritual action, the Celebrant erects their own formula to establish the third ritual level, which is the Gate of Light, where they project outward the powers and profound insights they have found from summoning the Bornless One. This structure should represent the Celebrant's personal spiritual directive at that point in their life.

The Invocation of the Bornless One establishes a permanent manifested link to one's Higher Self. Therefore, it is necessary for the Celebrant to fast, say mass, undergo rigorous purification, and participate in other ascetic practices to facilitate the process. I have written into the ritual gender-based verbiage for men, women, and others to facilitate the identity of the Celebrant. Thus, the celebrant can use the male, female, or other gender-based expressions to facilitate individual preferences.

The Celebrant performs the consecration of the Temple of the Goddess, the Mass of the Goddess, and all four Elemental Worlds of the Tetrapatronis, completing the power vortices with the fifth power vortex in the order of Assiah through Atziluth. In addition, there are invocations or calls taken from the *Ars Notoria of Solomon the King* (a thirteenth-century grimoire of great repute), seven of which are used to profoundly empower the four power vortices and unveil the mystery of the Eye in the Triangle, which is the central mystery of the Bornless One rite.

BORNLESS ONE INVOCATION
RITE OF STELLAR GNOSIS

The Celebrant performs the Consecration of the Magna Dea and the Mass of the Great Goddess and the associated Benediction rituals before performing this working. The temple environment must be super charged and thoroughly sacralized in order for it to be ready for the performance of this ritual.

Tetrapatron Power Vortex of Assiah

The Celebrant proceeds to the eastern watchtower and therein bows and gives salute. Then Celebrant draws the invoking pentagram of Earth and intones the letter *Yod*, projecting a golden energy into the pentagram.

The Celebrant proceeds to the southern watchtower and therein bows and gives salute. The Celebrant draws the invoking pentagram of Earth and intones the letter *Shin*, projecting a scarlet energy into the pentagram.

The Celebrant proceeds to the western watchtower and therein bows and gives salute. The Celebrant draws the invoking pentagram of Earth and intones the letter *Vav*, projecting an azure energy into the pentagram.

The Celebrant proceeds to the northern watchtower and therein bows and gives salute. The Celebrant draws the invoking pentagram of Earth and intones the letter *Heh*, projecting a green energy into the pentagram.

The Celebrant proceeds to the center of the circle and therein bows and gives salute. The Celebrant draws the invoking pentagram of Earth to the Ultrapoint and intones the letter *Aleph*, projecting a brilliant white energy into the pentagram.

The Celebrant draws the four points of the watchtower circle together with their sword to form a square, starting in the East, proceeding deosil, and completing in the East. The Celebrant then takes the staff and, holding it over their head parallel to the floor, begins to turn in a widdershins arc until reaching a climax of speed, at which point they project the power into the Ultrapoint with the tip of the staff. The positive vortex is thus established.

The Celebrant meditates for a short period of time on the Gnostic wisdom of Basilides, the Greatest of Gnostic Philosophers and the supreme Neoplatonic Adept.

The Celebrant proceeds to the southeastern angle and draws therein an inverted invoking pentagram of spirit receptive, vibrates the letter *Aleph*, intones the word *'Amoq* (mystery), and says:

> *The light that is not reveals itself and a vision is born of fire and spirit. And I saw a curtain part at the utterance of the secret word of power—IAO. Therein was revealed an ornate door surrounded by two pillars that support an engraved triangular cornice. The pillar on the left is made of black onyx and the one on the right is fashioned of white alabaster. But the door is dark and mysterious; it remains sealed except to the one who*

has the key and knows the password. The door leads to the places beyond the material universe, for it is the Door of Perception.

The Celebrant proceeds to the northeastern angle and draws therein an inverted invoking pentagram of spirit receptive, vibrates the letter *Daleth*, intones the word *Thavunah* (insight), and says:

> *The light that is not reveals itself and a vision is born of fire and spirit. And I saw the Eye of the Sun that casts away the shadows of doubt and purges the soul of despair. In this fashion are the secrets of the spirit made known and all ignorance is illuminated. For the Light is the life of the Spirit—and the mysterious Eye of the Sun is the channel for this immeasurable power of life.*

The Celebrant proceeds to the northwestern angle and draws therein an inverted invoking pentagram of spirit receptive, vibrates the letter *Nun*, intones the word *Sheriruth* (obduration), and says:

> *The light that is not reveals itself and a vision is born of fire and spirit. And I saw the lightning bolt that is wielded by the hand of the glory of the Spirit, they are also the wand of authority and the staff of wisdom. What this power has fashioned by the ordination of its will shall endure, continue to grow, and ultimately prosper. Only the will of the Spirit is eternal.*

The Celebrant proceeds to the southwestern angle, and draws therein an inverted invoking pentagram of spirit receptive, vibrates the letter *Yod*, intones the word *Gomey* (a papyrus reed), and says:

> *The light that is not reveals itself and a vision is born of fire and spirit. And I saw a veil parting, and revealed therein was an emblem of the sigil of the Opening of the Way, inscribed with gold upon a pure white marble stele. Those who beheld this sign were also shown the password and the key which opens the Threshold between Universes, for the initiate is drawn into the realms beyond by the inspiration of the intellect and the pursuit of the ultimate truth.*

The Celebrant proceeds to the center of the circle and therein bows and gives salute. The Celebrant then draws the pentagram of spirit receptive in the Infrapoint and intones the letter *Lamed* and the word *Teheir* (purity), projecting a brilliant white energy into the pentagram. The Celebrant says:

> *The light that is not reveals itself and a vision is born of fire and spirit. And I saw beyond the great door, the threshold between multiverses. Therein was a dais of five marble steps, and a small ancient altar stood upon its summit. On either side of the altar stood two*

bronze braziers, from which a delicate perfumed incense smoke perfectly fumigated the atmosphere. The chamber was bright with the light of the Spirit, shining in a great beam from far above the altar, yet from no discernable source. And I heard a voice, and it said: "I am the thought that said I am! The beginning is the end, and the end is beginning!"

The Celebrant draws the four points of the angle circle together with their sword to form a square, starting in the Southeast, proceeding deosil, and completing in the Southwest. The Celebrant then takes the staff and, holding it over their head parallel to the floor, begins to turn in a deosil arc until reaching a climax of speed, and then grounds the power into the Infrapoint with the end of the staff. The negative vortex is thus established.

The Celebrant, using the transmutar wand, joins pairs of watchtowers and angles together by drawing a pylon between them. Thus, the Celebrant draws the East and the Southeast, the Northeast and the North, the Northwest and the West, and the Southwest and the South together. The Celebrant then joins each pair to the Infrapoint, starting with the East-Southeast pair and proceeding deosil to the South-Southwest, West-Northwest, and North-Northeast.

The Celebrant stands in the center of the circle and faces North (Earth), then fuses the two pentagrammic devices set in the Ultra- and Infrapoints with a great invoking spiral, thus creating the central pylon. In the Mesopoint, the Celebrant makes the sign of the octagram (four-horns gesture), signifying that the double squares and interlocking pylons are joined. They hold aloft a small specially consecrated round shield or paten (with a special host upon it) and vibrates the letter *Tet*, and says the following, choosing the language appropriate for one's gender:

Tet: Aegis of the Masters, Crown of Glory, Holy Octagon Shield of Power, I set forth and establish the base of all powers, wherein the magus has defined (his/her/their) domain and (sent forth his power and light into the earth/received into her chalice the light and fire of heaven/envisioned the heavens and earth rejoicing in their union of life). And the Dragon of the World Tree shall encircle this place, and the Great Goddess shall bless it with life and eternal renewal. In this sacred place is formulated the Dawn Creation of all Kings, in this place is Eden and Paradise, the Blood and Host of the True Graal, the Cornucopia and Cauldron of Rebirth. The Wisdom of the Structure of the Emanation of Spirit is herein given as a Gnosis of Spirit and Mind conjoined—the Universal Intelligence. This power wards, protects, and guides the seeker on the path to realization and awards (him/her/them) the mastery of life. The Keys to Heaven, Earth, and Hell are herein given to the wise mage who knows the Mystery of the Grail, the three Questions and their Answers. And I give herein the exegesis of the Word:

Yod, Shin, Vav, Heh—Yeshuah!—the Deliverer. Behold, the image of Assiah, a world of the Holy Qabalah! Therein shall you find the expression of spirit as the powers of procreation and transformation. Between these opposing powers is poised the soul of humanity, which ever-strives to find a point of balance and resolution. There is desire and lust, which causes the eternal continuation of material existence. There is death and transformation, which continually alters and destroys existence. The Self navigates upon the path of life, feeling the pleasures of the fulfillment of gain and the pain of loss. The laws and structures of the physical reality bind the spirit to the individual body, yet this pattern, however complete, has within itself the means of release from the endless cycle of procreation and dissolution. The process of release is unlike death because it leads the self-aware spirit back through all the worlds of expression, formation, and creation to the source.

Then the Celebrant intones the following invocation from the Ars Notoria of Solomon the King:

Assaylemath, Assay, Lemath, Azzabue, Azzaylemath, Lemath, Azacgessenio, Lemath, Sabanche, Ellithy, Aygezo.[44]

The Celebrant then meditates and divines within this vortex power field, knowing that only truth and goodness shall exist within this domain. When the mystery is complete, the Celebrant and participants shall eat of the host of the Grail and be fortified thereof.

Tetrapatron Power Vortex of Yetzirah

The Celebrant proceeds to the eastern watchtower and therein bows and gives salute. The Celebrant draws the invoking pentagram of Air and intones the letter *Aleph*, projecting a golden energy into the pentagram.

The Celebrant proceeds to the southern watchtower and therein bows and gives salute. Celebrant draws the invoking pentagram of Air and intones the letter *Lamed*, projecting a scarlet energy into the pentagram.

The Celebrant proceeds to the western watchtower and therein bows and gives salute. The Celebrant draws the invoking pentagram of Air and intones the letter *Heh*, projecting an azure energy into the pentagram.

The Celebrant proceeds to the northern watchtower and therein bows and gives salute. The Celebrant draws the invoking pentagram of Air and intones the letter *Mim*, projecting a green energy into the pentagram.

The Celebrant proceeds to the center of the circle and therein bows and gives salute. The Celebrant draws the invoking pentagram of Air to the Ultrapoint and intones the letter *Aleph*, projecting a brilliant white energy into the pentagram.

The Celebrant then takes the staff and, holding it over their head parallel to the floor. They begin to turn in a deosil arc speeding up until reaching a climax, and then projects the power into the Ultrapoint with the tip of the staff. The cone of power is thus established.

The Celebrant meditates for a short period of time on the Gnostic wisdom of Simon Magus, the Great Magician-Bishop of Samaria. The Celebrant then sets the three

---

44 Banner, James, ed., *Ars Notoria: The Notary Art of Solomon the King* (Trident Books, 1997) p. 9.

talismanic gate keys: one in the northeast angle (The Fool 0), one in the southern watchtower (The Moon XVIII), and one in the northwest angle (Adjustment VIII), with the appropriate Tarot Trumps placed on each. One is also imagined in the secret node in the Ultrapoint (The Wheel of Fortune X).

The Celebrant proceeds to the northwestern angle and draws an inverted invoking pentagram of spirit creative upon the gate key placed therein, as well as an invoking spiral, then vibrates the letter *Lamed* and intones the word *Odos* (the Threshold), and says:

> *The way to spiritual realization is the hard and lonely path of the magus. The light has revealed the way and continues to point the seeker in the correct direction, yet there are many hazards and temptations along the road. The magical revelation of our True Will shall make firm our ambition and act as a mantle to protect ourselves from the elements, to warm our hearts and fortify our resolve so that we may continue onward in the face of all adversity.*

The Celebrant proceeds to the southern watchtower and draws therein an inverted invoking pentagram of spirit creative upon the gate key, as well as an invoking spiral, then vibrates the letter *Quf*, intones the word *Olbios* (good fortune), and says:

> *The blessings of the Spirit manifest in nature shall give forth its bounty unto you. Those who have found the means to unite within themselves the holistic expression of the fusion of light and darkness shall discover therein a means for the fulfillment of both the mundane and spiritual life. The arts of the magician are made known, for they consist of the potent expression of the uniting of opposites. All have become bliss in the ecstatic state of enlightenment.*

The Celebrant proceeds to the northeastern angle and draws therein an inverted invoking pentagram of spirit creative upon the gate key, as well as an invoking spiral, then vibrates the letter *Aleph*, intones the word *Lampros* (the shining one), and says:

> *The Light of the Spirit shines forth from the lamp held by the exalted adept, and if we look, we shall see this light dimly perceived amidst the tenebrous shadows and foggy labyrinths of life's desolation and despair. Hearken to this master's light! For it leads us to our destiny and reveals, when the source of light is discovered, the true vision of the world and our place within it.*

The Celebrant proceeds to the center of the circle and therein bows, gives salute, and draws an inverted invoking pentagram of spirit creative upon the gate key placed therein. They also draw an invoking spiral, vibrate the letter *Kaph*, and intone the word *Sporos* (production of progeny), and says:

> *"Be fruitful and multiply," saith the false god of those religious leaders who presume through ignorance. The true path is not of this earth, and those who deceive us would*

bury us in concerns of the material world. Yet we know that the true knowledge of the Spirit shall be revealed to the ardent seeker, for even the densest fog or the utter gloom of total darkness cannot keep the steadfast seeker in ignorance. Let those who have obscured the truth with lies and illusions beware of the painful end to their folly. The Light of Truth shall eternally illuminate the world and will ultimately conquer all iniquities and injustices, for Spiritual Truth is the great equalizer, and nothing can evade it for long. Therefore, those who have seen the Light shall come together in fellowship and the body of adepts shall grow until one day, when it will contain all of humanity! Those who attempt to stop this evolution shall come to nought and be ground down to dust by necessity.

The Celebrant then stands in the North facing the South and draws all of the gate nodes (northeast, south, northwest, and center) together to form a tetrahedron, and then draws the three gate nodes of the base gateway trigon together in a deosil arc. The Celebrant advances from the North to the South, making the sign of the enterer and the sign of silence as they approach the threshold of the southern gate. Then, as the Celebrant stands before the southern gate, they make the sign of the rending of the veil and the opening portal gesture, enter the threshold, stand therein to receive its blessing, turn around to face the North, and proceed to the center of the circle.

The Celebrant, standing in the center of the circle, then draws the pentagram of spirit creative in the Infrapoint and intones the letter *Lamed*, projecting a violet energy into it.

The Celebrant then proceeds to draw the four watchtowers and three gate nodes together along the periphery of the magic circle using the staff, proceeding in a deosil arc. Then, the Celebrant takes the staff and, holding it over their head parallel to the floor, begins to turn in a deosil arc until reaching a climax of speed, and then projects the power into the Ultrapoint with the tip of the staff, joining the cone of power and the tetrahedron gate.

The Celebrant stands in the center of the circle and faces North (Air), then fuses the two pentagrammic devices set in the Ultra- and Infrapoints with a great invoking spiral, thus creating the central pylon. In the Mesopoint, the Celebrant visualizes the sign of the invoking septagon of creative spirit, signifying that the power vortex and tetrahedral blade are joined to form the magic sword. They hold a small, specially consecrated crystalline sword of power aloft and vibrate the letter *Lamed*, then say the following:

Lamed—the Power of the Yod is joined with the Tetrahedral Gate of Fire to forge the Great Sword of Power or Veritis Gladius (Sword of Truth), a true weapon of the Holy and Sacred Gnostic Magician. The Gate of Fire has purified my Will. All spurious and deceitful works are herein cast aside, and the True Will of the Holy Guardian Angel is herein empowered and projected into the world! And I give herein the exegesis of the Word:

Aleph, Lamed, Heh, Mim—Elohim!—the beloved spirit behold, the image of Yetzirah, a world of the Holy Qabalah! Therein shall you find the formulation of spirit into the consciousness of form, for thus is the generation of meaning and the awareness of spiritual values. The spirit has become a body both beauteous and filled with love. Therein is beheld the compassion of judgement and execution of divine retribution. This is the god of the creation of individual consciousness and to whom the masses pray and give sacrifice. Yet the Spirit of Consciousness is aware of a higher source and translates the inspiration it receives from that great transcendence into a powerful creed, which leads the individual to true self-knowledge. Herein are also the limitations which contain the world of individual consciousness. The process of self-identification stratifies the entity of awareness and holds it in the body of spiritual formation.

Then the Celebrant intones the following invocation from the *Ars Notoria of Solomon the King*:

Lameth, Leynach, Semach, Belmay, Azzailement, Gesegon, Lothamasim, Ozetogaglia, Zeziphier, Jofanum, Solatac, Bozefama, Defarciamar, Zemait, Lemaio, Pheralon, Anuc, Philosophi, Gregoon, Letos, Anum, Anum, Anum.[45]

Tetrapatron Power Vortex of Briah

Note: Circle progression uses a widdershins arc.

The Celebrant proceeds to the eastern watchtower and therein bows and gives salute. The Celebrant draws the invoking pentagram of Water and intones the letter *Shin*, projecting a golden energy into the pentagram.

The Celebrant proceeds to the northern watchtower and therein bows and gives salute. The Celebrant draws the invoking pentagram of Water and intones the letter *Yod*, projecting a green energy into the pentagram.

The Celebrant proceeds to the western watchtower and therein bows and gives salute. The Celebrant draws the invoking pentagram of Water and intones the letter *Aleph*, projecting an azure energy into the pentagram.

The Celebrant proceeds to the southern watchtower and therein bows and gives salute. The Celebrant draws the invoking pentagram of Water and intones the letter *Daleth*, projecting a scarlet energy into the pentagram.

The Celebrant proceeds to the center of the circle and therein bows and gives salute. The Celebrant draws the invoking pentagram of Water to the Infrapoint and intones the letter *Lamed*, projecting a violet energy into the pentagram. The Celebrant then draws all of the watchtowers together to the Infrapoint, starting in the East and proceeding widdershins, and they proceed to the North, West, and South.

The Celebrant then takes the staff and, holding it over their head parallel to the floor, they begin to turn in a widdershins arc, until reaching a climax of speed. Then, they ground the power into the Infrapoint with the end of the staff. The outer vortex is thus established.

The Celebrant meditates for a short period of time on the Gnostic wisdom of Valentinus, the First and Truly Greatest Gnostic Bishop. The Celebrant then draws an inner

---

45 Banner, James, ed., *Ars Notoria: The Notary Art of Solomon the King* (Trident Books, 1997) p. 11.

circle within the outer circle, wherein the inner circle is at least one foot of the edge of the outer circle. This is done with the sword.

The Celebrant proceeds to the southeastern angle, and draws therein an inverted invoking pentagram of spirit receptive, vibrates the letter *Gimmel,* and intones the word *Magia* (Magic) and says:

> *O light, in whom I have trusted, hear my repentance, and let my voice come into thy dwelling-place. Turn not thy image of light from me but regard me. If they constrain me, haste thee, and save me, when I shall cry unto thee, for my time passeth away as vapor, and I am become as matter.*[46]

The Celebrant proceeds to the northeastern angle and draws therein an inverted invoking pentagram of spirit receptive, vibrates the letter *Resh,* and intones the word *Baptisma* (Purification), and says:

> *O light of lights, in whom I have trusted from the beginning, hearken now, therefore, O light, unto my repentance. Save me, O light, for evil thoughts have come upon me. I gazed, O light, into the void; I saw a light there, and I thought, I will go into that region to take that light. And I went forth and fell into the midst of the lower Chaos.*[47]

The Celebrant proceeds to the northwestern angle, and draws therein an inverted invoking pentagram of spirit receptive, vibrates the letter *Lamed,* and intones the word *Pneuma* (Spirit), and says:

> *Light of lights, in whom I have trusted, leave me not in the darkness until the end of my time. Aid me, and save me, in thy mysteries. Incline thine ear unto me and save me. May the power of the light protect me, and carry me to the aeons of the height; for it is thou who shalt save me....*[48]

The Celebrant proceeds to the southwestern angle and draws therein an inverted invoking pentagram of spirit receptive, vibrates the letter *Nun,* and intones the word *hOrama* (Vision), and says:

> *O light of powers, give heed and save me. Let them that seek to take away my light be destitute and let them dwell in darkness. Let them that seek to take my power be turned into chaos and let them be ashamed. Let them descend speedily into the darkness, who constrain me saying, "We have mastered her." But let all those who seek the light, rejoice and be glad.*[49]

---

46 Mead, G.R.S., *Pistis Sophia: A Gnostic Gospel* (1921) p. 51.
47 *Ibid,* p. 37.
48 *Ibid,* p. 45.
49 *Ibid,* p. 49.

The Celebrant proceeds to the center of the circle and therein bows and gives salute, then draws therein an inverted invoking pentagram of spirit receptive to the Infrapoint and intones the word *Telos* (fulfillment). The Celebrant then intones:

Save me, O light, by thy great mystery; pardon me my transgression in thy remission; give unto me the baptism; remit my sins and purify me from my transgression. And my transgression is this lion-faced power, which hath never been hidden from thee; for because of it am I descended. "Tis I alone who have transgressed among the invisibles, in whose regions I was; I have descended into chaos, I have transgressed before thee, that thy statute might be accomplished."[50]

The Celebrant draws the four angles together into the Infrapoint, starting in the southeastern angle and proceeding widdershins to the northeast, the northwest, and completing in the southwest, thus establishing the inner vortex. The Celebrant then draws in the Ultrapoint a hexagram—the sign of union—and intones the letter *Aleph*, projecting a brilliant white energy into it.

The Celebrant then proceeds to draw the four angles together along the periphery of the magic circle using the staff, proceeding in a widdershins arc. Then Celebrant takes the staff and, holding it over their head parallel to the floor, begins to turn in a widdershins arc, until reaching a climax of speed, then projects the power into the Infrapoint with the end of the staff. The inner vortex of power is thus completed.

The Celebrant stands in the center of the circle and faces West (Water). They fuse the two pentagrammic devices set in the Infrapoint with a great invoking spiral, then draws the combined force of these two pentagrams up to the hexagram established in the Ultrapoint, thus creating the central pylon. In the Mesopoint, the Celebrant makes the sign of the trapezoidal-cross, signifying that the double vortices are joined into a Grail structure. They place in the center of the circle a specially consecrated chalice, filled with a liquid sacrament and covered with a purple veil upon a trigon of the Graal. The Celebrant then projects a spiral of sealing around it and vibrates the letter *Heh*, and says the following:

Heh—I invoke and reveal the Double-Vortices of the Womb Matrix: the Grail of Power, the inner and outer vortices of the mysteries of Sophia, that conjoined shall act as my most Holy Vault of the Adepts. And I give herein the exegesis of the Word:

Shin, Daleth, Aleph, Yod—Shadai—the Almighty!

Behold, the image of Briah, a World of the Holy Qabalah! Therein shall you find the potency of the forces of creation. For creation began with the fusion of polarities and, as such, it shall also terminate when the polarities once again merge in their full potency. Yet at this time, the violence of that joining has been superseded by the gentle mind of the Absolute working through the Primal Will upon the body or Throne of the creative matrix, and

---

50 Mead, G.R.S., *Pistis Sophia: A Gnostic Gospel* (1921) p. 92.

therein issues forth the stream of pure consciousness differentiated in awareness but unified in its formlessness. This is a model of the ideal method of magic, the ever-creative impulse establishing new formulations through its eternal transformations. This process of creation perfectly balances the intellect with the manifested spirit and therefore represents the goal of the true theurgist.

This chalice of the Grail that resides upon the altar trigon of the Greater Mysteries contains the elixir of the Feminine Spirit: may it become, for all who partake of it, the salvation of inequality and the redemption of all erroneous presumptions. Through it are we all profoundly inspired with the hidden truth!

Then, the Celebrant intones the following invocation from the *Ars Notoria of Solomon the King*:

O most mighty God, Invisible God, Theos Patir Herminas; By thy Archangels, Eliphamasay, Gelonucoa, Gebeche, Banai, Geraboaia, Elomnit; and by thy Glorious Angels, whose names are so consecrated, that they cannot be uttered by us; which are these, Do. Hel. X. P. A. Li. O. F. & c., which cannot be comprehended by human sense.[51]

When the mystery is complete, the Celebrant and all else who has partaken of it shall drink of the chalice of the Grail and be fortified thereof. The Celebrant then performs the ablutions for the chalice.

Tetrapatron Power Vortex of Atziluth

The Celebrant proceeds to the eastern watchtower and therein bows and gives salute. The Celebrant draws the invoking pentagram of Fire and intones the letter *Aleph*, projecting a golden energy into the pentagram.

The Celebrant proceeds to the southern watchtower and therein bows and gives salute. The Celebrant draws the invoking pentagram of Fire and intones the letter *Heh*, projecting a scarlet energy into the pentagram.

The Celebrant proceeds to the western watchtower and therein bows and gives salute. The Celebrant draws the invoking pentagram of Fire and intones the letter *Yod*, projecting an azure energy into the pentagram.

The Celebrant proceeds to the northern watchtower and therein bows and gives salute. The Celebrant draws the invoking pentagram of Fire and intones the letter *Heh*, projecting a green energy into the pentagram.

The Celebrant proceeds to the center of the circle and therein bows and gives salute. The Celebrant draws the invoking pentagram of Fire to the Infrapoint and intones the letter *Lamed*, projecting a violet energy into the pentagram.

The Celebrant proceeds to draw the four watchtowers to the Infrapoint in the order North, West, South, and East, using the sword. The Celebrant then takes the staff and,

---

[51] Banner, *op. cit.*, p. 12.

holding it over their head parallel to the floor, begins to turn in a deosil arc until reaching a climax of speed, and then grounds the power into the Infrapoint with the end of the staff. The positive vortex is thus established.

The Celebrant meditates for a short period of time on the Gnostic wisdom of Honorius, the Master Magician of Thebes and author of the *Sworn Book of Honorius*.

The Celebrant proceeds to the southeastern angle and draws therein an inverted invoking pentagram of spirit creative, vibrates the letter *Lamed,* and intones the word *Thaumasios* (wondrous), and says:

> *The seeker must fast, pray, and meditate for thirty days, saying the prayers as prescribed in the Sworn book (the great Psalter) at the stated times, and then begin the seven-day ordeal. The seeker shall make a mattress of exorcized hay, mosses, and linen, and place these into a clean room where the operation is to be done. They shall surround the mattress with clean sifted and dampened ashes, and upon the ashes around the mattress, they shall write the one-hundred names of God. They shall then perform the proper ablutions, and then, clothed in a hair shirt, they shall don their outer vestments, and perform their prayers until vespers, when they shall retire to the prepared room and perform the final prayers, saying: "Zabuather, Rabarmas, Yskiros, Kyrios, Gelon, Hel, Techel, Nothi, Ymeinlethon, Karex, Sabaoth, Sella, Chiros, Opiron, Nomygon, Oriel, Theos, Ya...." Then, they shall sleep and say no more, and they shall see the celestial palace and the mystery of God in all his glory, the nine orders of angels, and the company of all blessed spirits.*[52]

The Celebrant proceeds to the northeastern angle and draws therein an inverted invoking pentagram of spirit creative, vibrates the letter *Quf,* and intones the word *Abrotos* (Immortal), and says:

> *Good Jesus for thy ineffable mercy spare me, have mercy on me and hear me through the invocation of the Holy Trinity the Father, Son and Holy Spirit and that thou wouldst accept and take in good worth the words of my mouth by the invocation of thy 100 Holy Names.*[53]

The Celebrant proceeds to the northwestern angle and draws therein an inverted invoking pentagram of spirit creative, vibrates the letter *Nun,* and intones the word *Nekros* (The Dead), and says:

> *In this work let man remember death, for through the virtue of prayer and the power of God, in whom you must trust, your body will be made over into a spiritual body, and must be fed with spiritual meat, such as that of young ravens or crows, as David said: "He doth give the ox meat, and the meat of ravens and crow."*[54]

---

52 Driscoll, Daniel J., *The Sworn Book of Honorius the Magician* (Heptangle Books, 1977) pp. 60–67.
53 *Ibid,* p. 13.
54 *Ibid,* p. 67.

The Celebrant proceeds to the southwestern angle and draws therein an inverted invoking pentagram of spirit creative, vibrates the letter *Quf*, and intones the word *hAgios* (Holy), and says:

> *I beseech thee O my Lord, lighten and purge my soul and conscience with the brightness of thy light, illuminate and confirm my understanding with the sweetness of thy Holy Spirit.*[55]

The Celebrant proceeds to the center of the circle and therein bows and gives salute. The Celebrant intones:

> *We call this book the Sacred or Sworn Book for in it contained 100 sacred names of God.*[56]

The Celebrant then draws in the Ultrapoint the pentagram of spirit creative and intones the letter *Aleph*, projecting a brilliant white energy into it.

The Celebrant then proceeds to draw the four angles together along the periphery of the magic circle using the sword, proceeding in a widdershins arc. Then, the Celebrant takes the staff and, holding it over their head parallel to the floor, begins to turn in a widdershins arc, until reaching a climax of speed, and then projects the power into the Ultrapoint with the tip of the staff. The negative cone of power is thus established.

The Celebrant stands in the center of the circle and faces South (Fire). They then fuse the two pentagrammic devices set in the Ultra- and Infrapoints with a great invoking spiral, thus creating the central pylon. In the Mesopoint, the Celebrant makes the sign of the hexagram, signifying that the double powers of the vortices are joined. They hold a small, specially consecrated wand of power aloft and vibrate the letter *Shin*, and says the following:

> *Shin—the Power of the Double Wand of Power is thus activated. I draw the double powers of the Brilliant Vortex and the Dark Cone of Power, and therefore, in this wand that I hold, the forces of Light and Darkness are tightly bound so that they are one. The Yod-lode is the thunderbolt of the Great God, the Power of the Father of Fire, and the Primal Emanation of Creation! And I give herein the exegesis of the Word:*

> *Aleph, Heh, Yod, Heh—Ehieh! I shall be! Behold, the image of Atziluth, a World of the Holy Qabalah! Therein shall you find the individual awareness of selfhood which precipitated all creation—the primordial "I am!" For the core of all being consists of the knowledge of Selfhood, which distinguishes that self from all that is subjective to it. Everything that exists in consciousness is based upon the precepts of the definition of the individual self! The "I am" that promises to "become" is the identity of potential from which all future creation occurs. The individual self is never static, but ever-changing*

---

55 *Ibid*, p. 29.
56 *Ibid*, p. 3.

and transforming. The individuality of God represents the source of all spiritual change but is itself unchanged and undisturbed by the continuous emanation of its Being!

Then the Celebrant intones the following invocation from the *Ars Notoria of Solomon the King*:

Achacham, Yhel, Chelychem, Agzyvaztor, Yegor, Heilma, Helma, Hemna, Aglaros, Theomiros, Thomitos, Megal, Legal, Chariotos, Amasiel, Danyihayr.[57]

Tetrapatron Power Vortex of Stellar Gnosis

Note: Circle progression has a deosil arc.

The Celebrant stands in the center of the center and feels all of the previous vortex power fields coursing together in the temple. They draw these powers into their heart and hold them there while meditating for a short period of time. They then say:

Through my heart and soul, I see and know the Gnosis coursing through my mind from my Greater Spirit—the Bornless One, that does not die but is always one in the Godmind of the Eternal Source. I have tasted of the four Sacraments of Wisdom and know whereof they are made and how, and having mastered this wisdom, I seek the Eye of Lucifer so that I will know the Universal Mind and the "I" that is and is not, which lives in the soul of the ineffable eternal now! Thus is the Stone of Sion, the Mysterious Jewel of the Stellar Gnosis, and the Emerald Eye that lives through the union of the Tetrapatrons and unveils the mystery of the Undecigram to the subtle of mind and soul.

The Celebrant proceeds to the southeast angle and therein draws the sign of the Rose Cross, fills it with a rose-colored fluid, vibrates the letter *Lamed*, and intones the word *Thelema*. Below this device, the Celebrant draws an inverted invoking pentagram of spirit creative, and joins the two devices with an invoking spiral, thus creating the pylon. The Celebrant says:

Iezoramp, Zazamanp, Sacamap, Zachamy, Iecornamas, Iecohoruampda, Salatihel, Gezomel, Zarachiel, Megalis, Nachama.[58]

Lamed—the Power of the Yod is joined with the Tetrahedral Gate of Fire to forge the Great Sword of Power or Veritis Gladius (Sword of Truth), a true weapon of the Holy and Sacred Gnostic Magician. The Gate of Fire has purified my Will, all spurious and deceitful works are cast aside, and the True Will of the Holy Guardian Angel is herein empowered and projected into the world!

---

57 Banner, *op. cit.*, pp. 21–23.
58 Peterson, *op. cit.*, p. 161 starting with tenth word.

The Celebrant proceeds to the southwest angle and therein draws the sign of the hexagram cross, fills it with a golden colored fluid, vibrates the letter *Shin*, and intones the word *Agape*. Below this device, the Celebrant draws an inverted invoking pentagram of spirit creative, and joins the two devices with an invoking spiral, thus creating the pylon. The Celebrant says:

Nechamyha, Sazamaym, Suphonaym, Lazamair, Mehisrampna, Hamamyl, Zamanyl, Sihel, Deloth, Hamamyn, Hazameloch.[59]

Shin—the Power of the Double Wand of Power is thus activated. I draw the double powers of the Brilliant Vortex and the Dark Cone of Power, and therefore, in this wand that I hold, are the forces of Light and Darkness tightly bound so that they are one. The Yod-lode is the thunderbolt of the Great God, the Power of the Father of Fire, and the Primal Emanation of Creation!

The Celebrant proceeds to the northwest angle and therein draws the sign of the Pisces cross, fills it with a violet-colored fluid, vibrates the letter *Heh*, and intones the word *Thanatos*. Below this device, the Celebrant draws an inverted invoking pentagram of spirit receptive, and joins the two devices with an invoking spiral, thus creating the pylon. The Celebrant says:

Moys, Ramna, Secoram, Hamasichonea, Seronea, Zaramahem, Sacromohem, Iegonomay, Zaramohem, Chades.[60]

Heh—I invoke and reveal the Double-Vortices of the Womb Matrix: the Grail of Power, the inner and outer vortices of the mysteries of Sophia, that conjoined shall act as my most Holy Vault of the Adepts. This chalice of the Grail that resides upon the altar trigon of the Greater Mysteries contains the elixir of the Feminine Spirit. May it become, for all who partake of it, the salvation of inequality and the redemption of all erroneous presumptions. Through it, we are all profoundly inspired by the hidden truth!

The Celebrant proceeds to the northern watchtower and therein draws the sign of the Rose Ankh, fills it with an azure-colored fluid, vibrates the letter *Tet*, and intones the word *Eros*. Below this device, the Celebrant draws an inverted invoking pentagram of spirit receptive, and joins the two devices with an invoking spiral, thus creating the pylon. The Celebrant says (choosing the language appropriate for one's gender):

Bachuc, Iezemeloht, Harugo, Semorgizechon, Malaparos, Malapatas, Helatay, Helahenay, Methay, Meray.[61]

---

59 *Ibid*, starting with twenty-second word.
60 *Ibid*, starting with thirty-third word.
61 *Ibid*, starting with forty-third word.

Tet—Aegis of the Masters, Crown of Glory, Holy Octagon Shield of Power, I set forth and establish the base of all powers, wherein the magus has defined (his/her/their) domain and (sent forth his power and light into the earth/received into her chalice the light and fire of heaven/envisioned the heavens and earth rejoicing in their union of life). The Dragon of the World Tree shall encircle this place, and the Great Goddess shall bless it with life and eternal renewal. In this sacred place is formulated the Dawn Creation of all Kings; in this place is Eden and Paradise, the Blood and Host of the True Graal, the Cornucopia and Cauldron of Rebirth. The Wisdom of the Structure of the Emanation of Spirit is herein given as a Gnosis of Spirit and Mind conjoined: the Universal Intelligence. This power wards, protects, and guides the seeker on the path to realization and awards (him/her/them) the mastery of life. The Keys to Heaven, Earth, and Hell are herein given to the wise mage who knows the Mystery of the Graal: the three Questions and their Answers.

The Celebrant proceeds to the center of the circle in the Ultrapoint and therein visualizes an inverted septagon of spirit receptive, fills it with a brilliant emerald-colored fluid, vibrates the letter *Aleph*, and intones the word *Astron*. The Celebrant then draws the device of Pluto (the Grail Sign) in the Infrapoint, and charges it with a violet fluid. They then draw a line of force, rising from the Infrapoint slowly and profoundly up to the Ultrapoint, where the power is expressed with a great exhalation of cool breathing and projection through the highest point and beyond. A central pylon is thus created. The Celebrant says:

Malocht, Otheos, Hatamagiel, Hataha, Marihel, Gezozay, Iezoray, Gezozay, Saziel, Sazamay.[62]

Aleph—Emerald Eye of Lucifer, Jewel Star of Gnosis, Crystal Stone of Sion, the Fifth Graal, which is the amalgamation of the Vortex Power Fields of the Tetrapatron—the Four Powers of Tetra-sacramentary of Gnosis. Through this Eye are all mysteries revealed. Through this Jewel are all awards, honors, and accolades given including the highest rank of the master adept. Through this Stone are all other symbols of the Graal, and their virtues and powers, derived. The Sacred Seven Stellar Gnostic Rays shine through the abyss of all time and space, radiating its glories and wisdom upon us all. Thus is the sacrament of the Stars, the One True Vision of all that was and shall ever be, and that which is nought. We seek the Power and Vision of the Spirit of God, through the aegis of the Bornless One, who is known and never known, understood and inexplicable, the mystery and the manifestation of the single individual sentient being, the Sorcerer of Time and Space, and the myriad infinite beings that have been and always shall ever be—the One that is eternal and unfathomable.

---

62 *Ibid,* starting with first word.

The Celebrant, using the transmutar wand, draws each of the four trapezoidal points of the circle together to form the grand trapezoid, starting in the Southeast and proceeding deosil to the Southwest, Northwest, North, and completing in the Southeast. The Celebrant then draws each of the pylon devices in the four trapezoidal points of the circle to the center of the circle in the Ultrapoint, starting with the Southeast and proceeding widdershins to the North, Northwest, Southwest, and completing in the Southeast. The Celebrant then takes the staff and, holding it over their head parallel to the floor, begin to turn in a widdershins arc until reaching a climax of speed, and then project the power into the Ultrapoint with the tip of the staff. The positive vortex is thus established.

The Celebrant stands in the center of the circle and faces the Ultrapoint (Spirit). They then fuse the two devices set in the Ultra- and Infrapoints with a great invoking spiral, thus establishing the Emerald Eye of Lucifer. In the Mesopoint, the Celebrant holds a small wooden platform, upon which is set a crystal pyramid.

The Celebrant focuses on the crystal pyramid and feels all the emanations of the five vortex power fields fuse into union within it. They then sense a great radiation of power rise up from the Infrapoint through the Mesopoint, enter their body, and travel up and beyond the Ultrapoint.

After sensing this for a period and soaking it into their body, the Celebrant sets the wooden platform with the crystal pyramid carefully upon the central altar. They then draw a sealing spiral around it, stands away from it in the center of the circle, and says:

Aleph, Lamed, Shin, Tet, Heh—AL-ShaTaH—The Great Star of the Bornless One!

A Dark Night: Not a star is visible, but presently the moon shines out through a rift in the clouds. And I remember; "The sorrows are but shadows, they pass and are done, but there is that which remains."

Yet is the moon but illusion.

A dull day; but presently the Sun is seen as the clouds are dispelled by His light.

Is He that which remains?

Night once more; the Sun is lost to sight, only the moon reminds me of His presence. The clouds scud swiftly across the sky and disappear.

Thy Star Body is visible, O Beloved; all the sorrows and shadows have passed and there is that which remains.

When the clouds gather, let me never forget Thee, O Beloved![63]

---

63 Achad, *op. cit.*, p. 33.

The Celebrant then sits in the center of the circle and ponders upon the mysteries of this rite. The Celebrant completes this final and fifth process with a period of meditation before beginning the invocation of the Bornless One.

Then the Celebrant stands and takes the consecrated ring from the previous working from out of the purple velvet cloth, places it on the ring finger, and intones the sacred word of the godhead. They will assume the full power of the ring just before performing the invocation of the Bornless One.

The Invocation of the Bornless One

The Celebrant, standing in the center of the circle, performs the centering exercise of the descending wave, drawing the energy from the Ultrapoint down to their crown chakra. The Celebrant says:

Thee I invoke the Bornless One.
Thee that didst create the earth and the heavens.
Thee that didst create the night and the day.
Thee that didst create the darkness and the light.
Thou art Osoronnophris, whom no man hath seen at any time.
Thou art Iabas. Thou art Iapos.
Thou hast distinguished between the just and the unjust.
Thou didst make the female and the male.
Thou didst produce the seed and the fruit.
Thou didst form men to love one another and also to hate one another.

The Celebrant should fashion a personal invocation based on the example below.

I am (sacramental name and magical motto) of the Order of Lux et Tenebris in the inner, the Egregora Sancta Stella Gnostica in the outer; I am thy prophet unto whom thou didst commit thy mysteries: the ceremonies of the magic of Light and Darkness.

Thou didst produce the moist and the dry, and that which nourish all created things. Hear me, thou, for I am the messenger of Pharaoh Osoronophris. This is thy true name, handed down from the prophets of the Sun.

The Celebrant, facing the Southeast, makes the sign of the Rose Cross and vibrates the name Yashua (Deliverer), then draws it toward themselves to connect with the heart chakra.

The voice of my Higher Self said unto me: "Let me enter the path of darkness, and peradventure there shall I find the light. I am the only being in an abyss of darkness; from an abyss of darkness came I forth ere my birth, from the silence of a primal sleep. And the Voice of Ages answered unto my soul: 'I am (he/she/they) who formulates in darkness, the light that shineth in darkness, yet the darkness comprehended it not.'"

The Celebrant turns to the Southwest, makes the sign of the Rose Cross, and vibrates the name Yashua (Deliverer), then draws it toward themselves to connect with the heart chakra.

Hear me: Arbathiao Rheibet Atheleberseth Arablatha Albeue Ebenphchi Chithasgoe Ibaoth Iao; hear me, and make all spirits subject unto me, so that every spirit of the firmament and the aether, upon the earth and under the earth, on dry land and in the water, of whirling air, and of rushing fire, and every spell and scourge of God the vast one may be obedient unto me.

The Celebrant turns to the Northwest, makes the sign of the Rose Cross, and vibrates the name Yashua (Deliverer), then draws it toward themselves to connect with the heart chakra.

I invoke thee, the awesome and invisible God who dwelleth in the void place of the Spirit. Arogogorobrao Sochou Modorio Phalarchao Ooo. The Holy Bornless One. Hear me, and make all spirits subject unto me, so that every spirit of the firmament and the aether, upon the earth and under the earth, on dry land and in the water, of whirling air, and of rushing fire, and every spell and scourge of God the vast one may be obedient unto me.

The Celebrant turns to the Northeast, makes the sign of the Rose Cross, and vibrates the name Yashua (Deliverer), then draws it toward themselves to connect with the heart chakra.

Hear me: Roubriao Mari Odam. Baabnabaoth Assadonai Aphniao Itholeth Abrasax Aeooy, mighty Bornless One! Hear me, and make all spirits subject unto me, so that every spirit of the firmament and the aether, upon the earth and under the earth, on dry land and in the water, of whirling air, and of rushing fire, and every spell and scourge of God the vast one may be obedient unto me.

The Celebrant turns to the center, makes the sign of the Rose Cross in the Infrapoint, and vibrates the name Yashua (Deliverer), then draws it toward themselves to connect with the heart chakra.

Hear me: Mabarraio Ioel Kotha Athorebalo Abraoth! Hear me, and make all spirits subject unto me, so that every spirit of the firmament and of the aether, upon the earth and under the earth, on dry land and in the water, of whirling air, and of rushing fire, and every spell and scourge of God the vast one may be obedient unto me.

The Celebrant turns to the East, makes a large invoking spiral, and vibrates the name Yashua (Deliverer), then draws it toward themselves to connect with the heart chakra.

Hear me: Aoth Abraoth Basym Isak Sabaoth IAO! This is the (Lord/Lady) of the Gods. This is the (Lord/Lady) of the Universe. This is (he/she/they) whom the winds fear. This is (he/she/they), who having made voice by (his/her/their) commandment (is/are he/she/they), who of all things, (King/Queen), Ruler and Helper.

Hear me, and make all spirits subject unto me, so that every spirit of the firmament and the aether, upon the earth and under the earth, on dry land and in the water, of whirling air, and of rushing fire, and every spell and scourge of God the vast one may be obedient unto me.

The Celebrant turns to the Center, makes the sign of the hexagram in the Ultrapoint, and vibrates the name Protonoia, then draws it toward themselves to connect with the crown chakra.

Hear me: Ieou Pyr Iou Pyr Iaoth Iaeo Ioou Abrasax Aabriam OO YY EY Adonai! Eide Eide (Immediately! Immediately!) Angelos Kalos Tou Theon! Anlala Lai Gaia Apa Diachanna Choryn.

(He/She/They) Come(s) in the Power of the Light.
(He/She/They) Come(s) in the Light of Wisdom.
(He/She/They) Come(s) in the Mercy of the Light.
The Light Hath Healing in its Wings.
Let Heart and Mind Be as One in the Spirit!

The Celebrant then faces the East and draws the energy of the circle up into their body until it reaches the heart chakra. Then, while assuming the body posture of the tau cross, the Celebrant focuses upon the fiery hexagram in the Ultrapoint and draws the power from the heart chakra up to the crown and beyond, then pauses to establish a potent trance state. When the resulting trance state has cleared somewhat, the Celebrant continues:

Out of the darkness, let that light arise. Before I was blind, but now I see. I am the dweller in the invisible, the reconciler with the ineffable.

For the male Celebrant:

I am the Bornless Spirit, always knowing wherever I am bound, for I have sight in my feet. I am the Mighty One who possesses the Immortal Fire. I am the Great Truth who hates that evil should be wrought in the world. I am the one that causes lightning and thunder. I am the one whose sweat falls upon the earth as rain so that it can fill the oceans and bring new life. I am the one whose mouth burns completely. I am the one who begets and destroys. I am the favor of the Aion; my name is like a heart encircled by a serpent. Come forth and follow!

For the female Celebrant:

I am she, the Bornless Spirit, having wisdom in the heart, enduring and the immortal love. I am she, the Truth. I am she who seeks to right all wrongs wrought in the world. I am she that emanates all light and love. I am she, from whom the bounty of the spiritual gifts of life is given. I am she whose lips bestow the kiss of peace. I am she, the creatrix and fashioner of the sacred light. I am she, the compassion and love of the world.

For other Celebrants:

I am they, the Bornless Spirit, having wisdom in the soul, neither one nor the other, but unified in both. I am they, the mystery. I am they, who seeks justice, equality, and equity for all, and the dignity to be acknowledged. I am they, who emanates both Light and Darkness, who are above and below, behind and in front, and who pervade through all manifestations. I give the gift of the sovereignty of the individual and the blessings of love everlasting. I am they, who both creates and receives, the holder of the grail and the protector of its mysteries. I wield the sword of justice and the balancing scales of peace.

All:

I am the Trimorphic Protonoia! Hear me, and make all spirits subject unto me, so that every spirit of the firmament and the aether, upon the earth and under the earth, on dry land and in the water, of whirling air, and of rushing fire, and every spell and scourge of God the vast one may be obedient unto me. Iao Sabaoth Adonai Abrasax, and by the Great God, Iaeo, Aeeioyo Oyoieea Chabrax Phnesker Phiko Phnyro Phocho Bouch Ablanathanalba! Such are the words.

The Celebrant performs the exercise of centering for a final time. The Celebrant may then sit in meditation in the center of the circle and enjoy the ambience of the resultant invocation.

Prior to working the assumption rite, the Celebrant shall intone the following invocation:

IAŌ IAŌ IAŌ I call upon you, Ptha Ra Ptha Iē Phtha Oun Emēcha Erōchth Barōch Thorchtha Thōm Chaieouch Archandabar Ōeaeō Ynēōch Ēra Ōn Ēlōph Bom Phtha Athabrasia Abriasōth Barbarbelōcha Barbaiaōch; let there be depth, breadth, length, brightness, Ablanathanalba Abrasiaoua Akramma Chamarei Thōth Hōr Athōōpō. Come in, lord, and reveal![64]

The Crossing of the Gate of Light

The Celebrant resets the three talismanic gate keys; one in the southwest angle (The Chariot Atu VII), one in the eastern watchtower (The Lovers Atu VI), and one in the northwest angle (The Sun Atu XIX), with the appropriate Tarot Trumps placed on each. The Celebrant then meditates on the cards, building up the energies and noting the significance of the Gate Tarot Trumps.

The Celebrant then stands in the West, facing the East, and say:

The Gate of the Mysteries of the Self as God begins with the establishment of the Destiny of the Individual Soul and the three questions (of the Grail Mystery) applied to oneself,

---

64 Betz, *op. cit.*, p. 159.

and these are: "Who am I?", "Where have I been?", and "Where am I bound?" These questions and their answers manifest the three dimensions of the individual self, the three I's, or the Eye in the Triangle—thus I invoke!

The Celebrant then makes the sign of the Eye in the Triangle (hands held flat before oneself, index and thumb of both hands touching to form the triangle, and either the left or right eye staring out through it.

The Celebrant draws a trapezoidal cross and seals it with an invoking spiral in the southwestern angle, charging the gate key therein, vibrating the letter *Chet*, and intoning the word *Chavav* (to love), and then saying:

> *[Atu VII] I have come prepared for the process of my greatest transformation, for I have taken upon myself the armor of love and compassion, and I hold the Grail of the Spirit of Light in my heart. I seek union with the Source of all Spirituality, the Absolute Spirit who has authored all conscious sentience though its emanations. And the four Cherubim form the Chariot or Sacred Arc (Vault of the Adepts), wherein the Holy Mystery is enacted for those who realized the Graal. Yet this Mystery is protected by the Cherubim from those who are unworthy or ignorant.*
>
> *Lamed, Rogum, Ragia, Ragium, Ragiomal, Agaled, Eradioch, Anchovionos, Lechen, Saza, Ya, Manichel, Mamacuo, Lephoa, Bozaco, Cogemal, Salauyel, Yesunanu, Azaroch, Beyestar, Amak.*[65]

The Celebrant draws a trapezoidal cross and seals it with an invoking spiral in the eastern watchtower, charging the gate key therein, vibrating the letter *Zain*, and intoning the word *Zarach* (to rise up like the sun), and then saying:

> *[Atu VI] I seek to know the Great Love of the Absolute Spirit: to be fulfilled through the Power of the Unity of All Being and touched to the core of my heart and soul with the Shining Brilliant Light of the Love of God. This light draws me nigh unto it, where I bask in the Eternal Sun of Inner Illumination. The soul, mind, and body are brought into union within the Bornless Spirit of the Aeons, called Protonoia, Atman, and the Holy Guardian Angel—the God Within the "I." The archetypal male and female are thus joined together at the Wedding of the Soul and the Spirit, and therein is the salvation of the Sophia that had become lost in the World of Darkness and Illusion.*
>
> *Hanazay, Sazhaon, Hubi Sone, Hay, Ginbar, Ronail, Selmore, Hyramay, Lobal, Yzazamael, Amathomatois, Yaboageyors, Sozomcrat, Ampho, Delmedos, Geroch, Agalos, Meithatagiel, Secamai, Sabeleton, Mechorgrisces, Lerirenorbon.*[66]

---

65 Banner, *op. cit.*, p. 18.

66 *Ibid*, p. 40.

The Celebrant draws a trapezoidal cross and seals it with an invoking spiral in the northwestern angle, charging the gate key therein, vibrating the letter *Resh*, and intoning the word *Ruach* (the Soul or breath of life), and then saying:

[Atu XIX] The Twin Souls of the Lovers are united in the bond of the One Spirit, and therein the Holy Kingdom of the Deity is revealed in all its splendor and glory. Within are the Holy Trees of Life and Wisdom, and the Great Temple of the Mysteries. Yet the Mystery of the Self and its eternal counterpart, the Bornless One, shall herein be revealed, as well as its higher purpose in the destiny of the Absolute Being of Light. Let me come to know this sacred personage, to utter its name as a word of great magical power, and to know it as I seek to know myself. Thus, in revealing its essence, I shall reveal the Brilliant Light of my Inner God to all—and I am reborn as the Aten Disk, blazing in the Eastern sky as the light of the First Dawn.

Ezamamos, Hazalat, Ezityne, Hezemechel, Czemomechel, Zamay, Zaton, Ziamay, Nayzaton, Hyzemogoy, Jehhomantha, Jaraphy, Phalezeton, Sacrampha, Sagamazaim, Secranale, Sacramthan, Jezennalaton, Hachenatos, Jetelemathon, Zaymazay, Gigutheio, Geurlagon, Garyos, Mega'on, Hera, Cruhic, Crarihuc, Amen.[67]

The Celebrant then takes the transmutar wand and draws the three nodes of the gate structure together through the center of the circle in the Ultrapoint. They then draw an exterior circle, unifying the three nodes of the gate within its arc.

The Celebrant makes the sign of the parting of the threshold while standing in the West and facing the East, then advances through the gate to the center of the circle. The Celebrant says the following formula of union:

Chavav—The Love of God Shall Fortify Me!

Zarach—I shall rise up like the Sun and be united in Perfect Blissful Love!

Ruach—The Marriage of the Soul and the Bornless Spirit reveals the Paradise of the Mysteries of the Absolute Spirit!

Chabab—Zarach—Ruach—Chazar! (To Return)

Behold, I have opened the gate to my destiny, and now I summon forth its vision into the manifested World of Formation. I shall ask the three questions of the Mystery and seek their answers in the Halls of the Greatest Mystikon, and these questions are: "Who am I—what is my eternal and true essence?" "Where have I been and Why?" All of the fortunes and calamities that have befallen me are perceived as the Greater Veil of Necessity, and I accept them as part of the path that has led me to the Gateway of the

---

67 *Ibid*, pp. 45–46.

Holy Spirit. "Where am I bound, what is my destiny?" With this question I am bowed before you, the Source of All, and the mystery of my destiny is made clear to me. For there can be only one True Destiny, and that is where the Soul and Spirit are joined as One. Thus is revealed the Eye in the Triangle—(Celebrant makes the sign)—the three "I's" that stand as markers to my Sacred Goal.

Thus is the Eye of Flesh, which shall see all the phenomena of the material world. The Eye of the Mind, which shall know all the mysteries of the inter-subjective structures. The Eye of Spirit (contemplation), which shall know the mysteries of the soul and the ineffable Gnosis. Each way of knowledge has its place and importance, and we shall never confuse one with the other; for such is the nature of the true apprehension of the greatest truth and the method of enlightenment. Thus is the Eye in the Triangle! So mote it be.

The Celebrant deeply contemplates the secret responses to the three questions until they are clearly known and perceived as a vision. The Celebrant then proceeds to perform the Lotus seven-breath, achieving a profound trance and climax at the end of this working.

Closing and Sealing the Gate of Light

The Celebrant says:

Be my mind open to the Spirit of the Absolute. Be my heart a center for the Light and the Love which blesses the infinite realms. Be my body a temple for the Eternal Flame of the highest spiritual purpose. So mote it be.

The Celebrant then stands and turns to the West, leaving the center of the circle, then turns again to face the East, standing in the West. The Celebrant performs the Closing Threshold gesture and then seals the three gate nodes, beginning with the Northwest, then the East, and finishing in the Southwest.

The Celebrant seals the four watchtowers, the four angles, and the Ultrapoint and Infrapoint. The ritual is completed. The Celebrant now silently meditates and ponders the meaning of all that has transpired—and does not perform this rite again until all is clear and realized.

CHAPTER SEVEN

ALCHEMICAL HIEROMANY RITE OF UNION

This ritual is the culmination of the Abramelin Lunar Ordeal, representing the point where all of the elements of this series of rituals are brought to perfect and harmonious completion. The mythic theme and structure for this ritual is based upon the critical Rosicrucian document *The Chemical Wedding of Christian Rosenkreutz*. Many have puzzled over this simple seven-part allegory, and its simplicity belies a deep and powerful mystery that is still relevant today, even though it was supposedly first written in 1604 CE. Still, I was fortunate in having in my library a copy of the book, with a new translation by Joscelyn Godwin and a powerful commentary written by Adam McLean.[68] It is due to Mr. McLean's brilliant commentary that the allegory was reducible to a format, which allowed it to be incorporated into this ritual. The sevenfold pattern of the allegory is analogous to the sevenfold stages of the alchemical magnum opus, which was meant to illuminate as well as obfuscate.

As a historical note to this entire ordeal and its presentation, this last ritual entirely eluded me when I assembled the rituals for the Abramelin Lunar Ordeal together back in 2009. I knew that some kind of ritual marriage or union was required, but exactly how to do this was completely opaque to me. Even so, I took what rituals I had and went ahead and performed them, with the exception of the Bornless Envisioning rite and the Assumption of Great Powers. By undergoing that ordeal in the late autumn and early winter of 2009, I was able to put a process of spiritual ascension into motion that has produced many amazing things. Still, I was not able to conclude the ordeal because I was missing the last and essential piece of the puzzle. This had a deleterious effect on me overall, and I had problems balancing what I experienced in the ritual and what I experienced in life afterwards.

---

68 Godwin, Joscelyn and Adam McLean, *The Chemical Wedding of Christian Rosenkreutz* (Phanes Press, 1991).

A goddess (Godhead of Water) was revealed to me in that working, as well as an image of myself as an ageless youth (my Bornless or Higher Self), but what I required was a method to ritually join them together where they could be reborn as a singular unified expression, living as my innate conscious being. Many months passed, and only a year after the time that I began the ordeal did the meaning and purpose of the final rite become revealed. It came in fragments, and then in whole pieces as I carefully read, studied, and meditated on the translation and the commentary on the Chemical Wedding, which had been the very first clue.

The key to this mystery is that the Chemical Wedding is not really a wedding as we would understand it. It is more like an allegory of death (a voluntary execution) and an alchemical rebirth of a young king and queen. In the process, their substances are fully commingled and jointly undergo the redemptive and creative process of complete alchemical rebirth, where their new forms are of the highest and purest nature—Spirit residing and incarnating in nature. A traditional wedding is wholly absent from this allegory, and so is any kind of Christian symbology or allegorical tropes. The story is completely alchemical and philosophical, but it hides a powerful mystery that is timeless and critical to understanding the higher processes of spiritual union.

Therefore, with this final ritual functioning as the most important keystone, I was able to complete this ordeal and proceed from that point forward. I had successfully acquired the powerful forces that freed and unleashed, for all time, my spirit and being. I wrote the accounts of this final working in my journal and noted the final combination of operations for this ordeal, which will also include the Bornless Envisioning rite and the Assumption of Great Powers.

This ritual working consists of a four-part layer of ritual structures that represent the Magic Castle of Mysteries, the Descending Tetrahedral Gateway or Underworld Tower of Transformation, the Inner Domain of the Crossroads and inner circle, which denotes where the core of the mystery is revealed, and then, finally, the Ascending Tetrahedral Gateway or Tower of Resurrection. The central or core mystery is a simple three-way handfasting between the three elements revealed in the Abramelin Ordeal: the archetypal feminine, the archetypical masculine, and the magician fused together in space and time. The elements of the ring, magic mirror, and the vestments of glory are blessed, empowered, and sacralized so that they may be used by the high adept to represent the union of Spirit, Mind, and Body—the Three-fold Initiation.

The rite begins with a powerful introit, where the Celebrant contemplates the invitation to the Alchemical Wedding of the Deity and Higher Self. These are depicted as polarities: the Divine King and Queen. After a suitable period of meditation, the Celebrant indicates that they truly will themselves to proceed with the mystery, knowing that to do so is to incur a transformation that cannot be reversed or taken for granted.

The Magic Castle of the Mysteries is a ritual structure that consists of the four watchtowers set with proper formulas and the device of the Rose Cross. The center of the circle is set with an inverted Rose Ankh, representing the Orb of Dominion, and the four Rose Crosses, which is a construct that represents the seat of the divine royalty, or

Sangreal. These five structures form the outer castle structure where the outer mysteries are revealed.

There are a number of correspondences that can be used at these five points, but most notable are the five classical stages in Alchemy (which predated the seven used in this rite). However, the theme of this outer vehicle is encapsulated in the formula that is used to spell the word *cruor*, which means "blood" in Latin. The Castle of the Mysteries is the divine Regnum, which exists everywhere but cannot be perceived except by the wise and the elect. The five-fold castle structure, which is determined by the operation of squaring the circle, represents the five qualities of the Castle depicted in the Chemical Wedding. It consists of the outer gates and antechamber, the dining hall, the garden, the library (room of the great globe), and the hall of the wedding. Omitted is the hall of the sun (where the play within a play is enacted) and the secret treasury, where the tomb of the sleeping Venus lies. This last item is alluded to in the outer rite. The Magic Castle could easily be seen as an analogue for the mythic Grail Castle.

The Descending Tetrahedral Gateway, or Tower of Transformation, is the first of the tetrahedral gateway structures that leads the Celebrant into the underworld core of the mysteries. The descent represents the first three steps of the alchemical process: calcination, dissolution, and separation. All three of these steps represent the reducing of the prima materia into its more elementary forms, symbolizing the death and reduction of the young king and queen in the Chemical Wedding. The three formula letters and Tarot cards are the Hermit (Atu IX, *Yod*), the Hanged Man (Atu XII, *Mim*), and Death (Atu XIII, *Nun*).

The central mystery chamber, which is the third structure, is derived from the combination of the erection of the four crossroads with a central inner circle. The theme of the mystery chamber is found in the Tarot card the Lovers (Atu VI, *Zain*). This is where the Chemical Wedding, or joining of the physical substances of the sacrificed king and queen, are combined to form the synthesis of material out of which they shall be reborn and resurrected. The inner mystery is also a simple wedding ceremony or "handfasting" between the Godhead aspect, the representative of one's Higher Self, and the Celebrant. It would be assumed that this mystery will be slightly different for each individual and may involve a God aspect instead of Goddess (as I have personally experienced it). The alchemical stage of conjunction is depicted at this point of the rite.

The fourth ritual structure is the Ascending Tetrahedral Gateway, or Tower of Resurrection. It is the second and final tetrahedral structure that leads the Celebrant out of the mystery chamber and into the light of the day. This is an evolutionary arc that uses the final three stages of alchemy, which are fermentation, distillation, and coagulation. All three of these steps represent the regeneration and reconstitution of the prima materia into its final formulation, the Great Work of the Philosopher's Stone, and the Universal Medicine. The formula letters and Tarot cards are Aion or Last Judgement (Atu XX, *Shin*), Art (Atu XIV, *Samek*), and the Star/Fisher King (Atu IV, *Tzadi*).

The circuit of seven alchemical steps represents the completion of the Great Work and the fusion of the three elements of the self into a three-fold initiatory mastery of oneself and Spirit. Once this operation is complete and stabilized over one lunar cycle, then the final rite, known as the Envisioning, can be performed to completion.

The barbarous words of evocation used in the Castle of the Mysteries ritual structure are taken from the *Greek Magical Papyri in Translation*, section *PGM V*, 1–53, which is the spell for the Oracle of Serapis.

ALCHEMICAL HIEROMANY RITE OF UNION

This ritual is performed immediately following the Bornless One invocation rite, so in preparation, all of the associated rituals established with that working would be performed ahead of this ritual. The Alchemical Hieromany rite of Union represents the final event in the exceptional body of lore, performed in a single working.

Introit and Erection of the Castle of the Mysteries (Grail Castle)

The Celebrant stands in the center of the magic circle and salutes the four cardinal directions, beginning with the East and proceeding deosil, turning in place. They say the following introit prayer while looking at and focusing on the Ultrapoint in the center of the circle.

> *We, the worthy, are invited to the Chemical Wedding of the divine queen and king, who await our coming with trepidation and relief. The Chemical Wedding is not a true wedding in the sense that we would understand it. It is an execution, an alchemical fusion, and a potent restoration. Each of us has an important part to play and, as the adept in the guise of Christian Rosenkreutz, we are integral to the process of resurrection. You must know that we shall undergo a perilous journey; we shall be tested in our humility and weighed seven times by the scales of spiritual necessity. Seven gifts are given to us and we must give up seven possessions in order to gain entrance to the sacred Castle of the Mysteries and the Twin Towers of Transformation and Resurrection. The alchemical process has seven steps: three descending, three ascending, and one to enfold them all. Thus, we now begin.*

Then the Celebrant stands in silent meditation for a few minutes, letting the substance of the introit prayer penetrate deep within.

The Celebrant proceeds to the eastern watchtower, bows, and then, using the transmutar wand, draws a great Rose Cross, sealing it with an invoking spiral. They then intone the magic word *Convivor* and say the following incantation:

> *Convivor: we are brought together in fellowship and initiatory zeal—the convocation of regeneration and renewal. Nigredo: this is the prima materia or black matter from which the art begins. All must be reduced to the most simplistic level in order to establish the worthiest of foundations for the Great Work. Thus, we cross the three gates and enter the antechamber in the Castle of the Groom.*

Abraal Bachambēchi Baibeizōth Ēbai Bēboth Seriabebōth Amelchipsithiousthipothoio Pnoute Ninthērou Iyey Eoō Aieia Eeoia.[69]

The Celebrant proceeds to the southern watchtower, bows, and then, using the transmutar wand, draws a great Rose Cross, sealing it with an invoking spiral. They then intone the magic word *Redemptio,* and say the following incantation:

Redemptio: we seek salvation and redemption from all errors and transgressions against our Higher Selves. As people of humble spiritual states, we seek wisdom with pure hearts and humility. Albedo: the silver-white light of the Lunar Goddess. The Great Feminine Spirit teaches us compassion, love, grace, and spiritual service. Thus, we come to the dining hall, and therein learn to be humble and deny ourselves any hint of privilege.

Eeai Eyēie Ōōōōō Eyēō Iaōai Bakaxichych Bosipsetēt Phobēbirōth.[70]

The Celebrant proceeds to the western watchtower, bows, and then, using the transmutar wand, draws a great Rose Cross, sealing it with an invoking spiral. They then intone the magic word *Ubertas,* and say the following incantation:

Ubertas: the blessings of the mysteries bequeath to us a great abundance—not to us individually, but to humanity as a whole. The Holy Spirit pours out its blessing onto the earth, and all we need do to receive any of it is to give of ourselves. In giving, we receive, and what we lose in the quest for the One shall be rewarded to us three times or more. Citrinitas: the golden-ocher of the Solar God. The Great Masculine Spirit teaches us charity, truthfulness, strength, and integrity. Thus, we come to the garden where a mysterious fountain shows us the inner truth of the Sun and the Moon.

O Dargazas O Darmagas O Daphar Yakiaboth Ephia Zelearthar Akrabaeōphiazale Abramenothiēō Samas Phrēti.[71]

The Celebrant proceeds to the northern watchtower, bows, and then, using the transmutar wand, draws a great Rose Cross, sealing it with an invoking spiral. They then intone the magic word *Opera* and says the following incantation:

Opera: the Work is the secret process whereby humankind becomes refined into an exalted state of being, that of the divine person. This work is known as the Great Work, the Magnum Opus, and its product is the greatest of all achievements—the Gold of the Philosophers and the Stone of Transmutation. Rubedo: when the Lady of the Silver Moon is joined to the Lord of the Golden Sun and therein mixed in fusion, then the

---

69 Betz, *op. cit.,* p. 101.
70 Ibid.
71 Ibid.

Scarlet Blood of the Spirit is produced. Behold, it quickly resolves itself into the summum bonum. The library is the place where all knowledge is stored, not the knowledge of the past, but of all time and all places—the universal knowledge of Spirit. Herein is the mysterious Great Globe and many other wonders besides.

Methomeo Lamarmera Optēbi Ptēbi Marianou Akrabaeō Ephiazēle Arbamenothi Ēō Namisphrēti Bainchōōōch.[72]

The Celebrant proceeds to the center of the circle, bows, and then, using the transmutar wand, draws a great inverted Rose Ankh in the Ultrapoint, sealing it with an invoking spiral. They then intone the magic word *Regnum* and say the following incantation:

Regnum: the Sacred Kingdom or Throne of Spirit in the manifested world. We have entered the core of the source of all emanations, the Well of Souls, and Font of All Creation, and in this holy place we shall discover our destiny, which is to be an agent of the Double Gateway of transcendental initiation. Lapidus: the Stone of the Philosophers is the greatest power of transmutation that turns flesh into spirit, lead into gold, and the universal solvent and medicine. It is the Pansophic panacea of all time, the Key to the Cosmic Destiny of the Universe. The Great Hall of the Wedding is assayed through a winding staircase but represents the very center and highest place in the Castle of the Mysteries. Therein the highest court is held, as well as execution, where the young King and Queen are executed by the Moor, and then he is himself decapitated. The blood is collected, the flesh temporarily entombed, but the spirits light the skies at night and travel to the Tower of Transformation.

Kypodōkte Pintouche Etōm Thout Thasināeak Aroutrongoa Paphtha Enōsade Iaē Iaō Ai Adiaō Eoēy.[73]

Then the Celebrant draws the four cardinal directions together to form a square, starting in the North and proceeding widdershins to the West, South, and East using the sword. The Celebrant then draws the four Rose Crosses set in the four watchtowers to the inverted Rose Ankh set in the Ultrapoint, starting with the East and proceeding deosil until all five crosses are joined to form a vault structure, which is the energy signature of the Castle of the Mysteries. The Celebrant draws an obverse Rose Ankh in the Infrapoint and says the following prayer:

Convivor, Redemptio, Ubertas, Opera, Regnum— C. R. U. O. R., Cruor—Blood.

Nigredo, Albedo, Citrinitas, Rubedo, Lapidus: thus is the Stone of Philosophers generated through the outward alchemical mystery.

---

72 Ibid.
73 Ibid.

Know that the House of the Sun and the Hidden Treasury are places where the mystery allegory is shown, and the tomb of the Goddess Venus is hidden from the sight of the vulgar. Be warned that looking upon the mysteries entails a great burden and responsibility, for the one who sees and knows them shall be bidden to silence and become the warden of its gates.

Descending Gateway: Tower of Transformation

The Celebrant meditates in silence for a while. Then, they set the three talismanic gate keys: one in the southeast angle (Hermit IX), one in the western watchtower (Hanged Man XII), and one in the northeast angle (Death XIII), with the appropriate Tarot Trumps placed on each. The Celebrant then meditates on the cards placed therein, building up the energies and noting the significance of the Gate Tarot Trumps. The Celebrant then stands in the East, facing the West.

The Celebrant draws a trapezoidal cross and seals it with an invoking spiral in the southeastern angle, charging the Gate Key therein, intones the letter *Yod* (the Hermit), and then says:

[Atu IX] Calcination: the first step is the required surrendering of the petty ego and false outer identity and its attachment to possessions, status, and personal volition. These things are all illusions and obstacles standing in the way of the perfect harmonious union with the One. Our illusions and delusions are burned away, as is our attachment to the past. Without a false past to tie us down to delusions, fictions, and false memories, we have brought forth the possibility of realizing our true destiny.

The Celebrant draws a trapezoidal cross and seals it with an invoking spiral in the western watchtower, charging the Gate Key therein, intones the letter *Mim* (Hanged Man), and then says:

[Atu XII] Dissolution: the second step represents a further breaking down of our illusions through total immersion into the very source of our being, the ground unconscious mind. We are reduced to the very building blocks and elements of our being, where the cohesion of our self is eliminated so that we are merely a solution of various self-aspects floating together. All intentions have been sublimated, all needs have been suborned, and all that remains is the bliss of just simply being and the singular awareness of that being. From this elemental state, all possibilities are re-engaged, and all limitations abrogated.

The Celebrant draws a trapezoidal cross and seals it with an invoking spiral in the northeastern angle, charging the Gate Key therein, intones the letter *Nun* (Death), and then says:

[Atu XIII] Separation: the third step is where the various elements of our self, without any ego-based identity or cohesion, become isolated instances of our being, like millions of shards of a fractal mirror. Each is whole and complete in itself but represents the

constituents of our multifaceted self. Now that disunion has completely conquered our being, we may dispassionately evaluate them all, choosing anew those elements that will build the optimal self. Reflected in each facet is the shadow-light of Union, the One. Through this unity is the possibility of the renewal of the self and the outer identity, which is made far greater and deeper than before.

The Celebrant proceeds to the center of the circle and stands in the East facing the West. The three gate nodes are drawn to the Infrapoint in the center of the circle, in the sequence of Northeast, West, and Southeast. The Celebrant then draws the three nodes together in an arc, thus generating a triangle in a ring. The Celebrant makes the sign of the parting of the threshold and, as the Enterer, crosses into the gate of the western watchtower, then turns to face the East and proceeds to the center of the circle.

The Celebrant draws therein an invoking hexagram (union of Fire and Water) in the Infrapoint, sealing it with an invoking spiral. The Celebrant draws up the energies from the Infrapoint to their crown chakra, and then performs the Mantle of Glory (Qabalistic Cross).

Then, the Celebrant says the following while pointing to each of the three nodes in sequence:

Yod—We are strengthened by atonement and internalization.
Mim—We are relieved of our needs and drives and given internal peace.
Nun—We are reduced to our elements so we may be remade stronger and better.
Y. M. N.—Yeman—We descend into the dark night of the soul to undergo the trials of transformation.

Telesterion of the Alchemical Mysteries

The Celebrant proceeds to the northeast angle and draws therein a hexagram cross device sealed with an invoking spiral using the transmutar wand. Then, they slowly walk directly across the magic circle to the southwest angle, where they draw a hexagram cross device, sealed with an invoking spiral.

Then, the Celebrant proceeds widdershins to the southeast angle and draws therein a hexagram cross device sealed with an invoking spiral using the transmutar wand. Then, they slowly walk directly across the magic circle to the northwest angle, where they draw a hexagram cross device, sealed with an invoking spiral.

The Celebrant draws an inner circle around the confluence of the crossroads, makes the sign of parting the threshold, and steps into the new domain of the inner circle. They then project the inner circle to the outer periphery of the outer magic circle, with both hands pressing outwards. Then the Celebrant draws a great Rose Ankh in the Mesopoint of the center of the circle, intones the letter *Zain*, visualizes the appropriate Tarot card (Lovers Atu VI), and performs the following mystery rite. First, the alchemical stage is revealed with the following incantation:

Conjunction: the fourth step is where the power of union that is refracted in all of the facets of our being is amplified and brought into complete conscious awareness. There is the supreme moment of bliss and ecstasy, where the domain of the numinous spirit is superimposed upon the fragmented self, effortlessly bringing all of the facets together through the power of spiritual Love. This blissfulness, this exultant happiness, is the first sign of achieving the final stage of union with the One. The Spirit of Love manifests, and all coalesces into a harmonious whole.

The specially consecrated magic ring (as empowered in the Bornless Ring Consecration) is placed on the altar, and before the altar is placed the shroud that is to be used in the Bornless Assumption of Great Powers. A Mass and Benediction have been recently said over both of these articles, so they are sacralized and ready for use in this rite. The Celebrant is dressed in the vestments for saying mass and acts as the hierophant in this ceremony.

Placing the ring upon their finger, the Celebrant internally says the activating formula word, and then silently calls the name of the Higher Self, the Bornless One, while holding the hand with the ring above the head. Then, the Celebrant picks up the shroud and places it across the shoulders and neck, where both ends are hanging down the front. Thus garbed and standing in the center of the circle, they raise up both arms and receive anew the powers of the Bornless One into their body. They say the following incantation:

Out of the darkness, let that light arise. Before I was blind, but now I see. I am the dweller in the invisible, the reconciler with the ineffable.

For the male Celebrant:

I am the Bornless Spirit, always knowing wherever I am bound, for I have sight in my feet. I am the Mighty One who possesses the Immortal Fire. I am the Great Truth who hates that evil should be wrought in the world. I am the one that causes lightning and thunder. I am the one whose sweat falls upon the earth as rain so that it can inseminate it. I am the one whose mouth burns completely. I am the one who begets and destroys. I am the favor of the Aion; my name is like a heart encircled by a serpent. Come forth and follow!

For the female Celebrant:

I am she, the Bornless Spirit, with wisdom in the heart, enduring, and the immortal love. I am she, the Truth. I am she who seeks to right all wrongs wrought in the world. I am she that emanates all light and love. I am she, from whom the bounty of the spiritual gifts of life is given. I am she, whose lips bestow the kiss of peace. I am she, the creatrix and fashioner of the sacred light. I am she, the compassion and love of the world.

For other Celebrants:

I am they, the Bornless Spirit, having wisdom in the soul, neither one nor the other, but unified in both. I am they, the mystery. I am they, who seeks justice, equality, and equity for all, and the dignity to be acknowledged. I am they, who emanates both Light and

Darkness, who are above and below, behind and in front, and who pervade through all manifestations. I give the gift of the sovereignty of the individual and the blessings of love everlasting. I am they, who both creates and receives, the holder of the grail and the protector of its mysteries. I wield the sword of justice and the balancing scales of peace.

All:

I am the Trimorphic Protonoia! Hear me, and make all spirits subject unto me, so that every spirit of the firmament and the aether, upon the earth and under the earth, on dry land and in the water, of whirling air, and of rushing fire, and every spell and scourge of God the vast one may be obedient unto me. Iao Sabaoth Adonai Abrasax, and by the Great God, Iaeo, Aeeioyo Oyoieea Chabrax Phnesker Phiko Phnyro Phocho Bouch Ablanathanalba! Such are the words.

Then, the Celebrant stands in the center of the circle, holding their arms raised forward and ascending, and, facing the West, summons the Deity aspect to appear before them to receive the blessing of union. They say the following summoning and blessing:

I am the invisible One within the All. It is I who counsel those who are hidden since I know the All that exists in it. I am numberless beyond everyone. I am immeasurable, ineffable, yet whenever I wish, I shall reveal myself. I am the movement of the All. I exist before the All, and I am the All since I exist before everything.

I am a Voice speaking softly. I exist from the first. I dwell within the Silence that surrounds every one of them. And it is the hidden Voice that dwells within me, with the intangible, immeasurable Thought, within the immeasurable Silence.[74]

IAŌ IAŌ IAŌ—(Name of Element Godhead), I call upon you, Phtha Ra Phtha Iē Phtha Dun Emēcha Erōchth Barōch Thorchtha Thōm Chaieouch Archandabar Ōeaeō Ynēōch Ēra Ōn Ēlōph Bom Phtha Athabrasia Abriasōth Barbarbelōcha Barbaiaōch; let there be depth, breadth, length, brightness, Ablanathanalba Abrasiaoua Akramma Chamarei Thōth Hōr Athōōpō. Come in, lord, and reveal.[75]

The Celebrant turns to the East, holding their arms raised forward and ascending, summoning the Higher Self aspect to appear before them to receive the blessing of union. They say the following summoning and blessing:

I invoke thee, the awesome and invisible God who dwelleth in the void place of the Spirit. Arogogorobrao Sochou Modorio Phalarchao Ooo. The Holy Bornless One. Hear me, and make all spirits subject unto me, so that every spirit of the firmament and the aether,

---

74 Robinson, *op. cit.*, p. 462.
75 Betz, *op. cit.*, p. 159.

upon the earth and under the earth, on dry land and in the water, of whirling air, and of rushing fire, and every spell and scourge of God the vast one may be obedient unto me.

Then the Celebrant turns to face the South, backs up two steps, and beckons the invisible personages in the West and the East to come forward to the center, where they draw a great hexagram, symbolizing the union of archetypal opposites. The Celebrant then holds their arms raised forward at an ascending angle and gives the pledge and bond, saying the following incantation:

Zain: I am like the Great Mediator, Metatron, who stands before the Archetypal Man and Archetypal Woman, with hands raised to them both, wielding the power that binds and draws together. Let this binding between the Bornless One and the great Godhead before me be enjoined, as they are in the Universal Reality of the Eternal Now. Let it be known in my heart and soul every hour and every day for the rest of my life, and even beyond. Let it be for me the joining of the Light and Darkness, the Fusion of the One in the eternal embrace of Godhead and Augoeides. Forever unto eternity—may we all three be as One!

Thrice Great and Threefold Initiate, Master of the Castle of the Mysteries, Mistress of the Tower of Transformation, and Adjudicator of the Eternal Light of Life and Love, beacon of the Spirit in the Shadowy Worlds of Twilight.

The Celebrant makes the sign of the Rose Cross and the Rose Ankh in the center of the circle in the Mesopoint. They say the final blessing of this sacred union, drawing the unified Godhead and Higher Self into a combined embrace, focusing and vibrating on the heart chakra.

ASCENDING GATEWAY: TOWER OF RESURRECTION

The Celebrant resets the three talismanic gate keys: one in the southwest angle (Aion XX), one in the eastern watchtower (Art XIV), and one in the northwest angle (Star/Fisher King IV), with the appropriate Tarot Trumps placed on each. The Celebrant then meditates on the cards, building up the energies and noting the significance of the Gate Tarot Trumps. The Celebrant then stands in the West, facing the East.

The Celebrant draws a trapezoidal cross and seals it with an invoking spiral in the northwestern angle, charging the Gate Key therein, intoning the letter *Tzadi* (Fisher King/Star), and then saying:

[Atu IV] Fermentation: the fifth stage is where the divine love is fully realized, manifesting as the golden effulgence of the embodiment of the indwelling glory of the Augoeides, the Higher Self, which consciously awakens to empower and uplift the mortal life, shaken of all impurity, distractions, and lower impulses. The past was swept away, including all of its trials, pain, struggles, and difficulties; it is neutralized but not forgotten. All is pulled into the center of this formulating being, where the consciousness of the Godhead begins to awaken.

The Celebrant draws a trapezoidal cross and seals it with an invoking spiral in the eastern watchtower, charging the Gate Key therein, intoning the letter *Samek* (Art), and then saying:

> *[Atu XIV] Distillation: the sixth stage is where the recombined self through the aegis of the Augoeides and the Greater Godhead forge a powerful and completed synthesis, which is refined and purified through a series of trials and progressive insights. This stage is the training of the over-soul that is learning to transduce reality through a single point of mortal existence. It is also the beginning of the creation of an avatar, the perfect union of God and Humanity.*

The Celebrant draws a trapezoidal cross and seals it with an invoking spiral in the southwestern angle, charging the Gate Key therein, intoning the letter *Shin* (Aion), and then saying:

> *[Atu XX] Coagulation: the seventh stage is where the union of Godhead and Human Soul is perfected and brought into its mature form. At this point, the visage and being of the mortal human shines with the light and power of the fully realized Avatar of the Godhead. In a single moment, the full realization of one's complete and total destiny is realized, and the newly made mortal being of Golden Light seeks to complete the Destiny of the Deity in its humble yet perfect manner. Mankind is thus uplifted into God, and through them the Deity indwells in the material universe, and all is One, perfect and good. Blessed are they who have received this great gift, and blessed are they who seek this one mortal light and, from it, receive their own enlightenment. So the cycle continues, ever turning, until all sentient beings are one with Spirit and Spirit is one with all life. As it was in the beginning, is now, and ever shall be: One with Unity!*

The Celebrant proceeds to the center of the circle and stands in the West facing the East. The three gate nodes are drawn to the Ultrapoint in the center of the circle, in the sequence of Southwest, East, and Northwest. The Celebrant then draws the three nodes together in an arc, thus generating a triangle in a ring. The Celebrant makes the sign of the parting of the threshold, and as the Enterer, crosses into the Gate of the Eastern Watchtower, then turns to face the West, and proceeds to the center of the circle.

The Celebrant draws therein an invoking hexagram (union of Fire and Water) in the Ultrapoint, sealing it with an invoking spiral. The Celebrant draws down the energies from the Ultrapoint to their crown chakra, and then performs the Mantle of Glory (Qabalistic Cross).

Then, the Celebrant says the following, while pointing to each of the three nodes in sequence:

> *Tzadi*—Where the divine love is fully realized.
> *Samek*—The beginning of the creation of an avatar.
> *Shin*—Humankind is thus uplifted into God, and the Deity indwells in the material universe, and all is One, perfect and good.

> *Tz. S. Sh.—Tzasesh—Thus ascension brings mortal humanity into union with the Godhead. This is the ultimate destiny of humanity, set in each individual and eventually realized in everyone.*

The Celebrant then points to the seven nodes of the double gateway and central crossroads, beginning with the western gate, then the center, and finally the eastern gate, and intones the following incantation, which draws all of the dimensions of the rite together into union.

> *Yod—We are strengthened by atonement and internalization.*
> *Mim—We are relieved of our needs and drives and given internal peace.*
> *Nun—We are reduced to our elements so we may be remade stronger and better.*
> *Zain—Universal Love—Spirit and Flesh—is the Key to this process!*
> *Tzadi—Where the divine love is fully realized.*
> *Samek—The beginning of the creation of an avatar.*
> *Shin—Humankind is thus uplifted into God, and the Deity indwells in the material universe, and all is One, perfect and good.*

> *Y. M. N. Z. Tz. S. Sh.—YemanZaTzasesh—We descend into the dark night of the soul to undergo the trials of transformation. Love is our redeemer, teacher, and initiator: the key to the mystery. Thus, ascension brings mortal humanity into union with the Godhead. This is the ultimate destiny of humanity, set in each individual and eventually realized in everyone.*

> *Thus are the seven steps of Alchemical Transformation: the three steps of the Involution Arc, the midpoint of Revelation of Love of the Godhead, and the three steps of the Evolutionary Arc. The secret is now revealed and unleashed. The Chemical Wedding is complete!*

The rite is now fulfilled, and the Celebrant, after a suitable period of time, draws sealing spirals to all of the cardinal directions, the cross-cardinal directions, and the three points in the center of the circle. The working is now completely sealed and done.

CHAPTER EIGHT

BORNLESS RING CONSECRATION RITE

The Bornless Ring Consecration rite is the third in the series to be used in conjunction with the Bornless One invocation rite, which is the version used in the Abramelin Lunar Ordeal. This rite was taken from the same source as the Bornless One rite, which is the *Greek Magical Papyri in Translation*, edited by Hans Dieter Betz. This particular rite is from *PGM XII*, lines 201 through 350, and is distilled and adapted from that original Greek manuscript.[76]

The purpose for the Ring Consecration rite in the Bornless series is to formulate a magical trigger or tool (link) to materialize the magical power of the Higher Self and project it into the world. The ring is therefore a linking device, not to be misconstrued as representing anything more than the symbolic and mythic quality that it represents.

The consecration ritual is simple enough since it is done immediately following a special Mass and a Benediction. The sacraments are used to directly bless and empower the ring, and the powerful invocations distilled from the *Greek Magical Papyri* supply the verbiage. Little else is required for this simple rite, other than a careful and fixed concentration on the difficult but sonorous words of power. After charging the ring, a vigil is performed until just before the first dawning light, which should shine upon the ring and further words of power said over it. There is also an invocation of the godhead Ouphōr, which is used the first time that one wears it. From that moment onward, all one needs to do is just say that godhead's name when slipping the ring on the finger.

Items required:

- One ring (as previously described)
- A purple velvet cloth (to enfold the ring when not being used)
- Sacrament: consecrated wine, oil, and holy water
- The energized temple from the saying of a Mass and a Benediction

---

76 Betz, *op. cit.*, pp. 161–163.

BORNLESS RING CONSECRATION RITE

The Celebrant performs the Consecration of the Magna Dea, the Mass of the Great Goddess, and the associated Benediction rituals before performing this working. The temple environment must be super-charged and thoroughly sacralized in order for it to be ready for the performance of this ritual.

Consecration of the Magic Ring

The Celebrant will have already performed a special Mass and a Benediction rite for the occasion. The temple will be charged with the holy sacrament in an octagon configuration (watchtowers and angles). There will be consecrated wine, oil, and holy water to be used, as well as an appropriate incense.

The ring should be sitting on a purple velvet cloth (three square inches). The Celebrant proceeds to incense the ring extensively, then applies a small amount of oil, holy water, and consecrated wine. Then, using the transmutar wand, the Celebrant makes three signs of the simple hexagram (symbol of unity) over it, then leans close to the ring and blows the breath over it three times. The Celebrant then profoundly bows before the altar, rises, and slightly bows to each of the four cardinal directions. Once this is accomplished, the Celebrant takes the transmutar wand in the right hand and holds it over their head while holding the left hand over the ring, saying the following powerful incantation slowly, sonorously, and with great intensity:

I charge this ring with the powers and authority of the highest and absolute Godhead, so that it will forge for me a link and a sacred conduit between myself and the highest god.

O lords and controllers of Kings, come, benevolent, for that purpose for which I call you, as benevolent assistants in this rite for my benefit.

I am Chrates, who came forth from the eye of the Sun. I am the god whom no one sees or rashly names. I am the sacred bird Phoinix. I am Krates the holy, called Marmaraōth. I am Helios, who showed forth light. I am Aphrodite, called Typhi.

I am Esenephys, called spring. I am the image resembling true images. I am Souchos, who appears as a crocodile. Therefore, I beseech you, come as my helpers, for I am about to call on the hidden and ineffable name, the forefather of gods, overseer and lord of all.

Here me, lord, whose hidden name is ineffable. The daimons, hearing it, are terrified—the name Barbareich Arsemphemphrōthou—and of it the sun, of it the earth, hearing, rolls over; Hades, hearing, is shaken; rivers, seas, lakes, and springs, hearing, are frozen; rock, hearing it, are split. Heaven is your head; ether, body; earth, feet; and the water around you, ocean, O Agathos Daimon. You are lord, the begetter and nourisher of all.

You, lord of life, ruling the upper and the lower realm, whose justice is not thwarted, whose glorious name the angels sing hymns, who have truth that never dies, hear me and complete for me this operation so that I may wear this power in every place, in every time, without being smitten or afflicted, so as to be intact from every danger while I wear this power.

Again, I call upon you—Phnō Eai Iabōk Adonai Sabaoth, "the King of all, ruling alone," Ouertō. Consecrate and empower this object for me, for the entire and glorious time of my life.

The Celebrant projects all of the power raised into the ring, then breathes the breath over it and places it into the purple velvet cloth. The ring now becomes part of vigil that lasts the night. Just before the dawn sunlight breaks, the Celebrant will take the wrapped ring out of doors, holding it and standing facing the east. As the first light breaks over the horizon, the Celebrant will open the cloth and intone the following incantation as the light blesses and further empowers the ring:

Greatest god, who exceed all power, I call on you, IAŌ Sabaōth Adōnai Eilōein Sebōein Saphtha Nouchita Chathathich Zeupein Nēphygor Astaphaios Katakerknēph Konteos Katout Kērideu Marmariōth Likyxanta Bessoum Symekonteu, the opponent of Thoth, Maskelli Maskellōth Phmou Kentabaōth Oreobazagra Hippochthōn Pyripēganyx Nyxiō Abrōrokore Kodēre Mouisdrō Malekh Thath Phath Chath Xeuzen Zeuzei Sousēnē Elathath Melasiō Koukōr Neusoo Pachiō Xiphnō Themel Nauth Ioklēth Sessōr Chamel Chasineu Xōchō Isllinōi Seisengpharangēs Mesichiōr Iōtabaas Chenouchi Chaam Phachiarath Neegōthara Iam Zeōch Akrammachamarei Cheroubeim Bainchōōch Eiophaleon Ichnaōth Pōe Xephithōth Xouthouth Thoothiou Xeriphōnar Ephinarasōr Chanizara Anamegar Iōo Xtouroriam Iōk Niōr Chettaios Eloumaios Nōiō Damnameneu Axiōthōph Psethaiakklōps Sisageta Neoriphrōr Hippokelephoklōps Zeinacha Iaphethana A E Ē I O Y Ō.

I have called on you, greatest god, and through you on all things, that you may give divine and supreme strength to this image and it effective and powerful against all opponents, strengthen friendships, produce all sorts of profits, bring dreams, give prophecies, cause psychological passions and bodily sufferings and incapacitating illness, and perfect all erotic filters. Please, lord, bring to fulfillment a complete consecration.

Then the ring is covered up once again in the purple cloth and the Celebrant retires to the temple, where the covered ring is placed for safe keeping. The incubation period is three days and nights from that moment.

On the third evening, the Celebrant will, in a consecrated and empowered temple space, take out the ring from the purple cloth and place it on the ring finger of the right hand. The Celebrant raises the right hand and shows the ring stone to the heavens, and then says the following incantation:

Bornless Ring Consecration Rite

Ei Ieou Marieth
Ei Ieou Montheathi Mongith
Ei Ieou Chareōth Monkēb
Ei Ieou Sōchou Sorsōē
Ei Ieou Tiōtiō Ouiēr
Ei Ieou Charōchsi Charmiōth
Ei Ieou Sathimōoyeēoy
Ei Ieou Rairai Mourirai
Ei Ieou Amoun Ēei Osiris
Ei Ieou Phirimnoun
Ei Ieou Anmorchathi Ouēr
Orchimorōipougth
Ei Ieou Machpsachathanth
Ei Ieou Moroth.

The Celebrant removes the ring and puts it back into the velvet cloth. Then, whenever it is put back on, hold the ring stone to the heavens and say the word *Ouphōr*.

CHAPTER NINE

BORNLESS ASSUMPTION OF GREAT POWERS RITE

The Bornless Assumption of Great Powers rite is the second in the series to be used in conjunction with the Bornless One invocation rite, which is the version used in the Abramelin Lunar Ordeal. These rituals were taken from the same source as the Bornless One invocation rite, which is the *Greek Magical Papyri in Translation*, edited by Hans Dieter Betz. This particular rite is from *PGM IV*, lines 154 through 285, and is distilled and adapted from that original Greek manuscript.[77]

This rite is used for the assumption of great powers and is performed at some point following the Bornless One invocation rite. It is used to assume the powers, authorities, and to quicken the manifestation of the Bornless One as the Higher Self. This rite is based on a simulation of death and rebirth, and therefore invokes the dark god of the underworld, Typhon.

The operator wears a plain black robe, wrapped in three yards of gauze, and lays upon the floor as if dead, yet crowned with ivy and blindfolded. A long incantation is intoned, then the subject rises up and is vested in pure white robes of linen, and the operator says an affirmation. Another incantation is read, this time before the rising sun. Later, in the temple, the subject performs divination to see the image or imago of the godhead assumption and speaks a final set of incantations. It would seem that the subject would have to perform a great deal of memorization in order to complete this rite, adorn oneself with the gauze wrapping, and so on.

To aid in the execution of this rite, there should be two individuals simultaneously performing it. One should be the candidate who is to undergo the process and assume the godhead of the Bornless One, and the other an assistant who performs the incantations, guides, and aids the candidate as needed. If two people are performing this rite, then they can take turns going through the death and resurrection ordeal. If one is performing

---

[77] Betz, *op. cit.*, pp. 40–43.

this rite alone, then I would recommend that they perform the incantation first, then wrap up themselves in the gauze covering and perform a deep trance-based meditation to simulate the process of death and resurrection.

The papyrus spell advises that the assumption of great power be done at midnight, and then the candidate may properly greet the rising sun as the resurrected and empowered one. I would also recommend that the rite be performed one to three days (or more) following the Bornless One invocation rite. The period of being wrapped up in gauze can last only as long as one can assume the deepest trance state, and then it is followed by the resurrection. However, one should then undergo an evening vigil, with light sleep and trance, then to arise and go outside to witness the rising sun, where additional incantations are said. Once that is accomplished, the candidate should immediately return to the temple to perform a mirror gazing, and thereby perceive the nimbus and vision of the Bornless One surrounding their person.

The empowered magic ring should also be used in this rite, the candidate invoking the sacred Godname (as during the Bornless One invocation) before being wrapped in gauze, so that, upon awakening, they shall be fully bonded with the power and glory of their Bornless One.

Items required:

- A white or pale blue gauze material, three yards in length, to act as a burial shroud
- Ivy crown
- Blindfold
- Consecrated magic ring
- White robes
- Black mirror, to be used instead of a bowl with dark liquid
- Special incense

BORNLESS ASSUMPTION OF GREAT POWERS RITE

The Celebrant performs the Consecration of the Magna Dea, the Mass of the Great Goddess, and the associated Benediction rituals before performing this working. The temple environment must be super-charged and thoroughly sacralized in order for it to be ready for the performance of this ritual.

Assumption Rite

The candidate is divested of robes changes into a plain black robe, is crowned with ivy, blindfolded, and is wrapped in gauze to simulate a death shroud. The assistant helps the candidate to wear this vestment. The candidate lays down in the center of the circle completely covered, with their head pointing toward the East and feet pointing to the West. Within the shroud, they assume the pose of a great pharaoh who is entombed, with arms crossed over the chest and feet tightly together. The candidate is also wearing the specially consecrated magic ring, which was activated in the Bornless One invocation. To aid in this state, the initiator may also tie the legs together and wrap the chest to secure the arms with additional strips of gauze. Once ensconced, the candidate enters as deep a trance as is possible, while the assistant kneels before the shrouded body and bows, passing the hands over it and projecting power into the staged corpse.

There should be an interlude of funeral music and the sounds of sobbing and weeping that grows ever-distant, as does the music. Then the assistant, who is kneeling at the side of the enshrouded body, shall say the following incantation with great force and power:

O mighty Typhon
Ruler of heaven and master
God of gods, O Lord
Aberamen thoou…,

O dark's disturber, thunders' bringer, whirlwind, night flasher, breather-forth of hot and cold, shaker of rocks, wall tremblor, boiler of the waves, disturber of the sea's great depth

Io Erbet Taui Meni

I am (he/she/they) who searched with you the world and found great Osiris, whom I brought to you chained. I am (he/she/they) who joined you in war with the gods (but others say "against the gods"). I am (he/she/they) who closed heaven's double gates and put to sleep the serpent which must not be seen, who stopped the seas, the streams, the river currents where'er you rule this realm. And as your soldier, I have been conquered by the gods; I have been thrown face down because of empty wrath. Raise up your friend, I beg you, I implore; throw me not on the ground, O lord of gods, Aeminaebarōtherrecthōrabeanimea, O grant me power, I beg, and give to me this favor, so that, whene'er I tell one of the gods to come, he is seen coming swiftly to me in answer to my chants:

Naine Basanaptatou Eaptou Mēnōphaesmē Paptou Mēnōph Aesimē Trauapti Peuchrē Trauara Ptoumēph Mourai Anchouchaphapta Moursa Aramei IAŌ Aththaraui Menoker Boroptoumēth at Taui Mēni Charchara Ptoumau Lalapsa Traui Trauepse Mamō Phortoucha Aeēio Ioy Oeōa EAI AEĒI IAŌ AĒI AI IAŌ.

Then the assistant shall pass their hands over the enshrouded candidate, and they shall say:

Rise up—for the Great God hath willed it so, and so it is!

The candidate is assisted to rise, the shroud and blindfold are removed, and they change out of the plain black robe to a brilliant white robe, but the ivy crown remains. Copious amounts of incense are burned at this moment, and the incense smoke is directed toward the candidate. Once this is done, the candidate shall say:

I have been attracted to your holy form
I have been given power by your holy name
Lord, god of gods, master, daimon.
Aththouin Thouthoui Thauanti Laō Aptatō.

Then, the candidate performs their sacred vigil, ensuring not to sleep deeply or completely until just before the dawning light. The candidate will proceed out of the temple and face the East, greeting the rising sun, whose first rays shall illuminate them. The candidate will say the following incantation:

I call you who did first control God's wrath, you who hold the royal scepter o'er the heavens. You who are midpoint of the stars above, you, master Typhon, you I call, who are the dreaded sovereign o'er the firmament. You who are fearful, awesome, threatening, you who're obscure and irresistible and hater of the wicked, you I call, Typhon, in hours unlawful and unmeasured, you who've walked on unquenched, clear-crackling fire, you who are over snows, below dark ice, you who hold sovereignty over the Moirai (Fates), I invoked you in prayer, I call, almighty one, that you perform for me whate'er I ask of you, and that you nod ascent at once to me and grant that what I ask is mine because I adjure you!

Gar Thala Bauzau Thōrthōr Kathaukath Lathin Na Borkakar Borba Karborbouch Mō Tau Ouzōnz Ōn Yabith, mighty Typhon, hear me, (name), and perform for me (the assumption of my Augoeides). For I speak your true name, Iō Erbēth Iō Parkerbēth Iō Bolchosēth Oen Typhon Asbarabō Bieaisē Mr Nerō Maramō Tauēr Chthenthōnie Alam Bētōr Menkechra Nerdōmeu Amōrēs Meeme Ōtēs Syschie Anthōnie Phra; listen to me and perform the assumption.

Then the candidate will return to the temple, which should be dimmed until there is only a small amount of light shining on the candidate's face. They shall take a consecrated black mirror and set it up in the place where they may gaze deeply into it, looking deep into their own face. The candidate shall speak over the mirror:

Amoun Auantau Laaimoutau Riptou Mantaui Imantou Lantou Lpatoumi Anchōmach Araptoumi, hither to me O Autogenes, O Osoronnophris, O Bornless One! Be attentive to me because as the god I wish and command this, Achchōr Achchōr Achachach Ptoumi Chachchō Charachōch Chaptoumē Choracho Ptenachōcheu.

Then the candidate will stare deeply into the black mirror and mentally summon the Bornless One to appear, and they will see it as a cloud or as rays of light that shall gently overlay the image of themselves. The candidate will stare and mentally commune with the Bornless One until the effect is ended, saying within their mind the following paragraph.

But you are not unaware, mighty king and leader of magicians, that this is the chief name of Typhon, at whom the ground, the depths of the sea, hades, heaven, the sun, the moon, the visible chorus of stars, the whole universe all tremble, the name which, when it is uttered, forcibly brings gods and daimons to it. This is the name that consists of one-hundred letters. Finally, when you have called, whomever you have called will appear, god or dead man, and he will give an answer about anything you ask. To dismiss— 'Depart, master, for the Great God, NN, wishes and commands this of you,' speak the name of 100 letters and he will depart.

CHAPTER TEN

BORNLESS ENVISIONING RITE

THE BORNLESS ENVISIONING RITE is the third in the series to be used in conjunction with the Bornless One invocation rite, which is the version used in the Abramelin Lunar Ordeal. The Bornless One rite was taken from the same source as the ring consecration rite, which is the *Greek Magical Papyri in Translation,* edited by Hans Dieter Betz. This particular rite is from *PGM IV,* lines 850 through 1226, and is distilled and adapted from that original Greek manuscript.[78]

The Bornless Envisioning rite takes a total of three days and requires three masses to be said, with an accompanying incantation to be read, known as the Hidden Stele and Death Delivering Stele. The third evening is when the actual rite is to be performed, begun with another magical Mass and a Benediction rite. The preceding two days are a time of reflection, meditation, and purification, with special baths and the elimination of all worldly concerns that might distract one from the work. The main operator should be crowned with a garland and have prepared a special phylactery that is to be worn around the waist. White robes are the preferred adornment, as is the optional controller crystal, to be worn around the neck. The Bornless One invocation rite ordeal should have been performed previously just before or on the full moon, and this rite should be performed on the next full moon that occurs.

The purpose of the Envisioning rite is to gather up the powerful visions that the operator experienced while invoking their Higher Self into manifestation. These are projected into a dark mirror as potent questions for the Higher Self, to be resolved as visions of confirmation for one's destiny and ultimate purpose. Having this knowledge, the operator can more unerringly live their life and proceed to accomplish the great work in a clearer and more efficient manner than would be otherwise. Therefore, this rite is not only a divination rite, but it's an active and powerful rite that literally generates the

---

[78] Betz, *op. cit.*, pp. 54–61.

future for the operator so that they may revel in glory of knowing and following their spiritual and material destiny, however that is revealed.

The specific ritual begins with a circle consecration rite, Mass, and Benediction. After a suitable period of deep meditation, the operator then proceeds to build up a powerful crossroads in the temple, using incantations from the *PGM* and the device of the inverted Rose Ankh. This is performed using a widdershins arc, starting in the Southwest and proceeding directly to the Southeast, then circumambulating to the Northeast and proceeding directly to the Northwest. The center of the circle is set with a great inverted Rose Ankh in the Infrapoint, and all of the four angles are drawn together through it. There are five specialized incantations taken from the *PGM* to empower this crossroads vortex ritual structure.

At this point in the rite, the Celebrant puts on the magic ring, summons the associated godhead, and then performs the macro-rite for the Bornless One. The Celebrant pauses to complete a full assumption of that entity before continuing.

The lamp and black mirror are placed on a small altar in the center of the circle, the lamp is lit, and the phylactery is put on, along with the garland crown and the controller crystal around the neck. At this point, the Celebrant intones four incantations: the light-bringing charm, the light-retaining spell, and the summoning of the Godhead (to the Bornless One, said three times), and then performs the envisioning using the black mirror.

Once the envisioning with the black mirror is completed, the Celebrant performs the farewell of the Godhead, the dismissal of the brightness, and an all-night vigil, greeting the sun's first light as it dawns in the morning.

BORNLESS ENVISIONING RITE

The Celebrant performs the Consecration of the Magna Dea, the Mass of the Great Goddess, and the associated Benediction rituals before performing this working. The temple environment must be super-charged and thoroughly sacralized in order for it to be ready for the performance of this ritual.

Envisioning Rite

The Celebrant, prior to this working, performs two consecutive evenings of the magical mass and, just prior to receiving communion, they shall recite the incantations known as the Hidden Stele and the Death Delivering Stele (included below). In addition, they will take magical baths, perform long periods of meditation, and determine what their actual destiny consists of, based on the previous Bornless One invocation rite. This must be fully formulated before performing the main rite; otherwise, if this knowledge is not forthcoming, the Celebrant will have to skip this working until a future full moon, to be determined by portends, dreams, and visions.

On the evening of the envisioning, the Celebrant performs a circle consecration rite, a third magical Mass, and a Benediction rite. These operations will set the stage for the actual envisioning. In addition, the Celebrant will ensure that a central altar is set up with a lamp and a black scrying mirror. They will also place the magic ring wrapped in a purple velvet cloth, phylactery girdle, and the control crystal beside the lamp and the mirror. The Celebrant sits in the center of the circle and meditates for a period of time.

Then, the Celebrant will perform the macro-rite for summoning the Bornless One.

The Celebrant rises, turns to the Center, makes the sign of the hexagram in the Ultrapoint and vibrates the name *Protonoia*, then draws it toward themselves to connect with the crown chakra.

Hear me: Ieou Pyr Iou Pyr Iaoth Iaeo Ioou Abrasax Aabriam OO YY EY Adonai! Eide Eide (Immediately! Immediately!) Angelos Kalos Tou Theon! Anlala Lai Gaia Apa Diachanna Choryn.

(He/She/They) come(s) in the Power of the Light.
(He/She/They) come(s) in the Light of Wisdom.
(He/She/They) come(s) in the Mercy of the Light.
The Light Hath Healing in its Wings.
Let Heart and Mind Be as One in the Spirit!

The Celebrant then faces the East and draws the energy of the circle up into their body until it reaches the heart chakra. Then, while assuming the body posture of the Tau Cross, the Celebrant focuses upon the fiery hexagram drawn in the Ultrapoint and draws the power from the heart chakra up to the crown and beyond, then pauses to establish a potent trance state. When the resulting trance state has cleared somewhat, the Celebrant continues:

Out of the darkness, let that light arise. Before I was blind, but now I see. I am the dweller in the invisible, the reconciler with the ineffable.

I am the Trimorphic Protonoia! Hear me, and make all spirits subject unto me, so that every spirit of the firmament and the aether, upon the earth and under the earth, on dry land and in the water, of whirling air, and of rushing fire, and every spell and scourge of God the vast one may be obedient unto me. Iao Sabaoth Adonai Abrasax, and by the Great God, Iaeo, Aeeioyo Oyoieea Chabrax Phnesker Phiko Phnyro Phocho Bouch Ablanathanalba! Such are the words.

The Celebrant performs the exercise of centering descending wave. The Celebrant may then sit in meditation in the center of the circle and enjoy the ambience of the resultant invocation.

Then the Celebrant intones the following invocation:

IAŌ IAŌ IAŌ I call upon you, Ptha Ra Ptha Iē Phtha Oun Emēcha Erōchth Barōch Thorchtha Thōm Chaieouch Archandabar Ōeaeō Ynēōch Ēra Ōn Ēlōph Bom Phtha Athabrasia Abriasōth Barbarbelōcha Barbaiaōch; let there be depth, breadth, length, brightness, Ablanathanalba Abrasiaoua Akramma Chamarei Thōth Hōr Athōōpō. Come in, lord, and reveal![79]

After a suitable period of time, the Celebrant will continue with the Envisioning rite.

The Celebrant proceeds to the southwestern angle and therein draws an inverted Rose Ankh device, fills it with a purple energy, and says the following incantation:

Ouriōr Amen Im Tar Chōb Klamphōb Phrē Phrōr Ptar Ousiri Saiōb Tēlō Kabē Manatathōr Asiōrikōr Bēeinor Amoun Ōm Menichtha Machtha Chthara Amachtha Aou Alakambōt Besinōr Aphesiōr Phrēph Amei Our Lamasir Chēriōb Pitrem Phēōth Nirin Allannathath Cheriōth Ōne Bousiri Ninouno Amanal Gagōsariēr Mēniam Tler Ooo Aa Etnē Ousiri Ousiri Ousiri Mēnēmb Mnēm Brabēl Tnēkaiōb

Hear me—hear my holy voice, because I call upon your holy names, and reveal to me concerning this great mystery.

The Celebrant proceeds directly across the circle to the northeastern angle and therein draws an inverted Rose Ankh device, fills it with a purple energy, and says the following incantation:

Barbēth Mnōr Arariak Tarērim Ōar Tērōk Saniōr Mēnik Phauek Paphorioumin Lariōr Etniamin Knōs Chalakthir Krōphēr Phēsimōt Prēbib Knala Eribētim Gnōri.

Come to me through the mirror darkly and show me the truth, since I speak your names, which thrice greatest Hermes wrote in Heliopolis with hieroglyphic letters.

The Celebrant proceeds widdershins from the Northeast to the northwestern angle and therein draws an inverted Rose Ankh device, fills it with a purple energy, and says the following incantation:

Arbakōriph Mēniam Ōbaōb Abniōb Mērim Baiax Chenōr Phēnim Ōra Ōrēsiou Ousiri Pniamousiri Phrēousiri Hōriousiri Naeiōrousiri Mēnimousiri Mnēkousiri Phlēkousiri Pēlēlousiri Onio Rabkousiri Aniōbousiri Amēaousiri Anōrousiri Amēnēphēousiri Amēniousiri Xōniōr Ēourousiri.

Enter into the blackened mirror and reveal to me concerning my greater destiny.

The Celebrant proceeds directly across the circle to the southeastern angle and therein draws an inverted Rose Ankh device, fills it with a purple energy, and says the following incantation:

IAŌ Elōai Marmachada Menephō Mermai Ieōr Aieō Erephie Pherephiō Chandouch Amōn Erepneu Zōnōr Akleua Menēthōni Kadakapeu Iō Plaitine re Aōth Iēi Ōēi Medchēnor

---

[79] Betz, *op. cit.*, p. 159.

Alachal Perechaēl Serenōph Dounax Anaxiboa Erebe Bō Bebōbia Anēsiodeu Iaōa Eniōeal Emerō Masaianda.

Hither to me, O lord, riding upon immaculate light without deceit and without anger; appear to me within this blackened mirror.

Marmariau Anapsichalaō Peoe Nipseoua Aiety Harrennōthēs Anerōphēs Ithyamarem Ōsiēr Anapsichyōn—appear! Appear! Appear!

Then, the Celebrant exchanges the transmutar wand for the sword and draws the four angles to the center of the circle in the Infrapoint. They take up the wand for the sword and proceed to the center of the circle, drawing in the Infrapoint a great inverted Rose Ankh device, fills it with a purple energy, and says the following incantation:

Phisio IAŌ Ageanouma Skabarō Skasabrōsou Asabrō, because I implore you this very moment to let the light and sun of the spirit appear in the blackened mirror. Mane Ouseiri, Mane Isi, Anoubis, the servant of all gods, and cause me to fall into a deep trance and see my inner god reveal itself in this empowered divination. Appear to me, O high minded god, Hermes thrice-great: may he appear, the Bornless One who made the four parts of the heaven and the foundations of the earth, Resennēethō Baseneraipan Thalthachthachōthch Chinebōth Chinebōth Mimylōth Masyntori Astobi. Come to me, you who are in heaven; come to me, you who are from the Orphic Egg. I conjure you, O Phanes by the Entō Tapsati Legēnisthō Ēlegē Serphouth Mouisrō Lege, having appeared and the two gods are about me, THAT. The one god is called SO and the other APH, Kalou Kagōēi Sesophei Bainchōōōch.

At this point in the ritual, the Celebrant will put on the control crystal, the phylactery, and the garland crown, and take out the magic ring from its cloth container and place it on their finger, silently invoking the godhead to activate the ring. Holding the transmutar aloft in the right hand and the control crystal in the left, the Celebrant shall say the preliminary incantation:

Hail, serpent and stout lion, natural sources of fire. And hail, clear water and lofty-leafed tree, and you who gather up clover from golden fields of beans, and who cause gentle foam to gush forth from pure mouths. Scarab, who drive the orb of fertile fire, O self-engendered one, because you are two-syllabled, AĒ, and are the first-appearing one, give me ascent, I pray, because your mystic symbols I declare.

Eō Ai Oy Amerr Oouōth Iyiōe Marmarauōth Lailam Soumarta.

Be gracious unto me, first father, and may you yourself send strength as my companion. Stay allied, lord, and listen to me through the charm that produces direct vision which I do this night, and reveal to me concerning my ultimate destiny through the blackened mirror. I (magic name)! IY EYĒ OŌ ARĒ IAEĒ AIAĒ E AI EY ĒIE ŌŌŌŌŌ EY ĒŌ IAŌIA.

The Celebrant makes three invoking spirals over the black mirror, and then says the following incantation:

I call upon you, the living god, fiery, invisible begetter of light, Iaēl Peipta Phōs Za Phthentha Phōsza Pyri Belia Iaō Eyō Oeē S Ōy Eoi a Eēioyō, give your strength, rouse your daimon, enter into this blackened mirror, fill it with a divine spirit, and show me your might. Let ALBALAL, who is the secret light. Let there be light, breadth, depth, length, height, brightness, and let the spirit within shine through, the lord Bouēl Phtha Phtha Phthaēl Phtha Abai Bainchōōōch, now, now, immediately, immediately, quickly, quickly.

Then the Celebrant lights the lamp that is next to the black mirror and says the following incantation:

I conjure you, holy light, holy brightness, breadth, depth, length, height, brightness, by the holy names which I have spoken and am now speaking…IAŌ Sabaōth Arbathiao Sesn Genbar Pharaggēs Ablanathanalba Akrammachamari Ai Ai Aio Axax Inax, remain by me in the present moment (that shall last for eternity), until I pray to the great god and learn about my ultimate destiny.

The Celebrant makes three invoking spirals over the black mirror and the lit lamp, and then says the following incantation to the Bornless One, using the secret name that they have learned to call it. (The first part is intoned three times.)

I call upon you, the greatest god, sovereign Hōros Harpokratēs Alkib Harsamosi Iōai Dagennouth Raracharai Abraiaōth, you who enlighten the universe and by your own power illumine the whole world, god of gods, benefactor, Ao IAŌ Eaēy, you who direct night and day, AI AŌ, handle and steer the tiller, restrain the serpent. You are good, holy Daimon, whose name is Harbathanōps Iaoai, whom sunrises and sunsets hymn when you arise and set. You who are praised among all gods, angels and daimons, come and appear to me, god of gods, Hōros Harpokratēs Alkib Harsamosi Iōai Dagennouth Raracharai Abraiaōth.

Enter, appear to me, lord, because I call upon you as the three baboons call upon you, who speak your holy name in symbolic fashion, A EE ĒĒĒ IIII OOOOO YYYYY ŌŌŌŌŌŌŌ (speak as a baboon). Enter in, appear to me, lord, for I speak your greatest names: Barbarai Barbaraōth Arempsous Periaōmēch Dera Kōnēthch IAŌ Bal Bēl Bol Be Srō Iaoēi Oyeēi Eēi Eoyēi Aēi Ēi Iaoēi.

The Celebrant then proceeds to the West, facing the East. They say:

The Gate of the Mysteries of the Self as God begins with the establishment of the Destiny of the Individual Soul, and the three questions (of the Grail Mystery) applied to oneself. These are: "Who am I?", "Where have I been?", and "Where am I bound?" These questions and their answers manifest the three dimensions of the individual self, the three I's, or the Eye in the Triangle—thus I invoke!

The Celebrant then makes the sign of the Eye in the Triangle (hands held flat before oneself, index and thumb of both hands touching to form the triangle, and either the left or right eye staring out through it).

The Celebrant proceeds back to the center of the circle and draws a circle over the black mirror, then opens it, as if opening a veil before it. They say:

Behold, I have opened the gate to my destiny, and now I summon forth its vision into the manifested World of Formation. I shall ask the three questions of the Mystery and seek their answers in the Halls of the Greatest Mystikon. These questions are: "Who am I—what is my eternal and true essence?" "Where have I been and why?" All of the fortunes and calamities that have befallen me are perceived as the Greater Veil of Necessity, and I accept them as part of the path that has led me to the Gateway of the Holy Spirit. "Where am I bound, what is my destiny?" With this question I am bowed before you, the Source of All, and the mystery of my destiny is made clear to me. For there can be only one True Destiny, and that is where the Soul and Spirit are joined as One. Thus is revealed the Eye in the Triangle—(Celebrant makes the sign.)—the three "I's" that stand as markers to my Sacred Goal.

Thus is the Eye of Flesh, which shall see all the phenomena of the material world. The Eye of the Mind, which shall know all the mysteries of the inter-subjective structures. The Eye of Spirit (contemplation), which shall know the mysteries of the soul and the ineffable Gnosis. Each way of knowledge has its place and importance, and we shall never confuse one with the other, for such is the nature of the true apprehension of the greatest truth and the method of enlightenment. Thus is the Eye in the Triangle! So mote it be.

Then the Celebrant sits comfortably before the black mirror and silently repeats the secret name of the Bornless One while looking into the mirror, seeking to make final contact with it, sensing the three secrets of their soul and their realization. When a vision appears, the Celebrant will say the following:

Hail, lord, god of gods, benefactor, Hōros Harpokratēs Alkib Harsamōsi IAŌ Aida Gennouth Raracharai Abraiaō. Let your hours which you traverse be welcome; let your glories be welcomed further, lord.

Thus, the Celebrant engages in the envisioning, projecting their envisioned destiny into the future; knowing all parts of it and what parts are yet unknown, the Bornless One shall reveal it once it is sought. This will go on as long as required, and then finally when it is at an end, the Celebrant shall stand, stretch, and reawaken themselves, and stand before the lamp and the black mirror. The Celebrant will draw a banishing spiral over the black mirror and the lamp, and then extinguish the lamp, saying:

The light is diminished, the Great God is joyously thanked for his assistance, and all is released and departed to the blessed realms of the domain of Spirit. There to await the next time of the summoning. Bainchōōōch Balsamēs—the matter is officially ended.

The Celebrant will then set sealing spirals to the four angles and the Infrapoint to seal the ritual patterns for future posterity. The Celebrant may also perform an optional all-night vigil and greet the morning light of the day with the confidence and expectancy of having gained the knowledge of one's personal destiny.

ADDENDUM INVOCATIONS AND ADORNMENT

Hidden Stele

Celebrant says:

Hail, God Aion and all of the aerial spirits, Phogaloa. Hail spirit who extends from heaven to Earth, Erdēneu, and from Earth which is in the middle chamber of the universe unto the borders of the abyss, Meremōgga. Hail, spirit who enters into me, convulses me, and leaves me kindly according to the will of god, Iōē Zanōphie. Hail, beginning and end of the immovable nature, DŌYGLAOPHŌN. Hail, revolution of untiring service by heavenly bodies, Rōgyeu Anami Pelēgeōn Adara Eioph. Hail, radiance of the universe subordinate to the solar ray, Ieo Yēō Iae Ai Ēōy Oei. Hail, orb of the night-illuminating, unequally shining moon, AIŌ RĒMA RŌDOUŌPIA. Hail to all spirits of the aerial images, Romidouē Aganasou Ōthaua. Hail to those whom the greeting is given with blessing, to siblings, to the holy. O great, greatest, round, incomprehensible figure of the universe, heavenly Enrōchesyēl; in Heaven, Pelētheu; of ether, Iogaraa; in the ether, Thōpyleo Dardy; watery, Iōēdes; earthy, Perēphia; fiery, Aphthalya; wind-like, Iōie Ēō Aya; luminous, Alapie; dark-looking, Iepseria; shining with heavenly light, Adamalōr; moist, fiery, and cold spirit. I glorify you, god of gods, the one who brought order to the universe, Areō Pieua; the one who gathered together the abyss of the invisible foundation of its position, Perō Mysēi O Pentōnax; the one who separated heaven and Earth and covered the heaven with eternal, golden wings, Rōdēry Oyōa; the one who fixed the earth on eternal foundations, Alēioōa; the one who hung up the ether high above the earth, Aie Ōē Ioya; the one who scattered the air with self-moving breezes, Ōie Oyō; the one who put the water roundabout, Ōrēpēlya; the one who raises up hurricanes, Ōristhaua; the one who thunders, Thephichyōnēl; the one who hurls lightnings, Ourēnes; the one who rains, Osiorni Pheugalga; the one who shakes the earth; Peratōnel; the one who produces living creatures, Arēsigylōa; the god of the Aions; you who are great, lord, god, ruler of the all, Archizō Nyon Thēnar Methōr Pary Phezor Thapsamydō Marōmi Chēlōpsa.

Bornless Envisioning Rite

Death Delivering Stele

Celebrant says:

I praise thee, O God Aion, the one and blessed of the aions and the father of the world, with cosmic prayers. Come to me, you who filled the whole universe with air, who hung up the fire from the heavenly water and separated the earth from the water. Pay attention, form, spirit, earth, and sea, to a word from the one who is wise concerning divine necessity, and accept my words as fiery darts, because I am human, the most beautiful creature of the god in heaven, made out of spirit, dew, and earth. Heaven, be opened; accept my words. Listen, Helios, father of the world; I call upon you with your name Aēō Ey Ēoi Aioē Yeōa Ouorzara Lamanthathre Kanthiōper Garpsarthrē Menlardapa Kenthēr Dryomen Thrandrēthrē Iabe Zelanthi Ber Zathrē Zakenti Biollithrē Aēō Oyō Eō Oō Ramiatha Aēō Ōyō Oyō Ōayō: the only one having the original element. You are the holy and powerful name considered sacred by all the angels; protect me, (magic name), from every excess of power and from every violent act. Yes, do this, lord, god of gods, Ialdazaō Blatham Machōr Phrix Aē Keōpheēa Dymeō Pherphrithō Iachthō Psycheō Phirithmeō Rōserōth Thamastraphati Rimpsaōch Ialthe Meachi Abrathanōps, creator of the world, creator of the universe, lord, god of gods, Marmariō IAŌ. I have spoken of your unsurpassable glory, you who created gods, Archangels, and decans. The tens of thousands of angels stood by you and exalted the heavens, and the lord witnessed your Wisdom, which is Aion, Ieoyēōē Iaēaiēōēyoei, and I said that you are as strong as he is. I invoke your hundred-lettered name which extends from the sky to the depth of the earth; save me, for you are always ever rejoicing in saving those who are yours. Athēze Phōi Aaa Daigthi Thēobis Phiath Thambrami Abraōth Chtholchil Thoe Oelchōth Thiooēmch Choomch Saesi Isachchoē Ieroutha Ooooo Aiōai (one-hundred letters). I call upon you, the one whose name is inscribed on the holy phylactery, before whom the unquenchable lamp continually burns, the great God, the one who shone on the whole world, who is radiant at Jerusalem, lord, IAŌ Ai Ē Iōē Ōiē Iē Aiōai Ai Oyō Aōē Ēei Ieō Eyō Aēi Aō Aōa Aeēt Yō Eiē Aeo Iey Aeē Iaia IAŌ Ey Aey Iaē Ei Aaa Iii Ēēē Iō Iōē IAŌ (one-hundred letters), for a blessing, lord.

The phylactery consists of a strip of linen wrapped around body. Upon it is written these words:

I am Hōros Harpokratēs Alkib Harsamosis IAŌ AI Dagennouth Raracharai Abraiaōth, son of Isis Aththa Baththa and of Osiris Oronōnnōphris; keep me healthy, unharmed, not plagued by ghosts, and without terror during my lifetime.

PART III

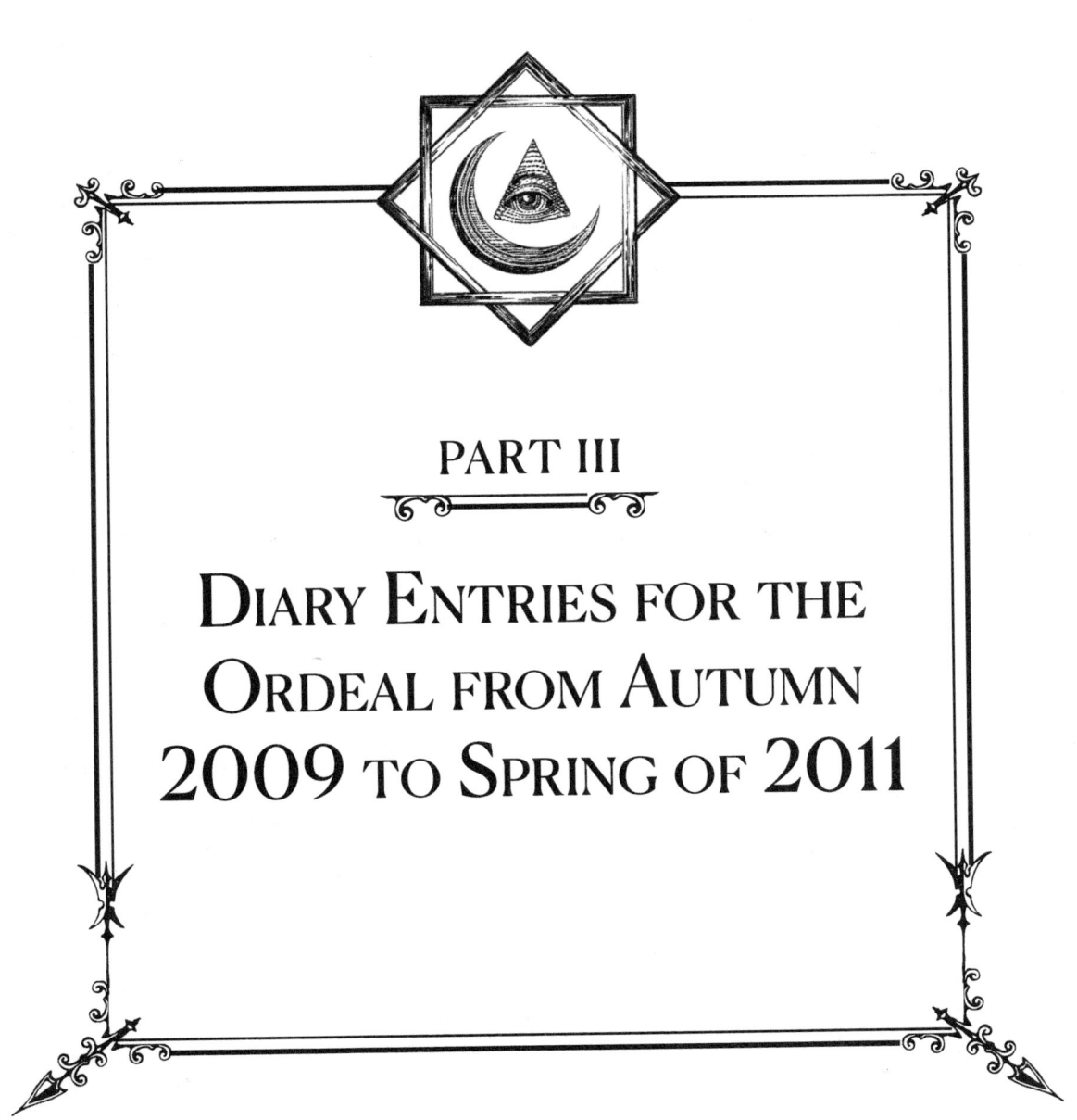

DIARY ENTRIES FOR THE ORDEAL FROM AUTUMN 2009 TO SPRING OF 2011

NOTE FROM THE AUTHOR

Diary Entries for the Ordeal Working from November 2009 to May 2011

Here are the diary entries that I wrote up when I performed the Abramelin Lunar Ordeal and when I had certain insights and thoughts concerning the working. Since it took me from November 2009 to May 2011 to fully complete this ordeal, there were moments of discovery that occurred in the interlude between when the last ritual was performed and when the ordeal officially ended some eighteen months later. The diary entries are taken from blog entries that I wrote up at the time, although I kept a diary of everything that happened as I was working through this ordeal. I will add some additional text from my diaries that I had kept out of my blog for personal reasons, but since that time I feel more disposed to reveal them.

I believe that it is important for anyone who is presenting a new variation on a tradition like the Sacred Magic of Abramelin to undergo it first and report on the results. It is just too easy to come up with all sorts of ideas and not actually test them. While these rituals and practices were something I had been developing and mastering over many years, the combination of them represented an entirely new approach to obtaining the K and C of the HGA. In presenting these personal observations while I performed this ordeal, I think that it might assist anyone who desires to follow in my footsteps. I have done the work, and I am presenting my personal experiences regarding it; therefore, it will not seem like such a radical departure from magical practices, traditions, or experimental approaches. It is not a fool's errand to consider this Lunar Ordeal as a means to obtain enlightenment, even briefly.

The dates for each section are when I posted the blog entry. Dates, times, and auspices are included for each step of the working, and all times are Central Standard or Central Daylight Savings Time. I have edited the entries for greater readability but not altered the content.

I have omitted the diary entries for the meditation and devotional sessions that were performed during the ordeal, as well as the weather conditions and other extraneous circumstances that I believe were not pertinent to the working as a whole.

CHAPTER ONE

Beginning of the Ordeal: Preparations and Consecrations (11/18/2009)

I have started the Abramelin Lunar Ordeal and will post articles at strategic points in the process to share with you how this ordeal is shaping up. One can spout platitudes and make theories about magic, but the real proof is in the performance of actual ordeals and experiments.

Since I have proposed an alternative path to the traditional Abramelin ordeal, joining it with the Invocation of the Bornless One, it is important for me to actually test my hypothesis and note the results for others to examine and ponder. What I have learned through my many years of practical experience is that one's intention has a powerful shaping influence on what one experiences in the practice of ritual magic. Even a highly flawed ritual performed by a mere novice can be as effective as one performed by an experienced magician if that novice has the right amount of passion, zeal, and an empowered and indomitable intention.

However, the difference between a novice and an experienced magician is that the experienced magician can repeat the phenomena produced and even share the rituals and ceremonies they used with others for their examination and experimentation. A novice is effective often as a matter of luck or the right combination of effects, and generally not because of their experience and knowledge. A novice may or may not produce effective results, but the likelihood is only somewhat slightly better than chance.

On Monday, November 16, at exactly 1:14 p.m. CST, day of the new moon, I began the Abramelin Lunar Ordeal with an extensive meditation session and later followed up that evening with a Mass of the Goddess. What I experienced was a potent affirmation that the path and action that I have chosen is the right one for me at this time. I sensed that I had engaged with a powerful spiritual presence—it was undoubtedly my personal aspect of the Goddess blanketing me with good will, anticipation, and joy at the beginning of what will prove to be a very challenging seven weeks of constant meditation, contemplation, and invocative ritual magic. So my personal aspect of the Deity is in positive accord with what I am spiritually and magically planning to do. That's a good sign, but there have been other signs that I have experienced that would also indicate that fate is positively disposed towards me.

Her message to me was in three parts. The first part she said to me: "Remember that nothing is free, and everything has consequences." Her second message was that "time heals all wounds and gently buries issues, and the secret is learning to let go and allow the constant flow of change transport you to where you need to go." She also said to me, "love is the key to enlightenment. Use this key and transform yourself." While some of this might seem like obvious platitudes, they were in direct response to thoughts and concerns that I had just prior to the working. Later that evening, after I had retired, I had many odd and strange dreams, but the message I deduced behind these dreams was to "be a mediator of the Gods."

The previous weekend (Saturday, November 7), I had invoked the Archangel Raziel (God's Mystery) using the new methodology that I recently assembled. Raziel is a spirit that I have invoked a number of times previously, since I have determined that he is the core of what I have discovered over the years as a very different Enochian system of magic, which incorporates the Nephilim as contra-Archangelic entities, as well as other variations. I intend to write extensively on this different approach to Enochian magic in the future, but for now, let's just say that I am quite familiar with Raziel.[80] I performed this rite with Soror Grace and Frater Arjuna in attendance. I ignored using planetary hours, so there wasn't any obligation to begin at a specific time.

Anyway, this entity, when invoked, had a profound effect on me and imparted some very fascinating information. The effect was one of acknowledgment, which empowered my intention and gave me a profound resolution that my desire to perform the upcoming ordeal is the correct thing to do. I had to recreate the sigil for Raziel, having misplaced the one that I made for previous invocations, and the Archangel told me that the new sigil was my passport and key for invoking the more potent and mysterious Seraphim and Cherubim, who I intend to invoke over the next four weekends. By the middle of December, I will have invoked all eight of these majestic spirits, and my intention for doing so has been strengthened by the favor and goodwill of Raziel. I still need to carefully build up my intention before attempting these invocations, but now I feel more resolved and compelled to do so, and less cautious and worried about the outcome. Invoking these Super-Archangels is no small matter, and approaching them with frivolous requests or unethical desires would be most disastrous for any magician.

Raziel also imparted to me that he had a hand in influencing and inspiring me to formulate this ordeal, even though the credit for doing so is still completely my own. So, now I have at least two patrons: Raziel and the godhead Hermes-Thoth Trismegistus. What this means is that a bit of angelic providence has inspired and guided me to

---

80   I wrote this book, titled *Liber Nephilim*, and it was published and released October 2024 by Crossed Crow Books. I would recommend that you purchase and read it if you haven't done so already.

formulate this working. I must admit that I am greatly intrigued, and it would seem that the spiritual hierarchy agrees with what I am about to do.

Additionally, I had asked Raziel about human personal decorum for the ordeal, and whether it mattered, such as diet, piety, mental hygiene, physical hygiene, and so on. He replied that the only really important issues were focus, discipline, and consistency. Things of the body do not concern spirits, only things of the spirit. Profane minds, poor hygiene, and poor diets may interfere with the intention of the focus of the magic, but holiness isn't a factor, since humans are of spirit, mind, and body and inherently flawed, as is all of nature. (That might be true purely from the perspective of the eye of spirit, but from a Pagan perspective, all nature is perfect in its variants and non-Euclidean qualities.)

That being said, I must still be disciplined and diligent in all of my efforts for this ordeal to be successfully concluded. I will refrain from eating red meat, eat sparingly, and adopt a vegetarian diet for the weekend workings. I am also meditating twice daily—once at waking, and again before bed. The weekends will require some vigils and a steadfast focusing on just the magic at hand to avoid any distractions. I must, therefore, complete all of my work before the end of the week so as to make myself ready for the major workings on the weekend.

So, all is ready for the first set of invocations this coming weekend, when I will invoke the Seraphim and Cherubim of Earth, whose names are Zahariel and Yofiel, respectively. I will write a report summarizing those encounters, and we shall see how all that plays out. Right now, I feel very confident about the outcome, since all the signs point to a powerful affirmation of the rightness of this working and its success.

CHAPTER TWO

ABRAMELIN LUNAR ORDEAL: FIRST WEEKEND, ATTRIBUTE OF EARTH (11/23/2009)

I HAVE COMPLETED THE FIRST WEEKEND WORKING for the Abramelin Lunar Ordeal and I was astonished at how powerful and amazing the experience was. I am still processing it, but it was a truly remarkable event, made all the more amazing by the fact that there are another six weekends to go. This weekend was dedicated to the Element Earth and the invocation of the Seraph and Cherub of Earth, Zahriel and Yophiel respectively.

First of all, the week started with the saying of Mass, meditations twice daily, and a special Mass on Friday. I have been maintaining a fairly strict diet, although not entirely vegetarian. Since I began this working, I have avoided all red meat dishes, and I have cut my consumption of other meat dishes (fish and poultry) down to a minimum. For the weekend of the working, I have avoided eating any meat at all. I think that this regimen is a good one, and it certainly means that I am not weighted down with food and drink when I am attempting to work magic. Correspondingly, I am not overly hungry or weakened by fasting either. I have found that it's important to maintain a balance, since a complete fast would make one overly weak and unable to accommodate the strenuous efforts of working ritual for two hours with little or no rest. I have also avoided any distractions, such as television, during the weekend as well. So, my focus has been quite on target with little to either distract or interrupt the workings.

My wife, Grace Victoria Swann, has been my companion and assistant for these events and will continue to work the entire ordeal by my side, assisting me in gaining an objective perspective on the nature of these workings. Her experiences, although different in quality and kind, seem to represent another way of receiving the impressions and communications from these entities. I can't in good conscience talk about her experiences, but she, too, is quite succinctly aware that "something" has been invoked and materialized in the magic circle, and that it has communicated with her. So, I know that I am not imagining things or experiencing a delusional fantasy regarding the outcome of each of these workings.

In performing these theurgic invocations, I do not subscribe to the belief that the manifestation of spirits must be accompanied with poltergeist phenomena or obvious material manifestations. While I may "see" something, it's generally altogether different from what another person would perceive. What is important to these workings, and how I determine that they work, is that the participants sense and experience something quite "other" than what is normally running through their heads. I usually sense the presence of the spirit, and in the case of the Super-Archangels, it's enough sensation to almost knock one completely over. This is what I call a "palpable" sense of the presence of the spirit, which includes visual and auditory paranormal experiences. One might see the vision of an angel standing before oneself or not. However, my experience with invocation and evocation so far has shown that it will almost always endow one with a powerful set of impressions that continue (in dreams, insights, and lucid visions) well beyond the moment of the manifestation of the entity.

What I seek from performing invocations is an immersion into the domain of the spirit, which has the power to affect one on many levels simultaneously. I may see and hear things, but other types of information are being communicated on levels that I am not immediately aware of until later. An invocation may have a finite duration, but its effects continue for some time afterward. Therefore, performing a suite of invocations over a period of just four weekends will cause these different angelic entities to blend together, building a powerful meta-spirit, which is the establishment of the Godhead Element, the goal of the first phase of this ordeal.

Also, it is my belief and practice that when a magic circle is set, the planetary hour is locked in. However time is perceived by one inside or outside the circle is irrelevant. Once the magic circle is set, time within that space is no longer "normal" —which is to say that the sacred space becomes essentially timeless. This is not an arbitrary rule that I made up for my amusement. I have experienced so much time dilation or contraction within a magic circle that I believe that the time-space continuum within a magic circle (or at least one's perception of it) is highly distorted. Therefore, instead of having to speed through a working in order to complete it within an hour's time so it is performed under the auspices of a planet, all I have to do is set the magic circle during that period and the planetary hour is locked into place until the magic circle is sealed at the end of the working.

Now that we have established these basic understandings about the nature of invocation in regard to how I work it, we can continue to explore what exactly occurred. These workings incorporate the Archetypal Gate Ritual, with corresponding Mass and Benediction rites. The overall working takes roughly two and half hours to complete.

November 21: Invocation of Zahriel, Seraph of the Elemental tetrad of Earth. The approximate start was around 6 p.m. during the planetary hour of Sol, which was locked into the working. Zahriel was a highly energized entity—so much so that I sensed it even before the invocation began. Performing the invocation only greatly intensified what was already present in the magic circle.

The invocation itself was performed by me, a little bit roughly since I hadn't performed this ritual in many months. However, it was accomplished correctly and efficiently. The ritual structure has been worked over for several years now and it flows very well, although I am sure that some would say that it's probably a bit wordy. When the ritual climax was achieved, the resultant manifestation was easily sensible and palpable to both Grace and me. We felt a highly energized and zealous entity, full of power and inspiration—so much that it was almost bouncing off the walls. My whole body was tingling with this energy, like electric sparks passing through it, and this phenomenon went on, although greatly diminished, even to the next morning's meditation session. What I felt was an intense joyousness, zeal, and exaltation—the joy of life. The following are some of the things imparted by Zahriel to me during the meditative period following the invocation.

Joyous existence—the happiness and great innocent pleasure in all of life—even when it seems like a burden were the feelings that went through my mind. I saw a vision of a gaily dressed entity, like the Ghost of Christmas Present in Dickens' story "A Christmas Carol," amidst a halo of golden and brilliant lights. I felt all of the goodness that I have ever done for others compressed into a single moment of ecstatic happiness—an illumination of joyousness! I realized that knowing and being grateful for life was an important foundation to enlightenment, which can't occur without that sense of gratification. All things happen for a reason, even tragedies, and looking for a single reason "explaining why" is an illusion. Life must be reckoned in its totality, from beginning to end. This angel gives the gift of knowing the essential totality of one's existence before it has even ended—a truly remarkable gift!

We realize the nature of spirit by projecting our minds deep into our unconsciousness—and that depth of self and the deep inward projection awakens us to what is essentially "spiritual" in our lives. So in this manner we realize that we are connected to everyone else, and that our joy is analogous to the joy of others—since it is so contagious and uniformly found everywhere.

Some other points that were communicated to me: a developed life is a great and precious gift, therefore, seek to develop oneself to the ultimate degree. All good that is done for others has a powerful multiplying effect. One can never know just how a good deed for another affects them, especially when they carry it for their entire lifetime in one manner or another.

I suspect that we spend too much time thinking about all of the bad deeds done to us by others without ever accounting for the good.

Learn to be grateful for the good that has happened to you, and then treasure it in the eternal ever present "now." Enlightenment is cold, empty, and meaningless without the joy and rapture of the realization of the good spirit active in one's life. Thus, we all have our own personal Agathodaimon. We should discover and celebrate it while we still are able to do so. Never knowing that part of us is a tragic loss! I can use the sigil of Zahriel to bring joy when it seems absent from my life.

November 22: Invocation of Yophiel, Cherub of the Elemental tetrad of Earth. The approximate start was a little after 8 p.m., locking in the planetary hour of Jupiter. Where Zahriel was highly energized, Yophiel was much more subdued but no less powerful—in fact, this angel was perhaps even a bit frightening at first.

The invocation of Yophiel produced an energy and a presence that was profound and very intense. At first, the angel appeared to me in a kind of threatening guise; it was silent and ominous. I then produced the sigil of Raziel and said that I had summoned Yophiel with the guidance and authority of Raziel, and that seemed to completely break the spell of silence. The angel spoke to me in a kindly fashion, but with great reservation and intense gravity. Instead of exuberance and zeal, Yophiel was thoughtful, deep, calm, and almost gentle, but I sensed that behind it was a great reservoir of power and might to be used to assist or punish as required. Needless to say, I was quite awestruck at the reserve and restraint that seemed to govern this angelic entity. However, I found that the information transmitted to me was full of benevolence and kindness, though strict and hard in its unyielding judgment.

This is some of what the angel communicated to me that night. The main point of his teaching was the importance of spiritual discipline, consistency, and devotion to the Deity. Devotion consists of the expressed and constant demonstration of the love of the Deity—giving offerings and purely worshiping it. This also includes forgiving the errors and follies of others, as well as giving alms to the poor and supporting one's spiritual community. One should give either service or money to those who are bereft as a demonstration of spiritual solidarity with the human race. (Those who practice magic are too insular and generally disconnected from the rest of humanity, and this gap needs to be bridged.) We don't need to live like monks or nuns, but we need to be consistent and disciplined in how we spiritually live. This must be observed as a precondition to true enlightenment. One should also teach and lead where they may, or to be an able follower and supporter—and, above all else, to listen to others. Important spiritual messages often have the strangest and most unexpected sources. A chance encounter with a drunken derelict might actually impart greater (but hidden) wisdom than spending years meditating and pretending to be spiritual.

Perhaps the most profound thing that Yophiel imparted to me was the lesson of how to seek spiritual knowledge. He said to me, "beware of those who espouse only the Light, for their hypocrisy will unleash their dark side, harming others and themselves!" He also said, "beware also, those who indulge in the Darkness, for their corruption is complete!" Then he revealed to me an interesting idea—the way to the truth is found neither in the Light or the Darkness. It is found in the balance between the two. Spiritual wisdom is found in synthesis, where light is the thesis and darkness the antithesis. After mulling over these and other important pronouncements, the invocation ended.

So, that's some of what I encountered as I invoked these two powerful Super-Archangels. I have much to ponder and think about, and that's just the wisdom imparted by these two angels. I also need to prepare for the coming weekend when the ordeal will continue with the invocation of two more angels. I wonder how intense all these workings will be, and whether I can endure them and digest all that is happening within them.

CHAPTER THREE

ABRAMELIN LUNAR ORDEAL: SECOND WEEKEND, ATTRIBUTE OF AIR (11/30/2009)

I HAVE COMPLETED THE SECOND WEEKEND of the paired workings for the Abramelin Lunar Ordeal, this time focusing on the attributes of the Element of Air. This week's working started out with me catching a cold that lasted throughout most of the week, complicating the process but neither delaying nor halting it. It was pretty difficult to meditate while being ill, but I made up for the lack with other acts of devotion, ensuring that I was quite focused on the working. Thanksgiving also occurred during the middle of the week. I had to maintain focus on the working amidst celebrations and the distractions of people preparing for the festive season of Christmas and the Winter Solstice.

Grace and I decided to change the workings to Friday and Saturday instead of Saturday and Sunday, which aids her staying focused on schoolwork. She is having to go through the last few weeks of the semester and all of the work and preparation for final tests that that implies. Always the able acrobat, she is managing to balance her mundane commitments to training and schoolwork as well as working these ordeals by my side. I feel blessed by her presence. Her impressions of the working parallel my own, giving me an objective perspective on them that I would not otherwise have.

November 27: Invocation of Yehoel, Seraph of the Elemental tetrad of Air. The approximate start was around 7:40 p.m., locking in the planetary hour of Mars. The circle was consecrated, and Mass and Benediction were performed. Yehoel was a mind-blowing entity, literally causing me to experience an internal expansion of my mind that left me rather dazed and muddled afterward. Nothing could have prepared me for what I experienced that night!

At first, after the invocation had been completed, I saw and heard nothing, even though the energy in the temple was considerable (there undoubtedly was "something" in the temple). Then, I showed the sigil of Raziel and I saw a blurry human form take shape above me, with a deep blue colored body and a large white head (turban?). This blurry form increased in magnitude until it revealed a giant golden-white illuminated crystal that seemed to enclose me in its light. Yehoel spoke clearly and concisely into my mind, giving me much to ponder and think about, but I also noticed that my very mind was expanding as he communicated to me. I saw all of the flaws and imperfections in my ritual structures and declarations and knew what to do to perfect them to a higher refinement. I also saw my own spiritual and magical path and the magical paths of many others who are working magic as I am. There were quite a number of these peers, all engaging in the issues of working magic from different but analogous perspectives.

Yet each of us are so narrowly engaged in our pursuits that we miss the bigger picture: the whole of the discipline of magic rather than the specific practice of one individual. I realized that each of these individuals were very close spiritual kindred of mine, and that it would benefit us greatly if we could but find a way to unite and share our hard-won knowledge with each other. Considering the egotistical nature of some—if not nearly all—magicians working magic, this would be a pretty tall order. However, in order to truly realize the totality of magic and its capabilities, all of these different perspectives need to be united, like the facets of a complex crystal coming together and into focus. I was seeing, for the first time, the unified perspective and discipline of all systems of ritual and ceremonial magic, and I was astonished at how profound and all-encompassing this united discipline actually is. I saw the union of science and religion under the banner of magic. Of course, I am not the first to see this vision (Crowley made it a motto of the periodical *The Equinox*), but it still eludes us even into the beginning of the second decade of the twenty-first century. What is required is a meta-system, but that will have to wait for a group of brilliant individuals who will be able to cross barriers of ego-based ownership and personal magical pride.

These are some of Yehoel's words of wisdom to me.

Yehoel is concerned with the nature and revelation of what Crowley called the True Will, and what I call a person's individual manifest destiny. Yehoel told me that the True Will is discovered through the resolution of parables, riddles, paradoxes, and puzzles about the nature of reality, chance (fortune), and inherent capabilities (and flaws) associated with the individual. So, the True Will is not something straightforward; it's more of a profound personal mystery—one that requires a constant focused inquiry. However, all personal destinies are resolved at the same point: ultimate union with the godhead, whether a person realizes that truth or not. Such a state is not guaranteed, but it's part of a person's birthright. Every human being has this as their birthright, whether or not they manage to realize it in a single lifetime. Enlightenment and union with the godhead is always right there in front of us, the most obvious thing. Yet it would seem invisible to almost everyone. It is a simple thing to acquire, but usually requires a lifetime of experience and hardship before that step is actually known, discovered by the resolution of the mystery of the self and the true will.

How do we resolve this mystery about our destiny, besides living an entire lifetime and making good and probably bad decisions? Yehoel says that undergoing ecstatic union with the godhead over time, even in small phases and brief encounters, will reveal the greater truth and wisdom to us. How do we approach ecstatic union with the deity? By complete and total surrender at the moment just before that merging occurs. In other words, by leaving our egotistical notions and pride of our accomplishments at the gateway of the celestial temple and enter therein as humble supplicants full of devotion, love, and the absolute surrender of oneself. This would seem to go counter to most of what is discussed and written about ceremonial and ritual magic. Often, such practices are accompanied by the hazards of ego inflation.

This would seem to be a very mystical approach and very unmagical. However, the objective of the magician and the mystic are essentially the same: union with the godhead. The real difference between them is what they do once that union is obtained. The mystic renounces the world, and the magician re-enters it to become the nucleus of divinely inspired change. Obtaining spiritual ecstasy through small operations and simple steps will shatter the tough hide of the ego and open the Self up to a greater spiritual perspective. So, the preparation is a form of god-intoxication, particularly for this ordeal that I have derived. Without the stages of god-intoxication, the ordeal will fail. Yohoel said to me, "I am the revealer and inspirer of your personal destiny! The difficult steps—discipline and their associated hardships—these will be covered by the Cherub of Air."

The overall working gave me what seemed like a powerful brain-boost. My ability to intellectually contain all of this knowledge and to see things at both the grandest and most minute levels was enhanced more than one hundred-fold. I felt like I was stoned or even kind of drunk—I couldn't articulate or think in a focused manner even after the gateway was closed, dismissing the spirit. Even attempting to ground myself by eating some food had little effect. I had to retire very soon after the working, so potent was the experience. During the evening, I dreamed about a vast sandy wasteland that made my mouth burn with thirst. When I awoke the next day, the effect was still upon me, although somewhat diminished. If I focused too long on something, I felt myself completely and totally pulled into that string of thought, abrogating anything else I happened to be thinking or doing. It was a strange sensation—and not particularly pleasant, either.

November 28: Invocation of Ofaniel, Cherub of the Elemental tetrad of Air. The approximate start was a little after 9:00 p.m., locking in the planetary hour of the moon. Grace performed the circle consecration and assisted with the Mass. However, before the Mass was even completed, she went off into a powerful trance state, apparently communing with Ofaniel before the invocation rite was even performed. This is not the first time that I have seen this kind of phenomenon, but it was certainly the most dramatic.

Once again, I sensed a great power in the temple immediately following the invocation, and again the angelic spirit was silent and invisible until I presented the sigil of Raziel as my bona fide. However, once that was accomplished, I saw above me an entity that was shrouded in an orange and reddish light, and the voice I heard was harsh and pointed. Ofaniel, once unleashed, proceeded to harshly judge me, pointing out all of my flaws, failings, and the various follies that I had devoted my life to and the misinformation that I had believed in. All of this was brought out, including all of the wrongs that I had done in my entire life so far, which was certainly not a pure and stellar record by any stretch of the imagination. I was greatly humbled by this powerful condemnation of me since all of it was indeed true. I admitted as much, with the lame excuse that I am just a flawed mortal and, like all things of nature, imperfect. I did take responsibility for everything that I had done, and that seemed to lessen the harshness.

The fact that I am learning from my mistakes and seeking to take corrective actions in order to perfect myself might give me some leeway. This admission and its associated contrition seemed to mollify Ofaniel. From that point on, his demeanor was much more compassionate and charitable to me. He told me that it was always wise to admit one's mistakes and never to shrink from taking responsibility for them, and it's also quite humbling. This is a critical mind-state required to approach the admirable but equally foolish quest to become one with the godhead. So, it would seem to be important to know one's limitations, but to strive for spiritual union nonetheless.

I felt as though I had just encountered a powerful test, and, indeed, Ofaniel indicated that my resolve and my intention had been tested all week, what with my cold and its dragging inertia which I had to overcome. He told me that I would be continually tested even more severely in weeks ahead as I attempted to complete this ordeal. If I chose to cease my activity now, he would forgive me and allow me to do so without any repercussions. I indicated that I was resolved to complete the ordeal no matter what happened, and that short of dire illness or death, I would complete it. My answer seemed to cause him to regard me in greater esteem. He told me that the requirements of the four Cherubim should be followed without failure in order to be allowed to accomplish the feat of bringing all of the eight angelic spirits together in an octagram of the empowered godhead.

Ofaniel then gave me an important key to the process of magically induced enlightenment, which is the faithful execution of devotion, love, and service to the godhead. One must covet union in a single-minded manner, analogous to a lover ardently and passionately seeking the object of their desires. The intensity of these devotions must become ever greater until they nearly consume one's mind, body, and soul, and this must be accomplished before the Bornless One Invocation is even to be performed. There should be no distractions, interruptions, or diversions—one should be completely one pointed and totally focused. This, then, is my mission and objective as far as Ofaniel is concerned. Thus, the Bornless One Invocation must be accomplished with this level of deep devotion and perfect egoless surrender. To achieve this objective, one is required to enforce a very rigorous discipline as the basis for the entire working. Failure to do this will cause the Bornless One invocation rite to be empty and meaningless, or at least certainly a lot less impactful than it otherwise would be. Devotion and discipline are the essence of the key and surrender at the perfect moment of manifestation of the god within is the required method.

This is what Ofaniel imparted to me at the climax of the invocation.

"You have reached the midpoint of the working, and the beginning of the more challenging and difficult parts of the ordeal. The Seraphim will inspire you, and the Cherubim will challenge you, as you have never been inspired or challenged before. The Cherubim are

the keepers of the gateway of the Godhead, and they will test and judge you as either worthy or unworthy. Fulfilling their requirements is extremely important. It must be done with an open heart and a transparent motivation—anything less will cause the ordeal to fail. You will not be able to bring all eight of these Super-Archangels together without incurring a kind of curse on yourself, so be warned and prepare yourself!

"When you perform your devotions to the Godhead, you should kneel before your shrine, give offerings and praise to the Deity, and open yourself completely to it. Give offerings of flowers, incense, sacraments (food and drink), and poetic songs and words of praise and adoration. Love the Deity with all of your heart and soul. While you do these things, hold my sigil in your hand to act as a witness to them, for it will act as a key to opening the gateway of the revelation of the godhead. Note anything that occurs and whatever is communicated to you. This you shall do every day, starting at the beginning of the week until the day that you perform the invocation of the Bornless One. Also, be aware of the astrological times of the event of your workings, especially its date of expected climax. You will find great mysteries revealed in the transits and progressions revealed."

Then when the spirit of Ofaniel receded, and the mind-numbing sensation that had afflicted me since the invocation of the Seraph the prior day disappeared completely. My mind was clear and peacefully reposed. The rite ended just around thirty minutes before midnight.

So far, I had been tasked with giving alms to the poor and had only done so in a token manner. I must show greater generosity than that and, in addition, Ofaniel gave me the requirement of daily devotions to replace the meditations that I was performing twice daily. I must spend more time giving devotion, offerings, praise to my godhead, and do so with the utmost sincerity and passionate desire for spiritual union. I should hold the sigil of Ofaniel in my right hand while I do these tasks. Faithfully executing these instructions (and the others that the next two Cherubim will require of me) will aid my cause in achieving enlightenment and union with the godhead. Failure to do these tasks will ensure that I fail in the overall working, so it is up to me to see that they are faithfully accomplished. I vowed to see them done, as I fully intended to do—starting Monday. My reason for one day of rest is that I had a number of other tasks to complete on Sunday and I would be quite exhausted from the weekend of workings. This decision was sanctioned by the Super-Archangel.

This is what I have experienced for these two workings, and they produced quite a lot to ponder and undertake. I feel resolved to complete the ordeal, but now I am beginning to realize the degree of my commitment, the challenges that I now face, and the ones that lie in the near future. This ordeal will not be accomplished without a great deal of effort and work—in fact far more than I originally anticipated.

CHAPTER FOUR

ABRAMELIN LUNAR ORDEAL: THIRD WEEKEND, ATTRIBUTE OF WATER (12/7/2009)

I HAVE COMPLETED THE THIRD WEEKEND working in the Abramelin Lunar Ordeal, and I found this week to be the most difficult and challenging so far. I am amazed at the extent of potential interfering factors that I encountered. Where the previous week I had to contend with a cold and use whatever means to heal myself as much as possible before the working, this week I had to contend with minor disasters erupting in my mundane life, including (and especially) my job and its associated responsibilities. I can see the wisdom of not working for the entire duration of the more arduous section of the traditional Abramelin ordeal, but on a practical level I can't afford to follow that path. I have too many worldly responsibilities and I need to continue to support myself and my household. However, by chance and perseverance on my part, I managed to resolve everything and accomplish my magical objectives as well. In the midst of these workings, it almost made me wonder if I was going to have to choose between completing either the magical or mundane job objectives. Luckily, I was able to complete both thoroughly and completely, much to my surprise and satisfaction.

The week began quietly enough. I was so exhausted by the previous weekend's working that I took Sunday off to get some much-needed work completed. I also retired early that night to prepare me for the week. As requested by the Cherub, I switched from performing a thirty-minute meditation sessions first thing in the morning and before I went to bed in the evening to a singular longer meditation and devotion session in the evening. I used a devotion session that included prayers to my personal Godhead, silently reciting a prayer saying that there is no barrier between my Deity and myself except the illusionary one that I have created in my mind, and that I ardently seek and want union with my godhead.

When I recite this prayer, I can feel a moment of powerful passion well up in my deeper being and then pass. I am unable to sustain it for long, but that seems kind of normal to me so far. With practice, I may be able to sustain it for longer periods of time. The week progressed without too much difficulty until nearly the end of the work week, when I was notified that my job would require some important diligence Friday night and very early Saturday morning. I decided to perform the workings on Saturday and Sunday instead of Friday and Saturday. This didn't present much of a problem and gave me time to prepare for the working. I knew about this by Wednesday, so it wasn't a complicated change.

However, the work-related task was jeopardized by a catastrophic failure, which required me to work most of the weekend to fix it. My other job account also required an unusual bit of maintenance too, so I ended up spending two nearly eight-hour days over the weekend doing this work, not to mention dealing with the stress. I also pulled a muscle in my back and was not particularly happy about these circumstances since I had fully expected to have a quiet weekend as far as work is concerned. Luckily, I do have the benefit of working from home, so I didn't have to throw away any time for commuting. Despite these complications, I was resolved to perform these invocations, since delaying them was out of the question if I intended to complete this ordeal. I was certainly being tested by uncontrollable events, that was obvious.

As a result of my work-related issues, I was not able to perform any devotions on Friday before the working, although I did manage to get all of the preparations completed. I worked up to perhaps a couple of hours before the working, and somehow managed to find a bit of time to eat and take care of my needs. My partner, Grace, helped greatly in this effort, even though she was intensely involved in her own ordeal of completing her semester at school.

December 5: Invocation of Metatron, Seraphim of the Elemental tetrad of Water. The approximate start was around 8:10 p.m., during the planetary hour of Mercury, which was locked into the working. I had been anticipating this invocation all week because Metatron is a very famous and well-known angel, being both one of the Seraphim and the chief of the Archangels of the Tree of Life. There are many legends about him, including that he may have previously been human—perhaps even the later manifestation of the undying patriarch, Enoch—but he is also known for being mysterious and quite unfathomable. Since I had acquitted my mundane tasks in a satisfactory manner, I felt fully prepared, eager, and ready for this invocation, but I could not have been prepared for what I was about to experience, so unusual and unique was the manifestation of that entity.

Invocation of Metatron and its associated rites was performed without any problems or issues, in fact with a certain degree of ease. My lady, Grace, assisted me with the Mass and the Benediction, and I performed the circle consecration and the invocation rite myself. As the invocation was being performed, I noticed that there was a great deal of power and energy being generated as the rite progressed—more than I had previously experienced. My body was vibrating with nervous energy, and it increased to a climax when the invocation was completed and the spirit of the Seraphim began to manifest. I held up the sigil of Raziel, but that didn't even seem to matter—what was occurring happened with or without any kind of assistance. I saw a great shower of sparks and points of light form before me, and a powerful presence emerged from it in cascading fountains of light that dazzled my eyes.

Then, this body of light that was hovering above me descended and seemed to envelope me. I almost lost consciousness. The light was a beautiful blue flame. From the midst of this form, a shaft of brilliant and dazzling light shot forth and passed into me, seeming to penetrate my very being. I saw within myself, and there had been planted in me a small round object the size of a pearl that was vibrating with energy and emitting light in pulses. I heard a voice say to me, "this is my gift to you, Oh sojourner of the spiritual paths of super-celestial magic. It is the seed of spiritual love and greatest wisdom. Care for it, nurture it with love and your passion for God, believe in it as the link between you and your goal. If you do this, then the seed will open and unveil its glory unto your soul. If you fail, then it shall become a dead thing, which shall embitter and curse your very quest to its source. You must choose your path wisely and carefully so that the gift is a great boon to you instead of a barrier."

So, I realized that I had been impregnated with a "seed" of wisdom, and that realization amazed me, since I have never experienced anything like that before. I didn't feel violated or intruded upon because, in a way, I had asked for this boon, whether I realized it or not. The seed is nestled in my soul, silvery white on the outside, but lavender and rose colored on inside. It waits for me to achieve the right degree of passion and angst for it to be released, like a trigger. Meanwhile, I have a precious thing within me that I must protect, care for, and build. One could also conceive of it as a kind of ticking bomb or a poison pill if I am not careful and diligent. If all goes well, then this seed will open at the right time and release its splendor and power as a god-intoxicating passion and spiritually induced ecstasy. I must find the key and know how to deploy it between now and when I perform the Bornless One invocation rite—a mere twenty-five days away.

Metatron's gift has many sides or facets. Like a fragile egg, I will need to nurture it and keep it "warm" with devotions and an ever-increasing and accelerating passion for spiritual union with my personal godhead. If I fail, then the planted seed will die, and it will cause me all sorts of troubles and difficulties. To let such a precious gift be wasted would be a sign of extreme bad faith—probably one that I wouldn't be able to overcome in this lifetime. This seed can open the domain of the causal levels of consciousness and facilitate union between my Bornless higher spiritual self and my lower conscious self. My actions are the determining factor, so I must maintain a high level of personal integrity and make certain that nothing deters me from my spiritual goal.

Thus, the wager of my quest has been greatly magnified, as I stand to gain everything or lose it in a single seven-week ordeal. Needless to say, I am quite amazed about all of this; it's not at all what I expected. Other than telling me that brief communication, Metatron had nothing further to say, indicating that I would have the basis of his wisdom if the "seed" bloomed within my soul. He also said other information would be forthcoming from the Cherub of Water, so I looked forward to understanding the nature of what has occurred to me from him. I have been given a rare gift (the likes of which I have never heard of before), but it is also a test and a riddle to be solved.

I felt giddy, full of energy, but also greatly exhausted. I felt drunk, but I was sober. My mind had problems focusing and it was buzzing with all sorts of disconnected thoughts. I couldn't think clearly, and I communicated in an impulsive and disjointed sort of way (more so than usual). I attempted to retire but had problems falling asleep. I had all sorts of vivid dreams, but they were also mixed up and confusing. After I awoke the next day, I was tired, as if I hadn't slept very deeply or got the rest that I needed. I wondered if I would have the energy to even perform the next working.

The next day found me performing tasks for my mundane job again instead of thinking about what had happened to me the night before. I managed to complete everything that I was working on, and there were no major problems that I was not able to quickly solve. Once again, I managed to get everything completed just a couple of hours before the working was to begin. A long meditation with votive offerings helped to get my mind focused on the magical work.

December 6: Invocation of Kerubiel, Cherub of the Elemental attribute of Water. The approximate start was at around 8 p.m., locking in the planetary hour of Jupiter. Despite my fatigue and the stress of work-related tasks, I managed to find a new store of energy within me. Grace and I split up the ritual work in the same manner as the previous night, except we didn't need to perform the Benediction rite. (The environment was already greatly empowered by the previous night's working.) The mass was probably the best attempt that I have made to date with the revised Mass of the Great Goddess, since I was doing some ad-lib on sections that needed revising but hadn't yet been revised. Once these changes are put in, the ritual should be closer to its final form.

The invocation proceeded smoothly, and I could feel the buildup of power, which seemed to be at a magnitude greater than anything I had experienced previously. When the invocation was completed, there was silence and stillness. I showed the sigil of Raziel, but nothing changed in any dramatic way. Instead, I heard distant chords of some kind of celestial music. The stillness was the gentle presence of Kerubiel, which soothed and poured a healing balm unto me, such was the beauty and wondrous love emanating from this being. He appeared to me like a warm embrace or a fragrant summer's night, warm, friendly, and inviting. I felt calm, blissful, and very much at ease. I was amazed at this manifestation, for I certainly expected to be harshly judged and found woefully inadequate. Instead, I found a powerful presence that emanated peace, compassion, and healing vitality. I felt refreshed and the stress of the weekend banished as if it had never existed. What a truly marvelous thing!

Then I heard Kerubiel speak in a gentle whisper, saying the following things.

"You have bravely passed these tests, although more will be forthcoming. Each step in this ordeal will be more difficult than the previous one, so prepare yourself for this battle, for it shall be a mighty undertaking if you succeed. Know that I am the gate keeper of the Heart of God, and I will guard this great treasure from all who are not worthy. I have judged your heart and your integrity. Although you are far from perfect or even an ideal level of perfection, you have consistently loved God from the beginning of your path. You have called the Godhead by the name of the 'Goddess,' but it is one of the many manifestations that I have served as an emissary of the One. You have maintained that

connection and have given devotion to your godhead all through the years, from your youth until now without any lapse.

"I have also weighed your ethics and measured your integrity. I have found them consistent and overall good, but not perfect. So therefore, as the Gate Keeper, I open for you the gateway and act as your guide in this ordeal, which shall last for the rest of your life. Also know that to those I have deemed unworthy, I appear in a terrible and deadly guise to frighten them away and, if they persist, to unsoul them. Since your heart is good, then to you I appear gentle and compassionate.

"I reveal this wisdom to you—a great seed has been planted in you, and only the greatest passion and love of God will cause it to open and reveal its secrets. When giving devotions to your godhead, remember the poetry of Rumi, Hafiz, and Kabir, and other poetry of the love to God, such as the Psalms. Sing praises to God, whom you love and adore, and the seed will reveal to you its inner most secrets and greatest glory.

"Also, you will need to incorporate some additional elements from the Book of Abramelin into your ordeal. Examine the last three days of that traditional ordeal, such as the fasting, prayers, vigils, anointing and atonement (ashes upon the head)—these you will need to work into what you already have completed. Choose four days before drawing the eight angels together and dedicate each to one of the four Elements. For each day you shall summon, meditate, and commune with the Seraph and the Cherub of that Element for an hour or more, so that whatever knowledge, wisdom, and power they might have shall be given to you to accomplish this great ordeal. Do this fully before you dare to merge them together into the spirit of the Godhead Element that you shall summon. Continue from this night forward to give your devotions, remembering to call upon any of the Seraph or Cherub that you might need to inspire or guide you. For having passed by me, you are given these keys to aid in the completion of your ordeal."

The invocation of Keburiel was completed then, and even though I felt glad of the outcome, I was greatly exhausted. I was surprised at being so readily accepted by the Cherub, but I knew that I had not wavered in my faith all of these years, and perhaps this was my reward for being such a creature of habit and so fixated on my magic and my Pagan faith. It all turned out to have a purpose, so I felt quite happy. Then I remembered the seed planted in my soul, realizing that the work had really only just begun, and any degree of complacency on my part was deadly to me.

CHAPTER FIVE

ABRAMELIN LUNAR ORDEAL: FOURTH WEEKEND, ATTRIBUTE OF FIRE (12/14/2009)

I HAVE COMPLETED THE FOURTH WEEKEND working for the Abramelin Lunar Ordeal, which is the final series of working for the first phase. All eight of the Super-Archangels are now fully invoked, and I am ready to begin the next phase. Since the new moon occurs Wednesday, December 16, there will be no further activity until after the Winter Solstice, when the moon passes the crescent lunation type heading into the first quarter. There is a minor action that I must perform on the eve of the solstice, which is the charging of the magic ring to be used as a material link to the Bornless One. I have also completed the rendering of twenty-two magic squares from the Book of Abramelin onto parchment, to be charged in the final working. I may add others in the future if needed, but these twenty-two seemed to be the most usable of the lot. I also discovered that the latest version of the book has errors in the definition of the magic squares, since I had to fix several of them to make them consistent and usable. Discovering inaccuracies in that version of the book was a bit of a blow, since I am now wondering what other typos and mistakes are published in it.

This weekend, I performed the invocations on Friday and Saturday, which helped to accommodate the schedule of my lady and partner, Grace. She's having to finish up her schooling and needs Sunday to study for finals. So, I made all of the preparations that were necessary for an early resumption of the work. Grace and I celebrated the last quarter of the moon on Tuesday night with a meditation, a fire in the fireplace, and discussions about the second phase of the ordeal. I have arranged to have those days off from work, and I will be sequestered during that time, which means no media connections whatsoever. That will be odd, since my email and web access are kind of like a permanent appendage for me. Work was not as trying and difficult as last weekend, but there were still tasks that I had to do on the weekend again, although they were not difficult or taxing.

A friend of mine suggested that the difficulty that I had had the previous week may have been because I was transitioning from the Element of Air to Water, and had it been the other way around, perhaps the problems would have been less severe. I believe that he is definitely on to some profound insight, but I am not sure if that was the cause of the difficulties, since the spirits said that I was being tested. This was the middle of the first phase of the ordeal, and such activities are usually more difficult than the beginning or the end. I will certainly take this into consideration when I examine and analyze the performance of the ordeal—a change may be made to the sequence of Elements.

I managed to perform some kind of evening devotion every night, starting with Monday, using my temple time to focus on my personal Godhead and seek to obtain a sense of union and one-ness with it. Something is working, because I am experiencing an answering resonance when I perform this kind of devotion. I am also aware of the seed or pearl that Metatron planted within my soul, and I can feel it kind of stirring and communicating with me, appearing in my dreams sometime as a giant seed, huge pinecone, black pearl, golden Easter egg, or some other similar guise. There is definitely something there and it appears to be gaining power from my daily devotions. The meditations are also very quiet and subdued, as if in anticipation of some more profound occurrence. I found the quiescence of activity not at all soothing; it seemed more ominous and portending of what was to come. As it turned out, there was something building to a crescendo for the final two invocations of this part of the ordeal.

December 11: Invocation of Seraphiel, Seraph of the Elemental tetrad of Fire. The approximate start was around a few minutes before 8:15 p.m., locking in the planetary hour of Mars. I was able to meditate almost an hour before the working, helping me to focus intensely and assisting me to disengage from mundane preoccupations.

The Mass and Benediction were said, with Grace's assistance, which turned out a lot better due to the changes that we have both made. However, a few more changes are needed, but the Mass of the Goddess is getting ever closer to the state of perfection that we both desire.

I performed the invocation of Seraphiel and felt a tremendous force build up as I proceeded through it. Once I had completed the full invocation, the power emanating from the angelic entity was so intense and tangible that it literally knocked me flat on my back for a few minutes. I recovered, sat up, and took the sigil of Raziel into my hand and began to say that I had the authority of that angel to perform this working, but my words seemed to be drowned out by the roaring sound of flames and fire. I was hearing these sounds, but they didn't seem to disturb Grace, so I must assume that I alone heard them. It would seem that the invocation was proceeding apace, whether I had Raziel's sigil or not—it didn't matter one whit.

It was then that I saw the vision of Seraphiel, and I was astonished at the clarity and magnitude of that vision. There in my inner sight I beheld a great towering pillar of flame, as if in the distance, although its heat and the sulfurous smell of burning came to me as if in a dream. Then, I remembered an old vision dream that I had when I was seventeen, a time when I was just starting out on my magical journey. It was uncannily similar to what I was beholding now. I had even made a colored drawing of this vision and still had it somewhere amongst my copious files. Could that be? I don't recall that the column of fire I saw in my vision years ago had any kind of name associated with it, or if it was even a spirit. You can be the judge, as I am including that an artist's rendition of that drawing in this diary entry.

Then I heard the voice of Seraphiel call to me, a voice that sounded like rushing air or steam, and the voice said: "Frater Barrabbas Tiresius, we have indeed met before—a long time ago in your perceptions, but only moments ago for me. Although which came first is unknown to me, for time is indeed strange and disjointed where I stand." I then saw a crystal-clear vision of everything that had been happening to me around the time that I first had the vision and made the drawing. It was a time of newness, adventure, extreme sexual awakening, and the desire to master life and find a fitting path for myself. Little did I know what would befall me during that short period of time, which I now know as distant memories of a long and lost time. Magic during those days was new and every occurrence was deemed great, majestic, hair-raising, and profound. I was transported momentarily back to that time and was able to see and sense what I knew then, although it was superimposed upon my memories and the wisdom of being able to judge myself as a middle-aged adult. What a strange sensation I had with all of this—almost as if it were possible to talk to a version of myself that was 17 years old, nearly thirty-seven years in the past. Then it was 1972, today it is 2009, and I remembered that I had that vision and made that drawing in probably the same month as I am doing this invocation. I felt that this was strange and weird, because the convolutions of those different times and the oddities of fate that had so impressed me back then were reflected back to the present moment.

When this peculiar phenomenon had passed, I was witnessed and experienced a new and even stranger phenomenon. I felt a great rush of power emanating from the pillar of flame, surrounding me and then entering into me. It circulated the pearl of wisdom planted in my soul and seemed to super-charge it so that it glowed brilliantly like a tiny star. I heard a voice say to me, sounding like rushing air: "So I have quickened this seed planted in you by Metatron. So it shall grow and expand until it reveals its mysteries to you soon. Take care to continue to nurture it with good deeds, compassionate intentions, and devotions of love to the Godhead. All will be revealed to you soon enough by my counterpart, the Cherub of Fire."

Then, I felt a great paroxysm of ecstasy and rising passion emanate from the seed, and the sensation grew to such a great extent that I thought it would cause me to pass out again. But it passed, leaving behind a sense of warmth, glowing love, and devotion. I felt deeply touched by this entity to the core of my being. I heard the final words said to me: "The seed now contains the poems and songs of God intoxication, and my wisdom. You will find all of this at your service once you gain access to the revealed pearl of wisdom within you."

Then the emanation of Seraphiel faded away and the vision grew dim until it was gone. But the sensations still continued for a while, and I was amazed by what I had seen and experienced.

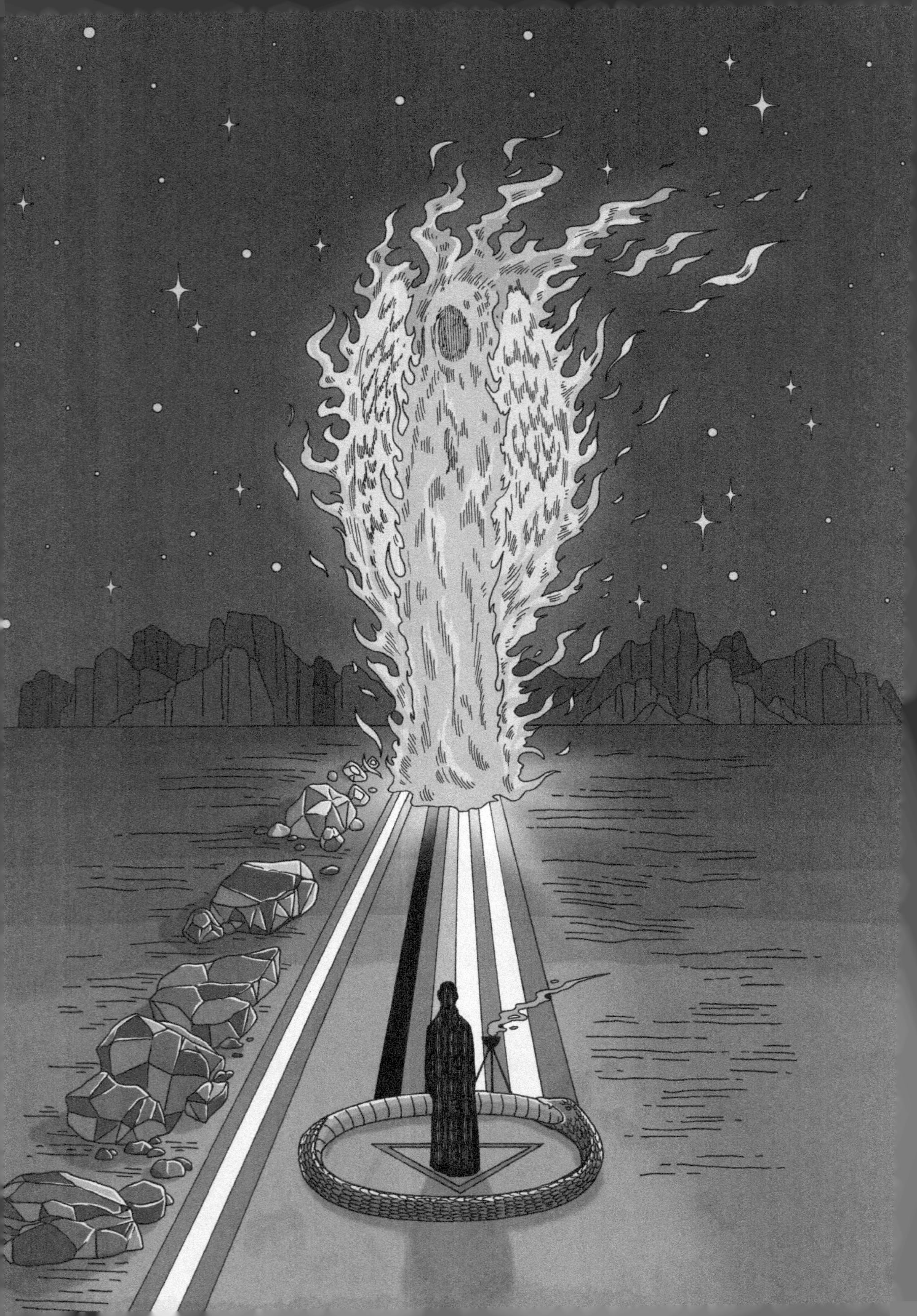

Abramelin Lunar Ordeal: Fourth Weekend, Attribute of Fire (12/14/2009)

The next day was another workday for me, even though it was Saturday. I was busy in the morning with work-related issues from morning to early afternoon, but nothing was difficult or unexpected, and all was completed without any difficulty. I seemed buoyed by the experience of the previous evening and everything felt like a blessed event, sweetened by some spiritual light that was yet unseen.

The evening meditation session was long and needful; however, I noticed that I was getting strong impressions of the future, especially the future of this very ordeal. I was listening to my journal entries and blog posts in my head as if I were writing them and had already passed through the entire ordeal. I felt elated at my apparent success, and how this was going to be perceived by other occultists and magicians. Then I came to awareness and realized that I had quite a bit of work ahead of me. No sense in celebrating something that would very likely challenge me to the core of my being. I also became aware of how harsh and difficult the final three days are going to be. I saw myself engaging in sessions of weeping alternating with sessions of ecstatic bliss—it was all very disturbing, as if the very boundaries of time had become momentary loose. It passed, and I was able to focus on doing the working, but the experience really haunted me as I attempted to shake it off.

December 12: Invocation of Rikbiel, Cherub of the Elemental tetrad of Fire. The approximate start was around 7:15 p.m., which locked in the planetary hour of Venus. I felt that the very martial spirit of Rikbiel would be moderated by that planetary influence, so that is why I chose it. I was hoping that the harshness of Rikbiel would be mitigated. As it turned out, no mitigation was necessary. Grace and I performed the Mass (but not the Benediction), and it was probably the smoothest and the most powerful iteration so far. I felt very pleased and happy with my performance, and things seemed to mesh between Grace and I quite well. Everything seemed to be going smoothly, and that mood carried me through the invocation.

The invocation was performed without any mishap, but I almost made a mistake in the execution and quickly corrected my action. I guess I was getting a little too carried away by my upbeat mood, and then strived to ensure that the rest of the rite was performed in a proper manner. The invocation came to climax, and I felt a great rush of power emanate from a presence that I could not see. That presence felt stern and very martial; there was no warmth or kindness in it at all. Then I saw orange and golden lights appear before me and take the form of a blurry outline of a human-like entity with shining golden eyes like two brilliant stars. Due to the malevolent nature of what I felt, I held up the sigil of Raziel and said that I had the authority of this angel to summon him, and then I began, unwittingly, to admit my faults, flaws, and how unworthy I was to even attempt this ritual. These admissions came unbidden from me, and I found myself almost groveling on the floor of the temple.

Then I heard Rikbiel's voice, a kind of tense whisper, say to me: "All your admissions and abasement are unnecessary, for I have already judged you as worthy of this ordeal. For the truth is that you would have been stopped by one of my seven colleagues if you had failed to prove your worth and the rightness of your intention. There are no delusions in your soul since you know your failings all too well. You are as other mortals are, and therein is nothing to be ashamed of. Rise up and face me." And so I did as I was asked. I then had vaguer and ghost-like impressions of the near future, and I felt strange, as if time had multiplied itself and everything was happening at the same time. Rikbiel said, "these are the ghosts of the future that will be happening soon. They represent the fact that I have appeared to you even before the invocation, due to the weight of having successfully invoked the previous seven of these great angelic spirits. I bless you on this chosen path of the ordeal, and I shall aid you in your quest. It will be another new path opened up for others, for that is what you must do once this ordeal is accomplished. Beware, though, for I must warn you that, having passed me, you are locked in this ordeal and cannot turn aside. It must be accomplished; there is no turning back, for madness and self-destruction shall overtake you if you would deem to quit at this time." He told me that what I must do is to intensify my devotion, increase the love and devotion that I feel for my Godhead, and seek ever more ardently spiritual union.

He also said this to me as parting words of wisdom: "If you believe that performing this ordeal is the conclusion of your work, then you are greatly mistaken. It is but a humble beginning of a lifelong aspiration that will continually test and challenge you. Most notably, you will take upon yourself a great yoke of spiritual and temporal responsibilities that will require you to teach and guide others. You must continue to give alms to the poor and support to your local spiritual institutions and volunteer yourself to your community. You may not be isolated or aloof, but fully engaged with your community. You will be shown a mission, and you must fulfill it as part of your spiritual true will. Such is way of enlightenment—there is no rest or time to accept the accolades of others, which in themselves, are meaningless. Vanity, delusion, jealousy, envy, spite, pride, and arrogance—these petty emotions will be no more since that part of you must die soon. Prepare for it. To be a servant of the people is the lot of one who is deemed a high adept by others, but you shall never know the fruits of your labors."

The emanations of Rikbiel departed. I gave it great thanks for appearing and felt a relief that the final invocation had now been completed. I was completely exhausted now, but the memory of his words was etched in my mind, and they did not cheer me up nor give me any pleasure.

CHAPTER SIX

Invocation of the Ogdoadic Elemental Godhead of Water (12/27/2009)

I have completed the next phase of the Abramelin Lunar Ordeal, which makes me ready to begin the actual Abramelin ordeal. This ordeal will consist of three days of fasting, meditating, and praying, with the final evening devoted to the revised Bornless One invocation and assumption of great power rites. I will become incommunicado during that period, so whatever happens to me will not be reported or written up until after the first of the year. Yet I am getting ahead of myself, since I have three separate workings to discuss with you and examine in detail.

Previously, I was told to perform a ritualized meditation session to reconnect and reestablish my alignment to the eight Super-Archangels before I attempted to do the rite that joined them together. I was going to do this in four separate evenings, one for each Element. However, due to the time of the season (it being just before Christmas), I decided to shorten this extra working to just two nights, focusing on the four Super-Archangels of Earth and Water one night, and Air and Fire the next night. I would also be able to test to see how these Elements behaved when I crossed from one Element to another using this revised methodology.

After the completion of the last working (weekend of December 11 and 12), I took a one-day break and then began to perform some short sessions of meditation and devotions to the Deity each evening. December 16 was the new moon, and all spiritual activity became very quiet and subdued, as if everything that had been done went into a brief hibernation. This continued all through the weekend, as I celebrated the Solstice with Pagan rituals on Saturday followed by a well-received feast. On Sunday, December 20, I performed the Bornless One Ring Consecration rite. This was done after consecrating the circle and saying the newest version of the Mass of the Goddess. The Ring Consecration rite was taken and adapted from the *Greek Magical Papyri* and was performed in two parts.

The first part was performed that evening, and the second part was performed just at the break of dawn, the sunrise of the Winter Solstice. The two rings that Grace and I are using for this working were consecrated with incense, holy water, sacramental wine and host, and holy oil. The rings seemed to glow with a strange golden and greenish light, although such a colored light wasn't anywhere in the temple. After the rings were consecrated and had the words of power said over them, I breathed the sacred breath upon them and placed them in their squares of purple velour cloth. They remained covered until the next morning, when we went out into our snow-covered grove and exposed them to the first light of dawn and said more words of power over them. Unfortunately, the day was very overcast and there were no rays of the sun observable, but I imagined them in my mind's eye and completed the consecration rite. I have left the rings incubating in their purple square cloths until they are needed, then the final ritual actions will be performed to fully activate them. I expect to do this the day before the Bornless One invocation is performed.

On the next day (Monday), I took a break from the activities to spend time with my wife, Grace, since she was leaving to spend Christmas with her parents. I was supposed to perform a kind of ritualized meditation session for each of the four Elements, re-establishing and re-aligning myself in preparation for erecting the Ogdoadic Tabernacle, consisting of the activation of all eight of the Super-Archangels. Since there was a lot of preparation that I had to do with the house and threats of a massive snowstorm, I decided to consolidate the working on two nights (instead of four) and join the Elements of Earth and Water, and Air and Fire. This consolidation worked out really well. So, instead of starting on Monday, I was able to defer the two workings to Wednesday (December 23) and Thursday (December 24). I performed a meditation session instead on the evening of December 22 after a day of many tasks, including some work-related ones.

December 23: I started the evening with a circle consecration and the newest version of the Mass of the Goddess. I would focus on the Seraph and Cherub of Earth and Water. I started the working around 9 p.m. but didn't need to use specific planetary hours. The energy of the temple after the Mass was intense, as if in anticipation of what I was about to do. I unsealed the vortex using unsealing spirals, established the eastern gateway set with invoking pentagrams of Earth and Water, then passed through a double gateway. I used the staff to re-establish the vortex energy field and then erected it as a pylon to re-establish the invocation of all four spirits. I had already set up the four consecrated and empowered sigils that were used to invoke the Seraphim and Cherubim; these were arranged on the four corners of the invoking trigon, with the sigil of Raziel in the center. I then intoned the Enochian invocation for all four spirits, and then re-read their visualized imago descriptions as I reconnected with each, touching the wand to the sigil, and then creating a line of force from it to my forehead. I contacted each one and then felt their combined power.

The first thing that was communicated to me was the name of the Godhead that I was to work with in the next major working—that name was Aset-Sophia (Isis-Sophia, or "Throne of Wisdom"). That combined Goddess aspect was to be superimposed on the Godhead of Water, Shadai El Chai (Almighty God of Life).

Invocation of the Ogdoadic Elemental Godhead of Water (12/27/2009)

This is what was communicated to me from the combined spirits of Earth and Water:

"Do not indulge in the sadness and death of the ego. Understand what this actually represents to one on your path. (Here, I got a sense to examine the writings of Ken Wilber on the Death of the Centauric level of development.) If you are bereft and overly mourn its passing, then you are greatly in error. Use your alignment to the Godhead to bring joy and bliss to your heart. The only necessary tears are those that are shed for joy, and not misery or unhappiness. Don't be dramatic or make this transition more difficult than it should be."

I was thinking about the implied reference to Ken Wilber—the Death of the Centauric level is actually the death or end of personal autonomy and the beginning of true spiritual service, which is the mark of the high adept. I felt compelled to know what this means in greater detail and focus on it as I undergo the ordeal of the vow of sequestering to be started next Monday. I also need to think more deeply about maybe changing the order of the Elements that I am using in the ordeal in the Bornless One invocation rite, since the combination of Earth and Water is very harmonious.[81]

December 24: I performed the ritualized meditation session of the invocations of the Seraph and Cherub of Air and Fire. As in the previous evening, I consecrated the circle, performed a Mass, and went through the same ritual steps to re-establish and re-align myself to the four Super-Archangels of Air and Fire. This is what they communicated to me:

"You have been thinking about what was missing in your thoughts about the article 'Magic and the Science of the Impossible,'[82] and it has escaped you. We shall reveal it to you, as a sign of our bond with you in this ordeal. The missing consideration is the mind model which you call the assumption of 'As If.' Occultism and magic are based on the mental game of imaginative creation—the 'As If' preposition. It can be projected out into the material world, held in the mind, or used as a probe to penetrate deeply within the unconscious mind. It is the real tool whereby a magician harnesses what is in the realm of the impossible, making their dreams become part of what is considered possible. The ordeal must remain structured as you have already determined it, for this ordeal is meant to be harsh and difficult, not harmonious and easy to accomplish. This is true for the transition of the Elements and in the Bornless One invocation rite. Change the

---

[81] After some years of deliberation, I have decided that the ordeal shouldn't be made easier or accommodating. Also, I doubt that changing the order would make the ordeal less challenging. So, I chose to keep it as it is.

[82] The referenced article does not appear to be found during a search. I believe that is based on the later works of Gustav Kuhn (whose book was published in 2019), who discusses the appeal of illusion and magical tricks as explanations for the malleability of the human brain. He dismisses the idea of magic as being real, however, staying close to the tenets of objective science.

transition only when working with consecutive Element invocations, not ordeals. The Elemental Godhead within the Angelic Ogdoad represents the full realization of the active Godhead, in which to create and destroy a universe—to destroy and recreate the self in the three days of the Abramelin Ordeal."

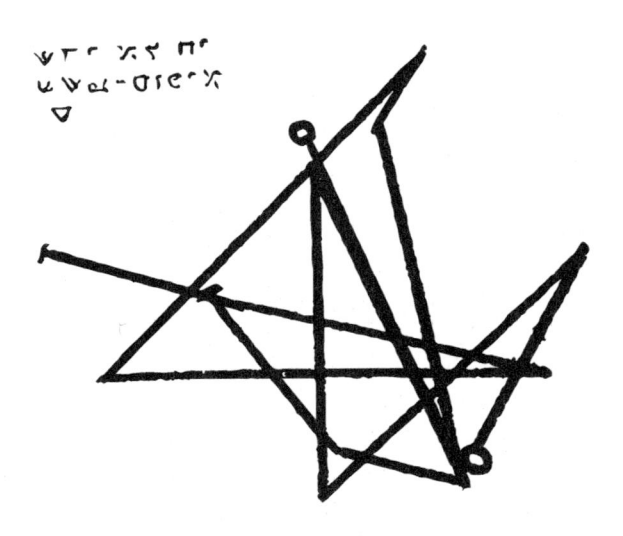

Sigil for Elemental Godhead of Water and Isis-Sophia.

I was also told to make a combined sigil of Aset-Isis with Shadai El Chai. Aset-Sophia is the mistress of Briah, the divine throne, or Khursia of Creation. I also looked up Ken Wilber's statements about extending human development beyond the Centauric level of conscious development, and this is what he wrote in the book *The Atman Project*.

> *If one can stand to differentiate from all that—if one can stand this new and demanding separation anxiety, ...stand to go beyond "self-actualization" and "autonomy"—stand, in fact, to let go personal life on the whole—then one is open to the transpersonal realms of the subtle and causal planes.*[83]

December 25: Christmas, reunited with Grace—no activity planned.

December 26: Invocation of the Godhead Element of Water and generation of the Ogdoadic Tabernacle.

I performed all three rituals: Invocation of the Godhead Element of Water, Ogdoadic Godhead Vortex, and the Triple Tetrahedral Gate rites. I decided to consolidate these rites that would have been performed on two consecutive nights into a single evening's working. The secondary rites are short enough, and so is the Godhead invocation. I felt that it could easily be accomplished in a single evening, thus freeing up Sunday, the

---

83   Wilber, Ken, *The Atman Project: Collected Works, Volume II* (Shambhala Press, 1999) p. 237.

Invocation of the Ogdoadic Elemental Godhead of Water (12/27/2009)

only day that I would have to finish up business before the ordeal begins. All in all, this was a fortuitous decision, and everything worked out quite well. I also had to spend an hour on the Pyradym instrument (a powerful sound-based therapy system) to alleviate feelings of extreme fatigue, which it did in an amazingly thorough manner. I was focused, alert, and ready for the working.

I set the magic circle at a little after 7:45 p.m., so the planetary hour of Venus was locked into the working. The Mass of the Goddess was performed with assistance from Grace. I decided to forgo the Benediction rite, since the Mass would create a sufficient foundation for the invocation of the Godhead Element of Water, and because I was already empowering the circle with the eight sigils of the Super-Archangels. I will relate what occurred at each ritual level after the Mass, starting with the invocation of the Element Godhead.

I performed the invocation of the Element Godhead of Water ritual, combining the summoning of the Godhead Shadai El Chai and the combined Goddess Aset-Sophia. The resultant energies and effects were gentle, warm, glowing, loving, and compassionate—I felt quite inspired. I sensed a kind of ocean or sea goddess aspect, and I even heard sea gulls in the distance and briefly smelled the salt breeze. It was quite real and profound, but quickly passed. The Godhead invocation seemed to blend with the invocations in the Mass of the Goddess, and I sensed that the combination was summoning something that was a lot like Aphrodite merged with Persephone—underworld and oceanic.

After a brief break, I went on to perform the Ogdoadic Godhead Vortex, which was the next ritual in the series. I set up the eight sigils of the Seraphim and Cherubim to the four watchtowers, mindful of the corresponding Element, and the Seraph sigil set above the Cherub. The Element Godhead of Water was still active and resident, with the erect staff still set next to and towering over the charged sigil of the Godhead of Water hybrid. I then proceeded to set empowered pylons at each of the four watchtowers, activating the Seraph and Cherub associated with the base Element. The first one (Fire to the East) actually caused a powerful nervous "thrill" to run down my entire body, centered in the heart chakra and the third eye chakra. This sensation was intensified at each subsequent watchtower until all eight of the Super-Archangels were fully activated and joined into four pylons of magical energy.

At this point, I felt as if a spike of empowered light was pushed through my skull, starting in the third eye and terminating somewhere in the core of my brain. I could use this "spike" to focus and look deep into things, promoting a kind of overpowering envisioning that threatened to keep me completely occupied, perhaps for far longer than I wanted, so I had to tightly control this new ability.

I then performed the Tetra-sacramentary Crossroads ritual structure, and this seemed to expand the power of the vortex energy field. I saw four distinctly powerful and seemingly autonomous spiritual pathways merge into a single meta-spiritual pathway, representing perhaps that all paths lead to one unified path that encapsulated them all. I continued on with the ritual and performed the central Pylon of Summoning, where I established the Element Godhead, which was already resident in the center of the circle (this part of the rite was probably quite redundant and had no additional effect).

It was at this point of the ritual that I performed the Summoning of the Holy Ogdoad of the Emissaries, where all eight points of the octagon ritual structure are joined together with the central Godhead Element. The result of this ritual action was truly incredible! At first, I saw the four outer pylons as pillars of golden fire, with a larger pillar of blue fire in the center of the circle and scarlet lines of force marking the crossroads. The four outer pillars of fire began to bow toward the center pillar of fire until they merged with it to become one massive pillar of fire, only its color had changed to green with a golden core and the crossroads became a deep violet color. This image faded away completely, replaced by a vision into which I was completely immersed. There was a diffused white light but no details, and in the midst of it all, I sensed the super-empowered presence of the Godhead manifest with accompanied sensations of complete awe and astonishment from me. I bowed low before this invisible presence and adored it; so much love, devotion, and compassion welled up from the core of my soul. I felt all of this passion and love reflected back to me and magnified a thousand times. I lay there in state of rapture and bliss, with all of these feelings rocking the very foundation of my being. Then it subsided to a gentle and loving beingness in me, and the vision went from misty and cloudy to one that was clearer.

I found myself standing on a beach just before the water, gently rolling in placid waves. The water was warm and inviting, and the sand was the purest white, while the waters of the ocean were greenish-blue and grey slate colored. There were no shells or debris on the beach, and the sky and surrounding area was completely obscured by a warm misty fog, which seemed to envelope everything. Then, a woman came walking forth from the ocean waves. She was obviously thoroughly wet and glistening with salty water. She was neither tall nor short but seemed around the same height as me. She wasn't naked either, instead wearing some kind embroidered white shift that was wet and clung to her body, leaving her legs and arms bare. She was pale but not exceptionally so; her face was incredibly beautiful. She had long hair that was braided into numerous strands, probably of a light brown but fitted with golden beads that made it look blonde. There were traces of seaweed in her hair, upon her shift, and on her legs. She looked natural and normal, except for her eyes, which were the most incredible shade of greenish-blue with very large and dark pupils, which made them look other-worldly. She smiled at me, and it seemed that the sun may have grown brighter in the misty sky. I walked into the water and approached her; she took my hands in hers and they were warm instead of cold. And then everything became silent, even the sound of waves and distant gulls. I heard her whisper the following words to me:

"I am here and have come, as you desired me so. I have been waiting for you to come for untold aeons. This place, where the water meets the earth, is the sacred meeting ground of mortal life and eternal spirit. In this guise that you see me now, I shall aid and help you to complete your quest. That quest is to awaken the God within you into full awareness, so that you and he, and me, might join in eternal embrace. I am your godly muse! Seek me in the days of your ordeal. Sing songs to me and recite mystical poetry. So shall the love of God arise and assume material form before you. Embrace it and love it fully.

Invocation of the Ogdoadic Elemental Godhead of Water (12/27/2009)

In this way, you shall begin the path of your total transformation. Know this, that you have known me before, many times, even in the dreams of your youth. I am the one who shall complete you. Never despair, for I am with you forever."

Then the vision receded, slipping away, and leaving me kneeling before the center of the circle, which was dark and cold. The memory of this moment was etched into my mind, and even now I can recall it with frightening clarity.

I then performed the last working, the Triple Tetrahedral Gate. This final rite did not cause any further visions, but it only intensified what had already been a fairly mind-blowing experience for me. I felt quite stunned at first when all of the rituals were complete, as though I were drunk or stoned, but a surreal inner clarity remained within me, which was profound and deeply moving. I could function, but just barely. I was haunted by sounds and sensations of the misty sandy beach that seemed so near, yet so far away. The ritual working was finally ended, and I felt beyond tired and exhausted. After properly grounding with a bit of food and drink and mindlessly finishing a few tasks, I went to bed, into an intermittent and dreamless sleep. I awoke still tired and affected by the rite.

Now that this final working is completed, all that remains is the ordeal itself, which begins tomorrow. During that time I will be completely sequestered, abstaining from all mundane cares as much as possible. I won't be answering the phone or replying to email, and I will avoid all forms of current events and the news. I will also be completely detached from all work-related tasks, having arranged this previously. It will be as if I were dead to the world, at least for the next three days. On Thursday morning, I will arise and experience the changing of the year as one who is beginning a new life—that is, if everything goes as I assume it will. For the completion of this working and the report of its results, you will have to wait until this coming weekend. I hope to be able to report some remarkable experiences at that time, so stay tuned until then.

CHAPTER SEVEN

ABRAMELIN ORDEAL AND BORNLESS ONE INVOCATION: FINAL ACTIONS (01/01/2010)

I HAVE COMPLETED THE ABRAMELIN LUNAR ORDEAL, and I must proclaim that it was not only a success, but also the three most difficult days of the entire seven-week process. Never have I been so thoroughly tested by an ordeal. After successfully concluding it, I was completely relieved and full of joy. I have performed the Bornless One invocation before, but I have not experienced the results so clearly and powerfully as I did this time. What I can say is that I have achieved the knowledge and conversation with my Holy Guardian Angel, whom I have perceived as my higher self or Augoeides. I have the magical name of this entity, which I can use to call and summon it to me whenever needed; the magical ring, which acts as a constant link to this being; and it also revealed to me its image and essence, all of which has never happened before. So, I would grade the newly developed ordeal as highly successful and much more accessible to individuals who don't have a large amount of time on their hands to perform the original ordeal as found in either the French or German versions of the Book of Abramelin. I believe that I have personally proven that this new ordeal not only works but could also represent a new and exciting path for ritual magicians to follow. It also brings to mind the issue of whether one must, as a rule, follow the dictates of the old grimoires in performing these workings, or whether a new and more accessible methodology can be developed to replace the older traditional ways. I will take up this issue in a future article, since I certainly have an opinion on the matter and experience to back it up. For now, we will focus on what I can tell you of the last three days of my ordeal.

December 28 through December 29: I began the Abramelin ordeal—the three days of atonement, purification, and spiritual surrender—at dawn on Monday. I anointed my forehead with scented oil and placed upon it a sprinkling of ash from my thurible. I spent probably a good forty minutes of prayer before my shrine, reciting over and over the mantra "I am unworthy to come nigh unto you, Oh my God!" I abased myself completely and felt loathsome and miserable, as I believed I should feel to accomplish the task of full and complete atonement. I was fully expecting to continue this process for some time when I felt a powerful presence come before me and a voice commanded me to cease this activity at once. Of course this interrupted what I was doing, and the voice continued to instruct me in a milder tone. It told me that when the *Book of Abramelin* was written centuries ago, the Jewish tradition of allocating "holy guardian angels" did not exist (it was developed as part of the unofficial doctrine of Christianity). God would set a guardian angel upon a prophet or a holy man, but not an ordinary person. Thus, one would be required to perform exceptional acts of piety and atonement in order to achieve this great boon from God. However, Christian doctrine had, in the fifth century, adopted the belief that everyone had a guardian angel who acted as an intermediary, so anyone could access their holy guardian angel as a matter of their birth right. The voice said: "You are only presuming to seek union with your higher self, which is your right, not attempting to assume and pretend to be God."

So, atonement in this ordeal does not have to be excessive, only to the degree to purify oneself and to prepare to surrender to the greater power of one's higher self. I can pray, meditate, make heartfelt and soulful devotions to the Godhead (which I have already invoked), enact fasting and purification, and seek to open myself completely to what will follow on the third day, but only to a degree that is sensible. The six previous weekends have already taken my measure, as it were, so there is little reason to abase myself at this juncture.

I acknowledged this wisdom, bowing my head, and proceeded to the next task, purification and devotion. I read the various poems of Rumi, Hafiz, Kabir, and others (such as the Song of Songs) to prepare my mind for the working. Other than some very mundane tasks (such as shoveling snow), I did nothing else for the duration of this time. I fasted the whole first day and ate only bread and drank water to break my fast after the sun had gone down. I also noticed that the ash had quickly disappeared from my head, so later that evening I performed a thorough ablution as part of the purification process.

I slept in the library annex of the temple all three nights to ensure that I would be close and resident to whatever transpired in the temple during the night. This meant that I had many really strange dreams and visions that haunted my sleep. I particularly remember meeting the young woman with the braided hair and strange eyes, who also seemed to be far older than she appeared. She took me to a pavilion up on the sands of the beach, which was open to the air but filtered the rays of the sun (which by now had become brilliant, driving away the mists and the fog). In the pavilion were many oriental carpets, pillows, plates of Middle Eastern delicacies, an oriental tea set, and a large hookah placed in the center. The hookah was quite ornate but was not burning, so it was hard to determine what it would be used for (tobacco or hashish). We sat down together, leaned onto the pillows, and proceeded to have an animated and pleasant discussion about philosophy, ancient history, and spiritual love. I noticed that she was wearing a beautiful pink coral necklace. A cool breeze blew through the pavilion, spiced with brine and exotic incense smoke. Perhaps we even made love, but I don't remember that part, if it even happened.

Day two began with body aches and a migraine headache, which abated somewhat during the morning's devotions. But the body aches continued and centered into my lower back (which I had previously injured), getting more severe as the day wore on. I continued to perform my purification exercises, including a deep cleansing bath and laxatives, which seemed to work somewhat, although not as well as I would have liked. I was also haunted by occasional visions of forbidden food (meat) since I was continuing my fast again until sunset. My wife Grace told me that I still seemed to be in my mind and not my body, and perhaps that was because I was becoming aware of a truly unfortunate pain and stiffness in my lower back. I was supposed to perform some rituals in the evening, but by that time, I was starting to be distracted by the pain and the stiffness. I medicated myself adequately, and then sought to perform that evening's working.

I performed the circle consecration, the Mass of the Goddess, and then performed again the Triple Tetrahedral Gate Ritual from the previous Saturday night. I discovered that the powerful Godhead aspect that I had invoked was still very much active and in force, and I communed with it for a time. I also completed the rite to consecrate the magic ring and proceeded to put it on my finger. I felt a powerful intense tingling from it, up my finger to my hand and into my body, making my head feel light and my mind giddy. I asked the Godhead of the ring to help me energize my body and temporarily heal it, although whatever I had done to my body was already powerfully affecting me. Perhaps all of the time I spent on the floor meditating and praying, reciting mystical poetry, and the moderately uncomfortable futon bed was taking its toll on my body—not to mention the fasting.

Day 3, December 30: This day began with the pain and stiffness in my back having reached a climax. It was difficult to stand erect for any length of time (or to sit for too long either), or else it affected my sense of balance. I felt like I had two left feet and had to stand in a kind of bull legged manner to remain upright for any length of time. This situation was not at all expected, nor did it bode well for the evening's climactic working—the Bornless One invocation—since that rite is very physically demanding, taking as much as three hours to complete. I began to wonder if I might have to postpone the working and I was quite dejected by having to consider this option. I wanted desperately to complete the ordeal, since the next day would be the full moon and the end of the period for the Lunar Ordeal. I was very troubled by all of these considerations and had to medicate myself as much as I could just to get through all of the preparations. The thought of attempting to complete the ordeal under such conditions seemed extremely daunting. Yet I knew that I had to at least attempt the ritual working, so I continued the preparations as best as I could.

Grace decided that she should attend that evening's working. She had previously decided not to attend, initially because she felt it was private and personal and wanted to give me as much privacy in these final operations as possible. Now, she felt instructed and compelled to help me complete the working that evening, offering whatever assistance was needed, and perhaps even helping me to do the ritual actions. I was profoundly grateful for Grace's help and support, and it made me a bit more confident that I would be able to complete the ordeal. The pain and stiffness of my back made it quite difficult to focus my mind on the objective of the rite. I attempted some further meditations and devotions, but these were not very successful because I was constantly being distracted and unable to find an asana that was comfortable enough to be endured for very long. That evening, I medicated myself as much as I dared and then sat down to meditate. I was wearing my magic ring, and I sought whatever healing power I was able to command from it to help me get through this evening and complete the working. I completely surrendered myself to the process, opening myself to whatever occurred that evening, but I would endeavor to work the ritual from beginning to end and not let my physical condition get in the way of my ritual performance and the reception of the HGA.

I began the rite of the Bornless One invocation, and at first, I felt a little bit shaky and not clearly focused, but that quickly changed as I got into the ritual. Despite the medication that I had taken, my mind became completely clear and all of the stiffness and pain in my back completely disappeared. I functioned as if nothing was wrong with me and proceeded to perform the ritual at the very best level of my abilities, which was quite a marvelous occurrence. I managed to effortlessly perform the first two stages of the rite without a break, proceeding up the steps of the concentric pylon pyramid, then went on with the next two stages after a short break of around fifteen minutes. The healing power that I had invoked from the ring had not only sustained me, but also allowed me to become loose in my body. I was riding a wave of ascending power that increased in intensity and was building up to a euphoric feeling of ecstasy. It literally pushed me through the final steps, so I went from Assiah to Yetzirah, Briah, and up to Atziluth, into the Eye of the Holy Dragon and beyond. Grace informed me that I was glowing, and that a tangible power was emanating from my body. I felt so exhilarated and greatly empowered, I could have danced a Scottish reel or even stood on my head—but I focused resolutely on performing the ritual, making hardly any errors, and enunciating all of the words of power and the descriptive text. Thus, I succeeded in building the four levels of the step-pyramid ritual structure and achieved the glorious apex at the Qabalistic world of Atziluth.

The final stage of the actual Bornless One invocation was performed as if I were on fire and fully empowered. I have never said this rite as well or in such a focused manner. I felt the closeness and intimacy of the Holy Guardian Angel, which I had never felt before, even before the invocation was completed. Once it was done, there were waves and reverberations of power as I felt and began to see the materialization of my higher self, the Augoeides, the one that is self-begotten (Autogenes) and eternal.

I have performed this rite many times (although not in its current revised form), but never have I experienced a manifestation of this magnitude or awesomeness. This was now the climax of six weekends of workings, resting as if it were on a foundation of eight Super-Archangels (Seraphim and Cherubim) who had become the emissaries of the manifested godhead of Shadia El Chai as the Goddess Isis-Sophia. At the apex of these six weeks of arduous workings, I erected the step pyramid-pylons of the four Qabalistic worlds, and upon its summit I generated the inner sanctum or etheric temple of my highest self, a veritable "vault of the adepti." Within that sacred vault, I intoned the powerful invocation of the Bornless or Headless One. Needless to say, it appeared to me as a pillar of rich azure light and gave me its name so I could summon it whenever I needed it. Within that blue pillar of light, I saw an idealized image of myself as a flawless and perfect youth, full of vigor, sweet happiness, optimism, love, and joy. It was a breath-taking experience to see myself in that guise, one that I had never assumed in life. I also felt the magic ring pulsing with power and the essence of the HGA flowing from it into me. I felt so very high and full of joy, having left my body of pain and imperfection far behind—at least for the moment. Then, I sensed and heard it speak of many things to me, and some of what it said I may impart to all of my readers.

The HGA, Augoeides, or Higher Self is an intimate spirit that is directly connected to a person. It is such for all human beings. The HGA is the sum of everything good that I have realized and accomplished in my entire life, from infancy to the last breath that I will draw—all that and much more. It is also connected to the Godhead and transmits all spiritual realization directly to me, whether I ask for it or not. It is like my future self that is wholly spiritual and beyond the moment of my death. All things of the flesh, emotions (except love), mind, and soul are part of the corporeal self and shall perish at the end of this lifetime, never to be seen or known in this world forever more. Through the HGA, I may sense and "see" all aspects of Spirit and the Godhead; without it I would be spiritually dead, a malady that is ironically called a "loss of soul." I may worship the Gods and Goddesses, feel them, and hear their words and blessings; venerate my spiritual ancestors; and summon angels, demons, spirits of the dead, and earth spirits, but always and only through the mediation of the HGA, whether I am aware of it or not.

Most religions, except those that are wholly occult- or mystically based, actually worship this personal Atman or Higher Self and never really engage directly with the Godhead, so there is a superficial and even delusional quality to exoteric religion, affecting its doctrines, dogma, and fixed practices. One can find many references to this idea, especially in the mystical poetry of Rumi, Hafiz, and Kabir, which I recited and read for hours before this final working. Only through occult practices and profound mystical experiences is this hidden nature of the Higher Self revealed. All outward practices, however engaging, are nought when compared to the revelations of the higher self, our personal intermediary of the Godhead.

So, what has been revealed to me is that the HGA is integral to one's being and functions as one's spiritual dimension. What I was seeking and attempting to connect with was always there. When I apprehended this truth, it was so simple and so familiar to me. It was all of the "good" that I have ever felt or shown to others, the love and devotion that I have shown the Godhead, my true spiritual self from infancy to death and beyond. It was such a miraculous and minor thing, always attached to me and a part of me, even though I was unaware of it most of the time. However, I needed to perform this massive and difficult ordeal to get me to detach enough from my mundane preoccupations and my ego to become truly aware of it, probably for the first time in my life—although I realized that it had been always there at the very pinnacle and edge of my being. As time goes forward from this point of realization, a greater awareness will unfold, teaching and guiding me, helping me to elevate my consciousness in an incomparable manner. The world has become my teacher, and my HGA is the master guide who will aid me in my lessons of life, death, and the Greater Spirit.

Through this divine union and awareness, I may experience a kind of immortality, though I shall be totally subsumed into the body of my HGA and nothing of the physical or mental Self will be left once I have died. This was quite a revelation to me, and I am still attempting to process it. It is not a death wish nor a desire to seek death, as much as it is a desire to live a long and productive life, however many years are left to me. I feel that, although I have already lived more than half of my allotted life span (or perhaps even more), the best and most productive years lie ahead of me, where the greatest challenges and accomplishments await. This pathway of the higher adept has not ended now or anytime in the future—it has only humbly begun, with the initial smallest steps: this simple realization. It's now up to me to make it grow into maturation so that I may know my full potential self.

I was also told that the rite of assumption does not have to be performed by me, since I have already completely achieved the assumption of my higher self. It is a ritual where the helpers or attendants of the rite may be empowered and blessed by its performance, sharing in a full measure of what the main Celebrant has been able to achieve. I will have to note this in the ritual and work it out accordingly.[84]

So, I have completed the ordeal, and it seems like I have achieved what was simply right in front of me all along, though I was unaware. Perhaps that is my folly, but I suspect that we are all so afflicted. I am now tied to spiritual service, but how that is defined and is worked out remains to be seen. There was much more communicated to me, some of it I have revealed, other secrets I have kept to myself because of their personal nature, and much that will be revealed as time goes on. I now feel very "other-worldly," and I need to reconnect with my body to be able to function. Grace has noticed this about me—I seem so much happier, joyful; there is a light in my person, perhaps a kind of illumination. But I am also distant and deep within my own spiritual process. I need to surface and re-examine my life, ironically, just as the New Year begins.

I have forged a new path and hopefully others will seek it, take it upon themselves and attempt to complete it. I have found it a daunting ordeal despite its brevity. For now, there is yet another method to invoking and manifesting the Holy Guardian Angel.

---

[84] Today, I believe that this rite, the Assumption of Great Powers, is relevant, but it should not be performed immediately following the Bornless One invocation rite. In fact, the apex of this working, the Bornless One invocation itself, will likely consume a person's attentions and focus, and attempting any other working immediately following might be difficult. Other appended rituals can be performed the next day, since the objective of the working is completed with the manifestation of the Bornless One.

CHAPTER EIGHT

SUMMARY AND CONCLUSION OF THE ABRAMELIN LUNAR ORDEAL WORKING (01/11/2010)

ENOUGH TIME HAS PASSED THAT I NEED TO EXAMINE all that happened during my seven-week ordeal and analyze and examine it from a higher-level perspective than I was able to determine after completing each individual working. I need to put the whole process together and study it using what I know about occult symbolism and spiritual phenomena to classify what I experienced during that entire period. I am certain that as more time passes, I may have additional thoughts and insights to report, but for now, it's important that I attempt to summarize what occurred and explain this process from a more abstract and theoretical perspective.

What I can deduce almost immediately is that this newly devised ordeal does indeed successfully achieve the same results that the traditional ordeal achieved, which is the Knowledge and Conversation with the Holy Guardian Angel. So, I can say that the new ordeal is efficient, succinct, and works quite well. That much I can say without any doubts or confusion—there is now a new way of undergoing this classic ordeal. What can't be said is that it produces *exactly* the same results or that it is in some way an analogous working. The Abramelin Lunar Ordeal working is quite different than the traditional Abramelin ordeal working, although I believe that they produce a similar kind of effect on the operator.

Since I have not worked the traditional ordeal (nor could I, even if I wanted to), then I really have little to compare between the two processes other than what I know about mystical and magical practices, since the Abramelin ordeal is entirely mystical and devotional. My version of this ordeal is almost entirely magical, with some elements of the devotional and mystical processes included in its formulation and deployment. These were added while undergoing the overall ordeal and were not really part of the original plan. The final mix of magical workings and mystical devotion produces the correct combination of actions within sacred space that produces the same result as the traditional ordeal. So, I can say with some degree of confidence that the Lunar Ordeal is in its final form. I will certainly rewrite and refine the specific rituals themselves, but the pattern of the ordeal is, I believe, complete.

I also believe that the invocation of the Archangel Raziel was crucial to the ordeal, even though that particular magical working wasn't part of the ordeal proper. For those who would want to duplicate this ordeal, it would be a requirement to perform this working as well as the rest in sequence. If we consider that the lunar ordeal covers the progression of Earth, Air, Water, Fire, and Spirit, then the pre-ordeal working would cover the "Self" and be part of the process that prepared one for the beginning of the ordeal. I will include this working in the structure of the ordeal, even though I consider it to be optional. Any magician who elects to undergo this ordeal may perform this working, an alternative working, or none.

The ordeal should be broken up into seven sections, starting with the pre-ordeal working, then proceeding through the four Elements, Spirit, and concluding with the Abramelin ordeal and the Bornless One invocation rite.

Ultimately, the intention nearly always outweighs the mechanism used in a magical working. If the intention is solid, then the working will be successful. This is true even if the ritual working or ordeal is imperfect or highly flawed. All of the required elements must be expressed in the working, yet the sequence of their expression is not that important. This means that a ritual working can be done in the wrong sequence and the end results will still be potent and valid. Of course, this is not an excuse for shoddy ritual design and poor execution. The better the design and the more esthetic the execution, the more profound and personally empowering the results.

This seems to be an important rule in the practice of magic, and it has some amazing consequences. Whether we use the traditional grimoires and lore to perform our magic or wholly and completely invent it anew, either approach will work if the intent is solid. If the magician understands what they are trying to do and realizes the mechanisms that are needed to trigger deep psychological states of consciousness and so cause a complete transcendental transformation of the personality. I believe that what I have fashioned in this new version of the Abramelin Ordeal is valid and works as advertised. Some of the things that occurred during this working were quite indicative that it was a true magical ordeal. These can be listed by the following points:

1. Structure of ordeal evolved while it was performed
2. Ordeal was dynamic and had a high degree of spontaneity
3. Spirits produced unexpected or unanticipated results
4. Ordeal had corroboration from objective observer
5. Ordeal candidate was challenged, almost to the point of failure
6. Ordeal followed expected patterns for spiritual enlightenment, even though many of those patterns were previously unknown

To complete the analysis, someone else needs to undertake the rituals of this ordeal and perform them, then compare their results with mine. When several individuals have completed this process, then and only then will I be able to say definitively that a new system of magic has been developed and proven to work in most cases. I look forward to that day.

CHAPTER NINE

Some Thoughts About the Abramelin Lunar Ordeal (03/01/2010)

It has now been sixty days since I completed the Abramelin Lunar Ordeal, and I am still waiting to perform the last piece, which is the Bornless One Envisioning rite. I celebrated a very powerful full moon rite the previous evening and not only received further insights into this working but was also able to reconnect to the previous ritual structures and their impressions. The temple still powerfully resonates with the achievement of that amazing ordeal since the base ritual structures consisted of vortices, which, in their sealed state, retain all of the energies and intelligences that were raised during the seven-week working. I only have to consecrate the space and say a Mass of the Goddess in order to experience harmonic resonances emanating from the sealed ritual structures. I am not yet ready to unseal these structures and continue with this ordeal, yet the information that I received last night would seem to substantiate that pause.

I also wanted to tie some loose ends up and share with you a new rendering of the picture of Seraphiel that I drew probably sometime in December 1972. My friend and associate, Rekhetra, produced this artwork based on the original-colored drawing that I did so long ago. It looks much more vibrant and interesting, having been redone by an accomplished artist. I have included this version in place of the crude drawing that I did so many years ago.[85]

Since I completed the primary ordeal in December, there has been a lot of internal processing, but only some outward indications that I am making some definitive progress towards my ultimate goal of union with the Godhead as the Unity of All Being. I believe that this process will be slow and evolving, with some intermittent but astonishing breakthroughs occurring over time. As all of the Super-Archangels seem to have said

---

85 The renewed color version of it can be found in the diary entry in this book for that particular working (see page 190).

to me, this is not the end of my spiritual path nor even the ultimate goal—it is merely the beginning of a more advanced and empowered stage.

One thing that is occurring with me that seems very clear is that I am pulling all of the powerful and strategic threads of my past together into a mosaic of the present. In order for me to determine the nature of my destiny, I must know where I have been and why. I must understand my own story in an intimate and magical manner so that I may realize the hidden forces that compelled me through my life's spiritual process. So far, the most compelling parts of my life happened in 1972 and 1973, when I established the foundation for the magic that I work on today.

While the techniques that I use to assemble my ritual lore were developed during the 1980s and 1990s, my actual beginnings occurred in the previous decade. Parts of my life's story have resurfaced after many years of neglect and forgetfulness, undoubtably due to the impact of the Abramelin Lunar Ordeal. A friend of mine confided to me that the Abramelin ordeal is not a working that can be resolved just by performing the required actions and observances for the required period. Often, the completed ordeal does nothing more than powerfully facilitate and impact the internal spirit of the magician, while the other facets of the process may take months or years to finally achieve full realization and mastery. He also told me that, in order to know one's ultimate destiny, one must first have complete recourse and understanding of the past. The past is the key to the future, so this is why I have become so haunted by occurrences that happened over thirty years ago.

Last night (February 28) was a strikingly beautiful full moon that mystically reflected on the ice and snow with a soft brilliant light, since it was a cloudless night. The moon turned the evening's darkness into a spectral landscape that seemed almost a dim reflection of a brilliant day. One could have easily navigated without any illumination whatsoever. In this mysterious and wondrous night, I performed the Mass of the Goddess and sought to reconnect to that magical ordeal completed two lunar cycles previously. I not only succeeded in reconnecting but was also amazed at how potent the atmosphere of the temple was after all that time. I was able to sense a connection with all four of the Seraphim, Cherubim, the Element Godhead of Water, and my HGA/Higher Self. All of these spiritual entities are very much alive and fully active in the temple, waiting for me to engage in further action.

What I received from this mélange of spirits was that I will need to perform two more iterations of the Bornless One invocation rite, but not until my greater wheel of fortune moves from being retrograde to going direct. This won't happen until July, so any future workings will have to wait at least until then, and more likely until the following autumn. I must also continue to work on pulling the most important parts of my past out of my living memories and weaving them into a unified expression of who I am and where I have been. This is the required foundation for determining the nature of my personal spiritual destiny. I believe that I will have to perform the Bornless One invocation rite once to establish this baseline of my present lifeline, and then work on projecting it forward, into the future. This action will produce many visions and begin to break up my present timeline, allowing me to perceive and project a future destiny that

I will be able to unerringly follow. Once that future is fully visualized, I will perform the Bornless One invocation rite for the final time.

That is what was communicated to me last night, and I believe there is much to ponder. I have never been much for believing in any kind of predestination or being tied down to a fixed future, so I will also have to think rather deeply about how one can project a future destiny and still retain a high degree of flexibility. Since it is probably impossible to collapse causality, I still may be able to build the rest of my life into an ideal by consistently following an empowered spiritual plan, sort of like living a self-fulfilled prophecy. That doesn't mean that I will be immune from accidents or any other kind of unexpected occurrences, but that such occurrences will neither deter me from my ultimate goal nor obstruct my path in any manner. Even death will not deter me since it will only hasten and complete the overall process of my life. Thus, I will achieve my goal of obtaining union with my Godhead no matter what happens in the future. If I leave behind a legacy of enough teachings, rituals, and lore, then others will not only be able to know what I did and how I got there, but they will be greatly aided in erecting their own spiritual apotheosis. Both tasks represent my true will, so whatever happens to me, both tasks will be accomplished, whether I complete all of my writings and teachings or not.

I was quite pleased with the results of my simple magical workings the prior evening. There is so much more to come, and I look forward to it. I also look forward to sharing some of this knowledge with you, my readers, as well.

CHAPTER TEN

DISCOVERY AND DEVELOPMENT OF THE MISSING RITUAL (11/10/2010)

AN IMPORTANT DISCOVERY OCCURRED TO ME regarding the Abramelin Lunar Ordeal. This is the missing piece that was given to me recently during a session of communing with my HGA. It was surprisingly simple and available, but also nearly inscrutable. That missing piece is to be found in the seventeenth-century story *The Chemical Wedding of Christian Rosenkreutz*. I am also boning up on my Alchemy, carefully examining a chapter from the book *Philosophy of Magic* by Arthur Versluis.[86] His fifteen-page chapter on Alchemy is probably the most succinct and brilliant that I have ever read anywhere. I am in the process of distilling that chapter, as well as using the information culled from it to see if I can crack open the Chemical Wedding and extract the required symbols and images to build a powerful mystery vortex.

There are seven steps or days to the Chemical Wedding, and this could be represented by a ritual structure consisting of the four watchtowers with a central double gateway, characterizing what I have called a spiral gateway. I have the clues and pieces; they just need to be put together to build a ritual working—the final one in the Abramelin Lunar Ordeal. I am looking forward to completing the work over the Solstice holidays, when I will be taking an eighteen-day vacation from work.

---

86 Versluis, Arthur, *The Philosophy of Magic* (Penguin Books, 1988) pp. 105–119.

CHAPTER ELEVEN

PLANS FOR WORKING THE FINAL RITES OF ALO (03/06/2011)

THE IDES OF MARCH HAVE COME, but outside the world is still locked in the frigid embrace of the frost giants, who have ruled this long winter with a cruel disdain for any human creature comforts. While the snows of December and January seemed proper and picturesque, they are unwelcome and tedious now in March. More snow is on the horizon, as we who live in the northern Midwest continue to endure a very arduous ordeal of cold, ice, and snow, and lack the solar blessings of warm and balmy breezes. Yet even as it seems like the middle of winter outside, I know that this time of darkness and frigid weather will pass to be replaced by warmer weather, the melting of the snow and ice, and the return of leaves, flowers, and all of the wildlife represented by the growing season. Each sunny day grows brighter and warmer, melting some of the ice and snow. My soul will certainly rejoice when I hear the sweet sounds of the spring peepers, the first indication that life has returned to the barren winter landscape. They usually are heard in the second or third week of April, around the time that I will be starting to complete the Abramelin Lunar Ordeal.

Now that I have completed the last ritual in the Abramelin Lunar Ordeal, I can plan for the final set of workings that will aid me in finally completing this ordeal. I started this working in November 2009 and completed the first phase in the last days of December of that year. Throughout 2010, I have experienced a series of remarkable events, all of which appear to have built up to this final magical conclusion. How odd that I have worked this ordeal for many months and experienced all of its intense phenomena at various strategic times, and now in April and May of this year, I will perform the final rites in this series. This mystical and magical journey has taken me nearly eighteen months, from beginning to end, which, ironically, is the same duration as the German version of the original Abramelin ordeal.

As I think and meditate on what I have experienced during the last eighteen months, I am amazed at all that has occurred to me. Certainly, I have opened doors that were not even conceivable to me. For instance, I now know that I am not alone on my spiritual and magical quest, having received more than qualitative hints that there are individuals who know vastly more about the occult and ritual magic than I. So amidst hints and dreams of the promise of the mysterious masters (those remarkable mortals), the acquisition of new knowledge, and the materialization and revelation of new friends and important contacts, I have started this year with a tremendous amount of anticipation and excitement.[87] There are many projects that I will seek to apply some final efforts so as to realize their total fruition, and I am looking forward to their completion.

Dates for the concluding Abramelin Lunar Ordeal have been set for the full moon of April (April 16 and 17) and just before the full moon of May (May 14 and 15). The weekend of the full moon in April will be when I'll perform the Ogdoadic Godhead Vortex Ritual and the Triple Tetrahedral Gate Ritual, then the next day I will follow with the Stellar Gnostic version of the Bornless One invocation rite. That will re-activate all of the components of this ordeal that had been previously established in the workings of December 2009. The weekend of the near full moon in May will be when I will complete the Abramelin Lunar Ordeal, first with the Alchemical Hierogamy rite of Union, and then, on the following evening, the Bornless One rite of Envisioning. The moon will be waxing gibbous and will have entered into the sign of Scorpio by the last night, which will be a most auspicious sign for the final rite. That final rite has been delayed all of these months, but in May, it will be finally completed.

It is my assumption that with the conclusion of this ordeal, the various powers, authorities, and prerogatives of the Bornless One will be completely mine to command. I will have envisioned my higher spiritual purpose and know the ultimate meaning of my life. The magical squares that I have chosen from the Book of Abramelin will be fully charged and activated, and I will begin to wield specific magical spells to achieve my long-term goals.

---

87 As it turned out, those contacts and individuals proved to be fraudulent, although it took me a couple of years to finally make that determination. I won't name any names, but the lesson here is that the only great teacher we have is our Higher Self, for only that being can know us as intimately as it can because it acts as a bridge between the Absolute Godhead and us.

CHAPTER TWELVE

PHASE ONE OF FINAL ABRAMELIN LUNAR ORDEAL WORKING (04/25/2011)

Not everything turns out as you would like it to, but most often, it turns out as it needs to be. This is certainly true about the first phase of the two-phase final part to the Abramelin Lunar Ordeal. As you may remember, I had scheduled to work magic for the weekend of April 16 and 17 during the full moon. I was going to re-establish contact with the previous structures of the Ordeal, which would include the Ogdoadic Godhead Vortex Ritual, the Triple Tetrahedral Gate Ritual, to be followed the next day with the Bornless One invocation (Stellar Gnosis version).

Typically, if I schedule myself to work magic on a particular day, I will move heaven and earth to make certain that it gets done on that date. This is part of my magical and spiritual discipline, and I am proud to say that most of the time, I adhere to this rule without prevarication. However, I found myself unprepared mentally and physically to do these rites for the scheduled weekend. Something seemed wrong about doing it then, and I felt very much compelled to spend the time instead with Grace, since she was leaving for nine days in the middle of the coming week. So, I decided to perform the two-day working the following weekend, since I would be alone and able to better focus on my intention to do the work. (It was also quite interesting that my plans intersected with the Christian observance of Easter and the Jewish observance of Passover.)

Changing the date to the following weekend (April 22 and 23) seemed like a good idea to me, but then I started to think about what I was going to do and the sequence of how I was going to do it. I had planned on doing the Alchemical Hierogamy rite of Union during the next month as part of the second phase, but for some reason I felt driven to add it to the Friday working, so its effect would be in place before I performed the Bornless One invocation the next day. Because I had previously performed these rites back in December 2009, I could make this change. I wanted to experience the joining of the Element Godhead with the HGA before I re-performed the Bornless

Phase One of Final Abramelin Lunar Ordeal Working (04/25/2011)

One invocation. I felt obligated to do this, and so I listened to my intuition and decided to act on it. I am very glad that I listened, since the end results were quite splendid.

I now realize how important that ritual was, and how fortunate that I was able to figure it out and write it up. Had I managed to develop this ritual back in the autumn of 2009, I believe that the period of the overall ordeal would have been significantly shortened. At any rate, often the pioneer and trail blazer has to do things the hard way and experience the creative process of developing an ordeal, with all of the haphazard, chaotic, and serendipitous occurrences that happen along the way. Had I not delayed the working, then I might have done it the way that I originally planned. By letting the date slip a weekend, I came up with a different, and I think better, plan. We shall see over time how it works out, but so far, I am very pleased with the results.

Additionally, I decided to dispense with using the planetary hours for the two workings. Since most of the rites have been performed before as part of the original ordeal, I felt that it wasn't necessary to enclose the working with planetary hours. I will, however, use planetary hours for the last working in May because it has not yet been attempted. I also felt that the Benediction rite was unnecessary since the temple was properly aligned and fully charged. Since I completed the first part of the ordeal back in December 2009, the sigils and other regalia for this working have been kept in the exact place where I left them. The forces and intelligences that were contacted back then are still quite active. I also felt that the auspiciousness of the dates precluded the need to somehow make the whole operation more sanctified and spiritually blessed than what it already was. The important part of this working was to perform the rite of Union, and to do it before the Bornless One invocation.

Needless to say, those (in the Order) who choose to undergo this ordeal as it has been established will perform it with the rite of Union after the Bornless One invocation. I also would recommend that it be executed very quickly afterwards, perhaps the day after the invocation. It was important for me to perform the Ogdoadic Godhead Vortex Ritual and the Triple Tetrahedral Gate Ritual in order to re-awaken and re-connect with the ordeal where I left it. Since the rite of Union was supposed to be worked while the HGA and the Element Godhead were active, I felt the need to re-immerse myself in this work. So, I assumed that the second time through these rituals wouldn't really be very illuminating. The key, of course, was with the rite of Union and the effect that it would have on the overall working. I was looking forward to that event with a great deal of anticipation.

Astrological considerations for the dates April 22 and April 23 were not particularly auspicious. The moon was in the sign Capricorn, and it was five days from the full moon, or two days before the last quarter. Moon in Capricorn is not an emotionally effusive aspect—it is, in fact, cold and inhibited. However, the lunation cycle for the moon was at type six, which is the disseminating type, useful for communication and guidance. I could expect a stable and placid, if not subdued, lunar impact, particularly with the sun having recently entered into Taurus. Still, this was the date for Good Friday and Earth Day, with next day of Saturday (Holy Saturday) representing the transition from death to rebirth, at least in Christian practice.

In the tradition of the Roman Catholics, the church altar was stripped on Holy Thursday after the Mass rite, and no mass was actually said after that event until Easter Sunday. Good Friday was a time of prayer, adoration of the cross, a procession of the Holy Eucharist, and a mass of the pre-sanctified, using sacraments produced on Thursday. Holy Saturday continued the abstinence of saying mass, but consisted of the blessing of the fire, reading of the prophecies, blessing of the baptismal font (in preparation for a special baptism in the old rite), and, at vespers, the first celebration of Christ's resurrection. All of these rites commemorated the execution, death, and rebirth of the founder and savior, Jesus Christ. So, I was undergoing my personal rites of the Abramelin Lunar Ordeal when the rest of the Christian world—orthodox as well as the other denominations—was celebrating their holiest weekend of the year, next to Christmas. Therefore, the timing was particularly auspicious, if one considers the impact of performing personal magic during a religious holiday.

On Friday and Saturday (starting during the evening on Friday), the Passover Shabbat is celebrated, representing the most auspicious moment in the eight-day celebration after the two Seder meals before its end, which is Tuesday. These are the fourth and fifth days of Passover, known as the *Choi Hamoed*, or "intermediate days." The intermediate days represent the Hebrews' deliverance from bondage in Egypt and their travels to the Red Sea. They are still in danger of being captured or killed by pharaoh's soldiers, and it is the seventh day when the miracle of the Red Sea splitting is performed by Yahweh, allowing the Hebrews to cross over and safely begin their sojourn to the promised land.

Let me now relate what happened to me during these two events, since we have established the reasons and the context for their operation. I will write up edited notations from my journal, excluding only those entries that I consider too personal to relate here.

Friday, April 22: Began the working at approximately 8:30 p.m. I completed setting the magic circle just after the clock signaled the half hour, so I was able to determine the start time. I performed the Mass of the Goddess to charge the temple, and the rite proceeded without any incident. I felt in high spirits for this work, and my body was without fatigue or any pain—not at all like the last time I did this working. I performed the Ogdoadic Godhead Vortex Ritual and found that the individual Seraphim and Cherubim had become completely fused into union. I received no sense of any individual messages or insights; instead they manifested as a powerful combination of force and intelligence, which was quite remarkable! I was nearly taken aback by the powers and the sense of the coalesced entities that I had awakened.

Once I had completed the invocation of the Element Godhead of Water, I reconnected and re-encountered the Goddess aspect that I had encountered nearly sixteen months ago. I found myself returned to the peaceful misty beach, where I had met a youthful barefoot woman with a white lace shift, tanned body and face, blonde hair in French braids, green eyes, and a friendly smile. I could once again smell the sea salt and hear the gentle sound of the waves lapping against the shore. I also heard sea gulls in the background but noticed that the sun was completely occluded by the enveloping mist. I idled with her a little while and felt comforted and refreshed by her presence. I had a strong sense of wellbeing and happiness, as if anticipating a time of joy. I now wonder if the Goddess was anticipating her wedding to the HGA, feeling the joy that one would expect to feel for such a glorious union.

The next ritual in the series for that evening was the Triple Tetrahedral Gate Ritual. I found this rite to be easy to perform and did so without incident. There were no striking visitations or other magical phenomena. I could feel the power of the ritual reach a kind of crescendo with the opening of the Great Gate, and I also sensed or even saw the Goddess and the HGA meeting each other on either side of the gateway. This rite set the stage for the next and final rite, having awakened and pulled together all of the elements from the last working. I was ready to proceed to the next level of the working.

Performing the rite of the Alchemical Hierogamy rite of Union was effortless, flowing, and nearly flawless. I marveled at how well the ritual worked, even though this was the first time that I had performed it. The first stage of the rite held an element of sadness, since that is where the young king and queen are executed and drained of blood, preparing them for the alchemical resurrection. However, instead of sensing the Goddess and the HGA going through this process, I felt myself going through it instead. I could visualize myself progressing through the three steps of alchemical dissolution, where my sense of ego-based selfhood was completely destroyed and made ready for distillation and regeneration. However, when I got to the central part of the rite and began to perform the rites of Conjunction, where the Goddess and HGA were to be wed, I found that they had returned to my sight, and I drew them together through the wedding rite.

I then envisioned a scene right out of the Lovers card in the Tarot, with me acting as the prelate who officially joins the two young lovers together. Once this act had reached its climax, I felt my heart filled with indescribable joy and a blissful happiness. It was a powerful sense of ecstatic union, and I even saw in my mind's eye where the two youthful lovers embraced and became one great being of light and love. I had to stop the working at this point for a while as I fully processed these new sensations. I fully sensed and felt the mysterious "lover within" as I had never sensed it before.

The rest of ritual proceeded without any further interruption but, as in the first part, I saw myself being reconstructed and made alchemically whole, fulfilled, regenerated, and renewed. The end of the rite had me feeling as if I were reborn and made completely new.

Once the final rite was finished, I had to sit and meditate for a while. I felt that the rite of Union was very likely the most magnificent ritual that I have ever experienced. I was so powerfully affected that I couldn't go to asleep right way. The rite had been completed at around 11:30 p.m., which was a three-hour period of intense ritualizing, but I was not at all tired. Later that evening, my dreams were very vivid and active, and I felt a blissful kind of joy and happiness that I hadn't felt in some time, as if the weight of all my cares and troubles had been completely removed from my shoulders.

Saturday, April 23: This time there was a bit of a delay before I was able to begin the working. I had some tasks to complete for the day, and then I wanted to take short nap afterward to catch up on my sleep. Unfortunately, I slept for about two hours, which meant that the time at my waking was around 7 p.m. It was still light out (because of daylight saving time, and because the days get so much longer in Minnesota the closer one is to the solstice), so I was at first confused by the time. I hadn't done the preparations for the Bornless One rite, so I had to focus on getting them completed before starting the work. I decided not to perform the Mass of the Goddess for this evening's work; instead, I would focus on just doing the Bornless One rite. I finally got everything ready, took a shower, and properly anointed myself. The magic circle was fully erected at around 10:00 p.m.

I then went through the five stages of the Bornless One invocation rite, where I set up the four Qabalistic Worlds as the platform steps to a raised energy temple, with the fifth stage functioning as a trapezoidal prismatic temple at the very top. I was able to pace myself and make it through these five arduous stages without difficulty or fatigue slowing me down. I felt ebullient, inspired, and fully empowered, so I managed to work through all of the operations until I got to the Bornless One invocation. I then went through this invocation and the final experience was far more powerful and remarkable than I have ever experienced before. The ecstatic feeling from the previous evening was greatly amplified, and by the time I had completed the invocation, I felt a truly great joy, and happiness overpowered all of my senses. I felt that the HGA and its apparent manifestation was supremely energized by the rite of Union of the previous evening. It was so apparent to my senses that I felt as if I were two individuals and not one. I could sense its thoughts and feelings as if they were my own.

The union between us was neither complete nor perfect, but it gave me a strange kind of doppelgänger effect, where I moved and sensed myself in two places in space and time at once, even though both bodies were very close. It's the oddest sensation that I have ever experienced, but it does represent to me that I am getting very close to my objective of being fully unified with the Higher Self. Once the rite had achieved its climax, I found myself blissfully enclosed in an absolutely wonderful state. I saw the world through the HGA's thoughts and could even engage in an internal dialogue with my higher self, even anticipating the answers! I wanted to know my destiny, at least for the rest of my life, and I saw that there was still so much more to experience and learn, even though I have lived more than half of my life so far. Could that mean that I have a long life ahead of me? I could interpret it that way, or it could just mean that my last days will be very busy, allowing me to complete my travels and studies in good order. I now realize that I have built a good, solid foundation, and the HGA showed me this, and so much more.

After I sat in meditation for a while, the superimposition of the HGA and myself merged until I felt it in my body, or perhaps I was in its body—I couldn't tell. It was talking to me inside my head as if it were just another facet of myself (or like friends in a casual conversation), and I felt just blissful, whole, and completely happy. Then, when there was nothing more to say, we both became quiet but fully aware of and delighted in our merged beings. This state of mind continued as I completed the ritual and finally retired to bed. I felt like I was a container for this being, sharing the space of my thoughts, feelings, and sensations with it. The whole thing was indescribable—and it is still very much active even now, many hours after it was completed.

Phase One of Final Abramelin Lunar Ordeal Working (04/25/2011)

One thing that I did ask my HGA was for help in determining a theme for the Theurgia-Goetia spirits. Looking at this problem through the eyes of my Higher Self, I found it to be all quite simple. The spirits of the Theurgia-Goetia are based on the sixteen directions of the winds, since they are winged air spirits who fly. Half of them are good, and the other half are demonic, so they would represent the spirits that ward the gateway of the Abyss: half of them are on this side, and the other half are on the night side of the Abyss. They form a circle whose center is the abysmal gateway. I am sure that this will help me develop a magical system to invoke and evoke those spirits, and I believe that more information will be forthcoming, but it was fascinating to ask this question and have it so easily answered.

The working was completed at around 1:15 a.m. Sunday morning, and after shutting everything down, I tried to sleep. I have to admit that it was difficult to sleep, even though I was tired, because another part of me (the HGA?) was still awake and processing everything at light speed. I even had the odd thought of: "So this is what it's like being in a body and seeking the succor of sleep—how interesting!"

On Sunday, which was Easter, I decided to rest somewhat, but I did feel moved to perform a thanksgiving mass, which I did after completing my journal entries. I had woken up late in the morning and still felt tired. I also felt like something was still moving around inside my head, inspiring me with all sorts of visions and insights. I said the Mass of the Goddess with all of the solemnity and joy of the moment, but I also was very tired. I cooked for myself a wonderful feast and thoroughly enjoyed eating it, since my senses had been so enhanced from my experience. I felt that I had successfully completed the first phase and felt a great deal of wonder and amazement at the magical process that produced these experiences. There was much to be grateful about, and I felt gratitude at the deepest levels.

I am looking forward to the next and final phase of this ordeal, which (unless something peculiar happens) will be Saturday, May 14. At that time, I will attempt to perform the Bornless One Envisioning rite. I will produce an edited version of my experience and also probably put together an epilogue for the whole ordeal.

CHAPTER THIRTEEN

Phase Two of Final Abramelin Lunar Ordeal Working (05/17/2011)

The strenuous labor and long period of discovery for this ordeal is now over, and I can begin to relate my final experiences of the last two evenings and Sunday morning. On Friday, May 13, I performed the Bornless One Envisioning rite in its entirety, even though the directions specified a three-day period of meditating before completion. I felt that, having undergone this process for over eighteen months, I didn't need to wait any further to complete this ordeal. Within myself, I felt as if everything was completely in order and in readiness. So, I followed my intuition, as is my rule in the art of magic, and was not disappointed with the results. It was wholly and completely mind blowing, and I am still reeling from its effects.

My dreams leading up to this event have been quite vivid and instructive, and they gave me a strong sense of completion and fullness. I was more than ready to begin this working, and therefore more than prepared to undergo whatever impact it was to have on me. I am delighted to state that I found the Bornless One envisioning ritual itself to be highly effective and more intense and powerful than anything that I have previously experienced. I had no difficulties in performing it, and was able to get everything worked out, particularly the substitutions that needed to be incorporated.

The Abramelin Lunar Ordeal, now a completed suite of rituals and workings, is not only highly effective, but is even more resplendent in its overall effects for the adherent than what I had originally thought. I can't but recommend this new method to others who are interested in experiencing a pathway to personal illumination through the art of ritual magic. With respect to those who have faithfully followed the traditional Abramelin ordeal, I believe that I have developed a suitable alternative that others, who do not have the privilege of devoting from six to eighteen months exclusively to this working, may follow and achieve a similar end. That is, of course, my opinion, and those who might be critical of my efforts will have to at least judge it by performing the rituals and experiencing them for themselves. Needless to say, I should report what

I experienced as part of my final engagement with this ordeal, since nothing more will need to be said afterward.

I have completed this long struggle, and I am so very glad that it is finally done—but what an amazing journey it has been! The total irony of this working is that it took me exactly, to the day, eighteen months to complete, which is the same amount of time specified for the German version of the traditional Abramelin ordeal. It has been something of a wild ride at times, where I seemed to be floating a foot or two off the ground, so intense was the overall impact and its effect on me. Presently, I feel quite grounded and completely sober, which is so unlike what I felt over a year ago. Prior to that final set of workings, I needed to process everything that hadn't been examined in my past, and I needed to figure out the final and most important ritual in the working, which was the Alchemical Hierogamy rite of Union based on the Chemical Wedding of Christian Rosencreutz.

Determining and developing that last rite took me over a year, but once I was able to deploy it, the other pieces all fell into place. I would assume that anyone else who would perform this ordeal, now that the complete suite of rituals has been written up, would take around seven weekends to complete. Then, of course, the envisioning rite would be performed at the next available full moon. Still, that final working shouldn't be performed until the magician's internal state is fully resolved and all issues, past and present, have been adequately processed.

For those who might not fully understand the functionality of this rite, the Bornless One Envisioning is used to both realize and project into the future the full nature of one's True Will, incorporating a charged and consecrated black mirror for this purpose. This ritual was distilled and developed from a group of rituals in the *PGM* (*Greek Magical Papyrus in Translation*), used for performing divination by scrying into a pool of ink. I had adapted these rituals into one monumental working that would divine, through the HGA, the nature of the magician's past, present identity, and future destiny. The divination rite is therefore split into three parts, representing the necessity for the magician to know their past, know who they are, and know what their future will be. Some of these questions can be answered by the magician; others require the intermediation of the HGA. This rite incorporates a two-way methodology in regard to divination as passive perception and active projection. The objective of this rite is to project the magician's desired and realized destiny into the future, thereby making it fully capable of being realized in the present.

Let me now relate all that happened to me on that last set of days when I performed the final ritual working in the Abramelin Lunar Ordeal.

Envisioning Rite. First Evening, Friday, May 13, 2011 (from 9:45 p.m. to around 12:45 a.m.): As I have stated previously, I decided to do the entire ritual the first night of the working. I would follow it up with smaller workings on Saturday evening and Sunday morning. On Saturday, I would just say the Mass of the Goddess and intone the Hidden Stele and the Death Delivering Stele. On Sunday, I would only intone the two Stele to complete the working. I would perform an impromptu scrying session on Saturday evening after the Mass, but only briefly connect with the black mirror on Sunday morning. Two other substitutions were also decided on for the working: I would forgo wearing a crown of ivy (because the season is still so early), and I would bless my cincture instead of using a strip of linen with words written on it, functioning as a kind of phylactery.

These are the order of the seven ritual actions to be performed the first evening before performing the Envisioning rite:

1. Perform ablutions and then set a consecrated magic circle.
2. Bless the cincture before saying Mass, intoning the invocation instead of wearing it around my waist as a phylactery. (This was well received, so I then completed the vesting for the Mass.)
3. Perform the Mass of the Great Goddess up to the point of performing communion, then perform the following operations while there is still sacrament available.
4. Intone the invocations of the Hidden Stele and Death Delivering Stele.
5. Bless the magic ring for a second time (the ring is the link to the HGA). I put on the ring, said the activating word, and then summoned the HGA. The result of these operations produced a highly enhanced sensation of the HGA, and the ring was tingling with magic power.
6. Consecrate the magic squares from the Book of Abramelin (selected squares printed on parchment) with sacral wine and charge with the directed power of the HGA.
7. Then, complete the magical Mass and proceeded with the Envisioning rite.

When I intoned the invocations from the Hidden Stele and the Death Delivering Stele (both of which are from the *PGM*) they produced an incredible intensity of magical power. I felt myself briefly enter into a trance state where I saw points of light form into various kinds of star formulations and even heard some kind of celestial tinkling, like some vast, distant glass wind chime. I felt intoxicated, and a rush of euphoria filled my heart. I had to rest momentarily while I processed these experiences. I thought to myself that this is certainly quite an auspicious occurrence for the beginning of this working.

Bornless One Envisioning Rite: I wrote this ritual more than eighteen months ago, but it has never been performed by me until now. I was amazed at how well it flowed and appeared to build up the power. The invocations taken from the PGM were astonishingly powerful. I could not believe how potent these incantations were, and their overall magical effect was completely amazing. I doubt that some of these incantations have been used in magic for nearly a couple of millennia, but they have lost nothing in the passage of time.

I performed the macro-rite to summon the HGA, but of course, it was already very much present. Still, I sensed it joyously respond to the remedial summoning, making me feel as though I were enclosed in golden column of light. I then set the inverted Rose Ankh device to each of the four angles and the center of the circle, and the accompanied incantations taken from the *PGM* made the performance vastly more intense and powerful. At this point in the ritual, the combined devices generated a kind of network of manifesting and empowering forces that seemed to transform the temple into some kind of royal emplacement. I almost expected to see the throne room and the royal chambers of some magnificent palace. The vortex had generated a kind of royal domain through its fused energies with the black mirror set at its core.

These final actions brought me to the place where the black mirror was ensconced, and as I sat before it, I made invoking spirals over it with my transmutar wand. As I did this, while intoning additional *PGM* incantations, the black mirror began to glow and pulsate, going from an obsidian black to a silver white orb at intervals. I felt myself pulled into this pulsating orb and it opened up, becoming like a vast tunnel or wormhole between worlds and revealing itself as a kind of silver lattice structure surrounded by inky blackness. I found myself drawn deep into it, and it was as if I was within a tunnel, but it simultaneously seemed like it was within me. When I got to the point in the incantation where I was supposed to utter a series of magical words like an Egyptian baboon, the illusion ceased for a moment due to my mirth, but then quickly reasserted itself. I then proceeded to contemplate upon the vastness of the black mirror, performing first an inquiry and projection for my past, present self-definition, and then my life's destiny. These were the three Eyes (or I's) in the Triangle, and I made this sign into the black mirror before starting each period of contemplation.

Contemplation on Where I Have Been: I saw so many images of my past, consisting of all of the most important and strategic moments, which led me to become who I am today. I saw these as a very rapid progression from the earliest memories to the present moment, yet each scene evolved slowly and fully while my mind's eye had already gone on to the next event. After a short while, it seemed that all of these memories were unfolding simultaneously, creating a vast illusion of time and events occurring all at once. It was an amazing thing to behold, and I imagined that one perceives this when death is fully realized. At that moment, I felt a powerful thought overwhelm me: "I must fully accept everything that has happened to me as a product of my True Will and the power of fate and necessity." I bowed to this wisdom and felt all of these memories coalesce into a single point of light, then enter deep into my soul. The black mirror became dark again, but only for a moment.

Contemplation on Who I Am—My True Identity: The mirror blazed forth again, but this time I saw and felt the full force of my HGA. It entered into my being and filled me with joy, happiness, wholeness, and an intoxicating euphoria. Because I had wed my HGA with the Element Godhead, it appeared to have a greater power and affinity for me, unlike the previous times when I had performed the Bornless One invocation. Through the HGA, I received a powerful and total sense of who I am, where I have been, and what I must do to complete my life. It told me that the key to my future spiritual enfoldment was to cultivate spiritual love, bliss, and ecstasy, and to realize this when summoning my higher self. Through this agency, I will experience the continual spiritual evolution that leads to mastery. Then the mirror went dark for the second time.

Contemplation on My Ultimate Destiny: I have accepted that I am now gone deep into middle age, and that I am passing into my final years of life. I have accomplished much, but so much yet remains to be done. My inner fear is that I will not have time to complete everything that I want to complete in order to leave behind an effective legacy—a true measure of immortality. Yet what I have seen is that the most interesting and amazing events of my life have not yet occurred, and that I must learn to live at a far greater level than what I have been doing lately. I asked for the time and longevity to complete my work and saw that, indeed, I could very well be long lived, if I worked at ensuring that my gift of life is not squandered. I must work at being healthier, and I can't take anything for granted. The future is indeterminate, so what I have left of my years of productive life may be a decade, two, or even three, but I can, by my actions, extend my life.

Yet death comes to all living beings, and I am no exception. Nothing is granted or pre-ordained to me or anyone; everything must be earned by steadfast commitments and hard, tireless work. I sensed that a number of procrastinating issues and tasks for me had been overturned, and I was now free to complete a number of outstanding tasks. I felt blessed, protected, loved, and wisely guided by the HGA that was now fully activated and enshrouding me like a luminous golden cloud. Yet this great spirit was also inside of me, looking at the world through my eyes, and feeling the joy of life through my heart.

Once these events had transpired, the black mirror seemed to turn silvery white, and I felt my will come from within me and project into the future that has not yet been determined. I sought to know, in the remaining years of my life, a profound stable simplicity, to be divested of all of the clutter and chaos of competing desires and ambitions, and to be refined and honed to one single aspiration. This aspiration was to be one with my HGA, to waken from death seeing through its eyes and thinking and feeling with its mind. I can't relate any more of these incredible phenomena, but it went on for seemingly forever, extending from my mere physical form into the infinity of the Godhead itself, where the boundaries of time and space melted away to nothing, revealing a single blazing supernova that filled my eyes and mind with dazzling and brilliant light. I sensed during this extended moment that the HGA was with me and in me, my eternal companion in all things.

I pulled myself away from looking into the black mirror and laid down to rest, closing my eyes so that they wouldn't see anything more. But still, I saw the brilliant light and felt the bliss and ecstatic happiness until I passed out for a time. Finally, I woke up, and the temple atmosphere was alive with tiny sparks of barely perceived light. I marveled at these for a moment, but then sealed the circle, covered up the black mirror and magical tools, extinguished the lamps and candles, and retired for the night. Yet I was given so little peace that evening afterward, for the visions continued in my head deep into the night.

Continuing the Working. Saturday, May 14, 2011 (from 9:55 p.m. to around 11:28 p.m.): The second evening came, but I was exhausted from the previous evening's working. I stumbled through the day's activities, but after a couple of naps and a good meal, I felt more refreshed and ready to start the next part of the working. In truth, the greater part of the working was already completed, and it seemed that the next two incidents were merely the final parts of an already magnificent conclusion.

I said the Mass and then intoned the two Stele incantations, which were just as powerful as they were previously, and after the rites were completed, I unsealed the vortices and sat before the black mirror. I uncovered it, expecting that it would be dark and lusterless, but I was surprised that it was still luminescent, just not as startling as it was previously. What was imparted to me indicated that the greater manifestation had already occurred, but what remained was just as important.

I was told in some manner (perhaps in my head) that the past is now completed—there is no more to be extracted from it other than memories of what had once been. The future potential is there for me to harvest, since so much has already been established by years of practice, work, and research. I have not been lax all these years of my life. Still, the key to it all is the present moment—what I do here and now will give a final shape to my remaining years. There is so much to do before I finally experience an end to this life, and previously I had so much doubt and despair as to whether all of it could even be completed. Now, I am not alone or without an important powerful spiritual ally.

The HGA has now engaged itself to me in my quest for completion, and the addition of that magic should make the future quite interesting. Whatever my work brings to fruition, the greatest work is the simple process of bringing my higher self incrementally closer to me until there is no difference. I have already begun this process, but its maintenance and continuation are both simple and succinct. It is wholly up to me to ensure that it is brought to complete manifestation and total realization. So, what I felt from this revelation was the impending urge and need to get to work—there is so much to do, but the joy is in the doing!

That is all I received this night, and the next day, I just performed the intonation of the Hidden Stele and the Death Delivering Stele in the morning and lit a stick of incense. I felt completely resolved. The working was completed, and so was the ordeal. I collected all of the sigils that had been placed in the temple so many months ago, and now I could move on to other, newer challenges. I am grateful for what I have experienced, and I feel optimistic and blessed for what the rest of my life has in store for me.

PART IV

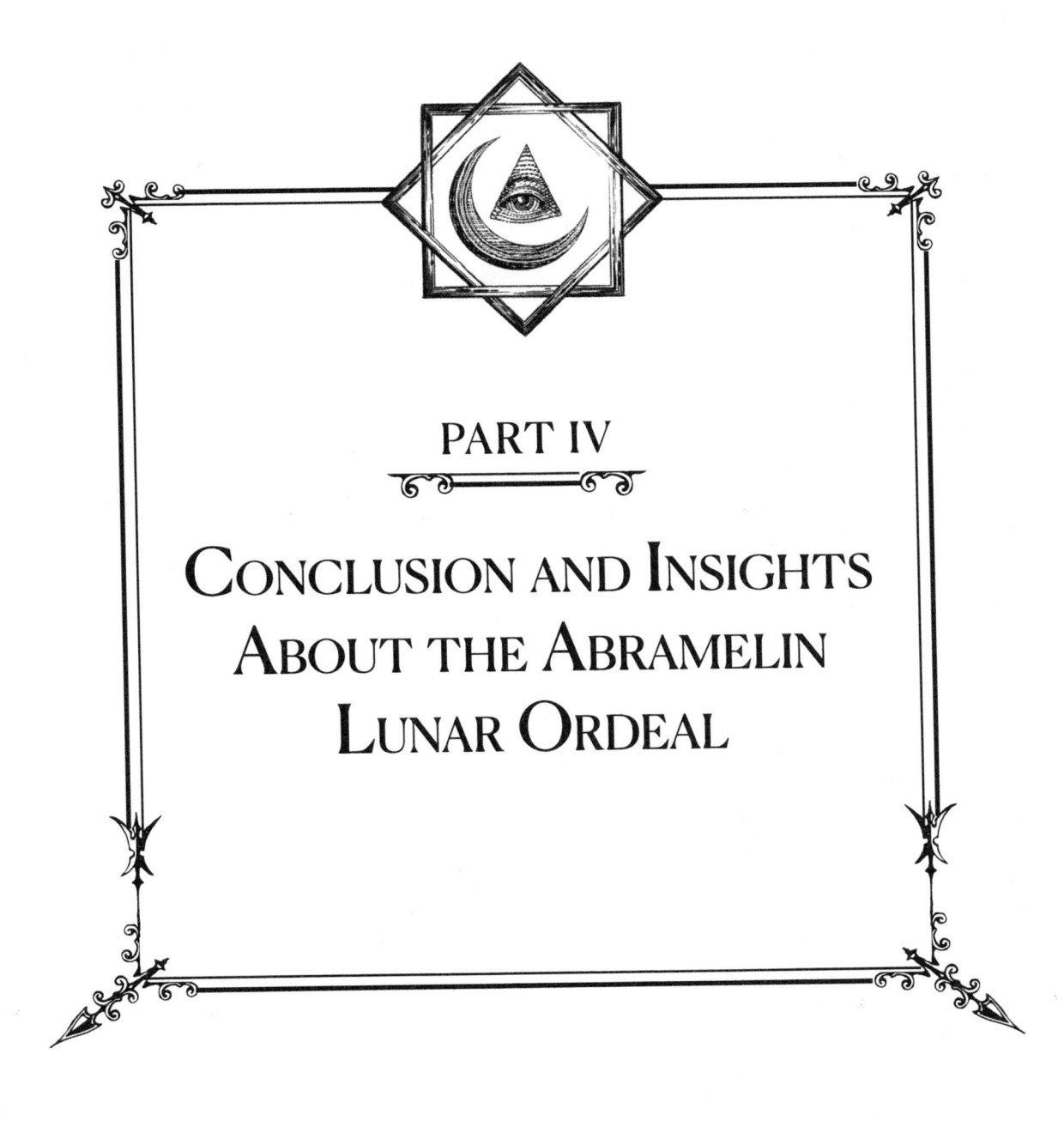

Conclusion and Insights About the Abramelin Lunar Ordeal

CHAPTER ONE

SEEKING ALTERNATIVES AND BREAKING WITH TRADITIONS

It has been my lot to always find a way to accomplish an objective in the art of magic that extends what I already practice and adds to the continuity of lore that I maintain. What I have tried to avoid is developing or adopting a methodology that doesn't fit with what I am already doing. When I was early in my studies and practices, I maintained that I had my own magical system and whatever materials I discovered were used to fill out and maximize that system. What this means is that I was loath to attempt to adopt other magical systems that required me to establish an entirely new basic foundation. I was particularly stubborn about this kind of approach, so I was able to avoid working with different magical systems that were unrelated and incompatible. I knew Witches who practiced Golden Dawn magic or grimoire-based magic who had to adopt lore that was completely different than what they were doing in their basic practices, and even had to have a separate location and tools to perform them.

Because of my attitude and conduct, I investigated a grimoire or tradition of magic and adapted anything that I found useful. I would then add that method or technique to my own system, thoroughly adapting it so that it appeared seamless with my own. I was behaving in this manner decades before the advent of Chaos magic made it something of a feature in the approach to developing magical systems without any respect or decorum towards the traditions that were being adapted. While I did have respect for these other traditions from which I was adapting lore, it didn't stop me from borrowing from them anyway.

When you examine the magical rituals in this book, you will see other traditions represented in the lore, most particularly the Golden Dawn. However, the level of complexity and the specifics of an energy model expanded and extended far beyond what anyone else is doing makes this lore uniquely my own. I am not the only ritual magician who uses experimentation and creative adaptation to build singular magical systems, but only with the popularity of Chaos magic has this approach become a more frequent occurrence among magical practitioners. When I was following this methodology decades ago, I was the oddball, and my approach was considered troublesome or annoying by traditionalists.

The last couple of decades has also seen the rise of those who espouse the traditional approach to magical practice, beginning with Joseph Lisiewski's book that directed magicians to use the old grimoires exclusively because only they could produce material manifestations in magical evocation. While that book was met with mixed opinions, it started a trend in the practice of magic that has only grown over time. It has produced what I call "grimoire-only traditionalists," or purists who believe that only the old ways of practicing magic actually produce results. Scholars were also at this time discovering obscure manuscripts hidden in various collections that were ostensibly books of magic and then translating and publishing them, which has fed the fire for this approach to magic. Back in the 1970s and 80s, there were very few of these translated grimoires available to the occult community to use in their magical practices. Now, there is a plethora of different translations of the various grimoires, and new ones come to light every year.

Those who espouse the traditional grimoire-only approach to magic have a lot of published works to use in adopting a more traditional approach to performing invocations and evocations. They have proposed a strict spirit-only model of magic and they strive to reconstruct the practices of ceremonial magicians in the sixteenth and seventeenth centuries as accurately as possible. There is also a kind of arrogance, conceit, and exclusivity in their community, where they tout their own approach to magic while denigrating those who are seeking to create their own magical traditions through creativity, innovation, and experimentation.

While I appreciate the many grimoires and magical books translated and published by scholars or individuals who have the language skills and historical insights, I have found these works to be curious and interesting, but typically not very useful. I also find it strange that someone who has taken pains to reconstruct a practice and mindset of a time and culture that has long since passed away would begrudge those of us who creating systems based on modern occult practices. I believe that accurately reconstructing a culture with beliefs and perspectives that existed nearly five hundred years in the past is practically impossible. Thus, attempting to engage with a system of magic that would require this kind of reconstruction in order to make it work as it did in the past is a fool's errand. What a reconstructionist does is approximate and invent in order to fill in the gaps that time has created, and that is nothing less than creating and experimenting with something that is actually new. The further in the past that a relic practice or ritual has as its origin, the more gaps there are to be filled in order to give it a healthy social context in the modern age.

That approach to using a grimoire as it was originally written had a precedence with the book of Abramelin the Sage, and magicians in the early twentieth century up to the present have approached it with that perspective. The grimoire-only crowd has latched on to this book and made it part of their practice because it fits with the idea that only the old grimoires, practiced as they were intended, would produce any results. This is a currently celebrated practice that would seem to prove what Lisiewski had proposed in his writings: the old ways are the best and only ways to perform ceremonial magic. Of course, what is omitted is that there was a very engaged cultural and temporal context that made these grimoires work as they did, and no one can reconstruct that mindset in this modern age.

Still, here I am continuing to develop my magical system, as I have been doing since the 1970s, only borrowing those pieces of lore that seem useful and then validating my rituals and workings through experimentation and creativity. I have benefited greatly from the writings of past occult scholars and magicians, but I have maintained my own approach, knowing that what I am doing is based on modern occult principles and practices. Of course, once I started to write my books and publish my opinions, there was bound to be trouble with the grimoire-only purists, who saw what I was doing as completely contrary to their beliefs and expectations. I was working on modern forms of magic that were quite effective and produced results. My very existence was likely a threat to their hubris and prejudice, and I am sure that many saw me as a kindred soul to Chaos magicians. As long as I kept to my own magical domain, many in that crowd could ignore me entirely, and my early books proposed a system of magic that had no connection to their practices.

However, once I declared that I had an alternative methodology or approach to a magical practice that was considered sacrosanct by the grimoire-only crowd, then the fur did fly, and I encountered a very angry backlash from these individuals. This was particularly true when I published in my blog that I had not only developed an alternative to the Abramelin working, but that it appeared to be quite successful. My solution was to ignore them entirely and continue with my work. Engaging with them on the internet was only frustrating and unproductive. I decided to take a lesson from my studies of Zen and not engage them or attempt to change their minds. That has given me a modicum of peace that I felt I needed so that I could continue living my life without the social drama of dealing with highly opinionated traditional magicians. I think that the message I gained was that it is okay to pursue your own path, to creatively invent and experiment with magical practices, to selectively acquire the lore of the past, and to seek to adapt it to the modern world regardless of who takes offense.

When an alternative methodology presents itself to me, I will explore it, develop new or revised lore, and then test it so that it is validated. I believe that this is the best approach that any modern magical practitioner can take, particularly with all the newly published magical material from previous ages. I also believe that all practitioners of magic in these modern times must adapt, adopt, derive, develop, experiment, and validate their practices—even those who espouse a grimoire-only perspective. While there might have been a kind of traditional approach to magic centuries ago where masters took on apprentices, we no longer have a culture that supports what was done in that age. I also believe that magicians have always invented their magical lore in each age, and that we must do the same thing today. We just have a lot more materials at our disposal than at any previous time.

This is the approach that I took when considering the practicalities of the Abramelin Sacred Magic and adopting a rigorous ordeal that could transform and transfigure any individual who seeks to perform it. I believe that I have been successful in this approach, but that it represents only one of many methodologies to achieve the same results. The steps I took to develop this lore were both practical and down-to-earth. I am not proposing something that is either too personalized or hair-brained to consider. It is a practical alternative to achieving a specific goal: K and C with your HGA.

Working with a system that is relevant to our current age is so critically important. Magical systems, methodologies, and practices that fit with the obligations and expectations of living in the post-modern age make them more accessible and manageable for us and others.

Alternatives can never be realized unless they are somehow shared, and that is why I have written this book. Aside from publishing, there are a myriad of media where such alternatives can be shared with the magical community and discussed in an impersonal and objective fashion. If someone has a good idea and it can be proven to be effective, then we should consider it, particularly if it fits in with our magical practice. I don't believe that I know everything, nor do I have the answers for every problem I might encounter in the practice of magic—and I believe that is true for everyone. If we share our beliefs and practices with other magicians, then we realize a whole new paradigm for magic, or at least see all of the possibilities that are available for us to use. I am hoping that the partisanship, cliques, and exclusive members-only approach to magic disappears and is replaced by acceptance, open-mindedness, and creative innovation. Such a place and time would be a brave new world for the discipline of ceremonial and ritual magic.

CHAPTER TWO

JOURNEY AND DEVELOPMENT OF THE LUNAR ORDEAL

My magical journey for the Abramelin Lunar Ordeal has been long and arduous, if you consider that I started this path back in 2009 and that I am just now, in 2025, publishing a book on it. Getting this work out to the public was one of the affirmations that I made thirteen years ago in 2011, and I can say that this objective has been met. Yet I had actually started this journey years before 2009, since there was an earlier version of the Archetypal Gate Ritual that invoked the four Element Archangels, a concept that I have long since discarded. This is because the Archangels are better represented by the ten Sephiroth of the Qabalah than by breaking out only four and assigning them to the four Elements. That original ritual was developed back in the early 90s when I was working with the Nephilim spirits. Over that decade, the ritual was expanded to include the four Qabalistic Worlds and the Enneagram, which I used to conjure one of the ten Sephorah and, in combination, invoked one of the Archangels on the Briatic level. That ritual was modified to invoke the Seraphim, Cherubim, and the Element Godhead, a critical component of the Abramelin Lunar Ordeal.

To ease my passage through the first phase of the Lunar Ordeal, I used the Archetypal Gate Ritual that incorporated the Enneagram to invoke the Archangel Raziel, and used the sigil of that angel as a pass-card to show that I had the authority to invoke the Seraphim and Cherubim. I actually didn't need to perform the invocation of Raziel to gain passage through the ordeal of these Super-Archangels, but it gave me a certain amount of confidence that I would succeed.

Of all the spirits that I have ever invoked or evoked, including Goetic Demons, it was the Seraphim and Cherubim that I found to be the most intense and frightening. They are not to be trifled with, and only fools approach them with no good reason or purpose. They challenged me, tested me at every point, and even inflicted illness and infirmity upon me to dissuade me from my objective. I found that my path forward was blocked by many trivial mundane occurrences, but I knew that the ordeal was testing my resolve, and as Chief Dan George said in the movie *Outlaw Josey Wales*, "I endeavored to persevere." I would suspect that anyone else performing this ordeal will experience similar obstacles to completing it. This is a pattern to be overcome, since even the traditional Abramelin working throws obstacles and distractions into the path of the operator.

The rest of the lore that I used in the Lunar Ordeal was invented based on what I knew or adapted from existing lore that I already possessed. The Bornless One invocation rite had gone through three versions before the final version was adopted. That version was derived from another suite of rituals which I developed for my Seven-Rayed Gnostic workings to establish myself as a seventh-degree initiate, standing at Chesed on the Tree of Life, and as a full-fledged magical Bishop. I had written up that lore in the late 80s and found the Bornless One rite to be acceptable for the Lunar Ordeal. Similarly, the Triple Tetrahedral Gate Ritual was based on a Qabalistic rite for Tarot-based pathworking named the Double Tetrahedral Gate Ritual. The Gateway of Ascension was a new concept, but some of the lore used to build it had been around for several years.

Still, it was 2009 when the idea and impetus for rewriting and revising the Abramelin working was born, and in a few months, I had written up all of the lore needed to perform the Abramelin Lunar Ordeal. Even so, when I was performing the rite, I was making corrections and adding elements to the rituals as I discovered missing attributes or erroneous structures that needed to be refined. In fact, I had omitted an entire ritual that was critical to the successful outcome of the Ordeal, and I suffered for months afterward trying to figure out what was needed to remedy the feelings of incompleteness that I experienced.

All of that was resolved when I performed the missing ritual in the context of redoing the ordeal by using macro rituals or a couple of strategic rituals in the suite of Ordeal rituals to return to the state of working when it was originally performed. Once I completed the final two phases of the working, I felt the process was completed and fulfilled. This is probably why I did not perform the Bornless Envisioning rite one month after the ordeal was completed. It didn't feel right to try to complete something that was still processing in my head.

What I can say now that this process is completed with all of the available lore, so that if someone were to take these rituals and perform them in the manner that they are supposed to be performed, the results would be far more conclusive and the ordeal would be experienced as completed and fully realized. I can guarantee that all of the rituals required are included in this book, and if they are performed in the correct sequence with the proper mindset, they will produce an astonishing personal transfiguration. If you elect to perform this ordeal for yourself, you will not be disappointed with the results. That is a fact I genuinely believe to be true, but if you want your own proof then you should perform the ordeal.

My path and journey were a crooked one because I was developing this lore as I was performing it to prove that it actually worked. Everything was being done on the fly, and I was inventing and refining it as I proceeded. That was not the optimal way of performing this ordeal, but since I was the trailblazer for this new working, the responsibility for ensuring that it was written in the best possible way was all my mine.

However, the pathway has been engineered and completed, and now I present in this book the completed version of the ordeal. I have validated it for myself, but now I will need to determine if others will have a similar experience when performing it. Only when there is a group of magicians who have successfully performed this ordeal can I safely say that it is now part of the overall tradition of the ordeals of transformation and transfiguration. Until that time, only I could say that it worked, and only then that it worked for me.

I have written about my journey and even produced my diary entries to show that I did indeed work it as I claimed. My journey has, for all practical purposes, ended with this book. The lore has evolved with editing and modifying the rituals so that they were brought up to date with my practical magical knowledge. While I may be continuing to work with what I started back in 2009, particularly regarding my HGA or Higher Self, that work is not part of this journey. It is just the never-ending journey of the itinerant ritual magician wending their way through life, learning, growing, and hopefully always creating new lore until that final day of destiny when death claims them.

What is important now is the journey that you will have if you want to adopt this ordeal and perform it. That will be quite an undertaking, as you can imagine, but it will not be one that slowly proceeds with months of preparation. You will complete it, if you persevere, in around seven weeks. In that short time, you will experience the full breath of what this ordeal can achieve for you. It seems like a small sacrifice to ask someone to engage in an intense set of workings spanning seven weeks, but those weeks will seem like months of experience compressed into days. The moon will travel its course, and you will be challenged in a manner that you may never have experienced before. That is all good and it is expected. What you need to do is to write up these rituals, practice them, develop your periodic liturgical practices, choose a date, schedule some vacation time away from your job, and then perform the ordeal during the allotted timeline. When you have completed the ordeal and completely processed it, I would like to hear from you and listen to your tales of power and paranormal experiences. I want to know the story of your journey, and I hope to hear it sometime in the future—that is if you decide to share it.

Here in this book is the challenge of a lifetime, and I hope that you will seek to realize it.

Chapter Three

Ultimate Destinations—Where Does This Path Lead Us?

Every ritual magician, no matter what kind of magic they perform, should perform ordeals and workings that completely challenge them and pull them out of their comfortable niche at some point in their career. Complacency is a curse, and so is hubris or believing that you have mastered something without risk, catastrophe, or challenge. It is also important to try new approaches to solving old problems and to think outside of the boundaries that we place on ourselves. If we don't experience challenges or take risks, we can never really grow or evolve, and this is especially true for the practice of magic. We evolve and grow through a process of transformative initiation, but we can also hide from our obligations and create a comfortable cocoon for ourselves. If there is no one who can externally challenge you, then it is important to force these challenges through the performance of ordeals.

Since I am no longer a member of a group, coven, or magical lodge, and that is a state I have often recently experienced, I am responsible for my own growth and periodic initiatory transformations. I have used this approach in the Order of the Gnostic Star, where initiatory degrees past the second are fulfilled through the performance of ritualized ordeals. An ordeal, as defined in the Order, is a challenge to perform a set of rituals in given period of time and document the results. They grow progressively more difficult as one advances up the path of initiations, passing through the four Elements to Spirit, where the lesser abyss is transcended. I have used the Tree of Life and the Sephiroth to qualify how I perceive the degrees, but I have found that the symmetrical structure of the Tree does not align with life experiences that travel in a spiral and seem to have multiple concurrent branches. Instead of a Tree, I would propose a bush, or perhaps, to eliminate any sense of linear space, an involuted tumbleweed. Making models and using them can be helpful, but one must never mistake the model for reality, which is always much more complex.

The pathway is not a linear progression, yet it has qualities that are like fractals, where a lesser ordeal can be the pattern or model of a higher ordeal with a different level of expertise and developed consciousness. It is, therefore, the understanding of the progressive layers of consciousness as mapped out by the Buddhists centuries ago that could, at least, provide us with a roadmap of where we are, where we have been, and where we must go.

Most of us function in the egoic state of consciousness with a strong, fixed awareness of self. We belong to a culture, occupy an economic class, belong and identify with specific social groups, and exist within a temporal matrix of events and occurrences. For those who are more creative, insightful, and not wedded to social group or class, who think and perceive independently and view themselves as autonomous, then this is a half-step above where most people reside. I believe that ceremonial and ritual magicians would occupy this half-step above most people. This doesn't mean that those occupying this half-step plane are somehow superior to everyone else. It means that they just don't fit into a reliable category and forgo basing their identity with a group. In some ways, they are deficient; in others, they are individuals free to create and move outside of expected norms.

However, above this half-step are whole levels of consciousness that are rarified and seldom achieved by human beings. These occupy the strata of the Subtle and Causal levels of being, and they can be split into four domains: the Low and High Subtle, and the Low and High Causal. The Low Subtle is represented by paranormal experiences, such as what I had experienced working the Ordeal. The High Subtle represents the ceiling for any kind of individuality. The Causal levels are where individuality disappears and the distinction between Self and Godhead dissolves altogether (Low Causal). This is a state that the Buddhists call *Nirvikalpa Samadhi,* where subject and object are replaced by the unitary experience of oneness and emptiness—the void. I believe that the dedicated aspirant should seek out the mechanisms and methodologies that will lead them to the Subtle and Causal levels of consciousness. The Lunar Ordeal is a model used to not only achieve a lower level of samadhi, but also even higher states of consciousness.

While I have experienced the levels of consciousness that would be defined as Low and High Subtle, I have only a sense of what the Causal level would feel like. I have approached it at the very perimeter of my magical and mystical experiences, but I have not been able to proceed to the next level or even maintain what I have achieved. These experiences of higher consciousness, although profound and impactful, cannot be maintained except for a brief time. My challenge is to lengthen and stabilize my toehold on to the Subtle with an eye towards the Causal, but I might not achieve that goal in my lifetime. As a man living in my final years of life, there is less time for me to work out this challenge. Still, this is the ultimate goal of all magicians, whether they realize it or not.

As I said previously, achieving the K and C of the HGA is a great responsibility. A magician experiences this ordeal as just the beginning of their work. It opens a door, but it is the responsibility for the magician to maintain that connection, and to do this, they must periodically revisit this working. This is not a one-time ordeal that a magician experiences and then is free to do whatever they feel like. There is an obligation to continue to work with this bond and eventually obtain complete conscious union with the HGA. This is a grave responsibility and forms an obligation to re-engage with the HGA again and again for the rest of one's life. There will be distractions, obstacles, and one can lose their way for a time. A magician can lose contact with their HGA, but it is truly always there, and since once an ordeal is successfully completed, it is only a matter for the magician to reconnect and re-engage.

Over the years since I completed my Lunar Ordeal, I have created and invented a lot of new lore, explored other ordeals, and now I have published quite a number of books that seek to deliver this knowledge and share my experiences with the public. However, I have gone through a period where my career completely distracted me from my magical and spiritual work, and undergoing a period of magical retirement, or, as Taylor Elwood calls it, "wintering," caused me to lose contact with my HGA. I know that it is there, since I feel it at peak moments and meet with it during sleep in my dreams, but I am not actively working with it in a magical temple. In writing this book, I have found myself pulled back to the time that I performed this ordeal and the journey that I experienced. I believe that this is the first phase or step to recover what has been lost and bring it forward into the present. I look forward to that time.

The seed that was planted in me by Metatron has now grown up to become this book—the wisdom of the Sacred Magic, delivered to others who might seek to experience it for themselves. It is my hope that this seed falls on fertile soil and grows to become a forest of trees. May your Holy Guardian Angel bless you and reveal itself to you in the near future.

Frater Barrabbas

APPENDIX III

ABRAMELIN MAGIC SQUARES: CONFIGURATION, CONSECRATION, AND USE

Since there are over two-hundred magic squares associated with the book of Abramelin the Sage, I quickly realized that, when consecrating and using these squares, I couldn't seek to use them all. To make a more manageable system for myself, I chose to use just twenty-two of them, and selected those that I thought would be more useful to me from the entire collection. These twenty-two magic squares I would draw on parchment and affix them in my Liber Spiritus, which I would charge and consecrate during the Bornless Envisioning rite three-day working.

These magic squares are the most famous part of the Sacred Magic of Abramelin, and they have beguiled magicians ever since they were first published by Mathers. However, without the attainment of the knowledge and conversation with the Holy Guardian Angel (or the Bornless or Headless One), the squares would not be active. A magician had to achieve this objective before being able to consecrate and charge the squares so that they might become activated. Originally, the magician through their HGA summoned and coerced demons and their servitors to active the squares and to wield them as desired. However, I have found this to be strange considering the power, authority, wisdom that the HGA possessed, that it could not by itself activate the squares when requested by the magician.

Another minor issue is that the magic squares were incomplete in the French edition, but fully developed in the later published German edition. For this reason, I used the Dehn-Guth edition of the Book of Abramelin to copy out the magic squares that I wanted to incorporate in my own workings. Still, what I discovered is that achieving the K and C of the HGA seemed to be more than sufficient to meet all of my magical needs, especially when one considers some of the magical work that I performed after I had achieved my own version of this ordeal. The magic squares are active, and they may have been unleashed in my favor without me being completely conscious of the fact, but I have not had recourse to use any of them since I activated them in 2011.

Here is the index of the list of the magic squares that I selected for my specific working. All of the squares are grouped in Book Four and contained in many chapters in that section. I have listed chapter and the number for the square in the following index. (See Dehn-Guth, pp. 147–188.)

CHAPTER ONE, DISCOVER ALL PAST AND FUTURE THINGS—
NOT DIRECTLY AGAINST GOD'S WILL:
 1. To know all past things
 2. Future things
 3. Future things
 4. Futures things in war
 5. Past and forgotten things
 6. Foretell coming sorrows
 7. Future things
 8. Past things
 9. Foretell wondrous and miraculous things
 10. Future things
 11. Future things

CHAPTER FOUR, TO CREATE VISIONS:
 1. In mirrors, glass, and crystals
 6. Through fire
 7. In water

CHAPTER SEVEN, TO MAKE ALCHEMY WORK VIA SPIRITS:
 3. To learn all sorts of alchemical arts from spirits

CHAPTER TEN, TO PREVENT AND REMOVE ALL OTHER MAGIC:
 1. To heal magical sickness

CHAPTER FOURTEEN, INVISIBILITY:
 4. To not be seen or thought of

CHAPTER SIXTEEN, TO RECOVER LOST TREASURES:
 5. Treasures in general

CHAPTER NINETEEN, TO ACHIEVE ALL SORTS OF FRIENDSHIPS:
 11. Peace in General

CHAPTER TWENTY, FOR ALL TYPES OF ANIMOSITY:
 5. To quiet gossip
 9. Against gossip

CHAPTER TWENTY-FOUR, FOR THE RETURN OF THINGS:
 3. Everything

Abramelin Magic Squares: Configuration, Consecration, and Use

The following are the designed impressions of the twenty-two magic squares as taken from the Dehn-Guth version of the Book of Abramelin.

Square index numbers are in the format (chapter.square number).

M	O	R	E	H
O	R	I	R	E
R	I	N	I	R
E	R	I	R	O
H	E	R	O	M

1.1

M	I	L	O	N
I	R	A	G	O
L	A	M	A	L
O	G	A	R	I
N	O	L	I	M

1.4

N	A	B	H	I
A	D	A	I	H
B	A	R	A	B
H	I	A	D	A
I	H	B	A	N

1.2

L	O	S	E	M
O	B	O	D	E
S	O	F	O	S
E	D	O	B	O
M	E	S	O	L

1.10

Conclusion and Insights About the Abramelin Lunar Ordeal

T	H	I	R	A	M	A
H	I	G	A	N	A	M
I	G	O	G	A	N	A
R	A	G	I	G	A	R
A	N	A	G	O	G	I
M	A	N	A	G	I	H
A	M	A	R	I	H	T

1.3

N	U	D	E	T	O	N
U	S	I	L	A	R	O
D	I	R	E	M	A	T
E	L	E	M	E	L	E
T	A	M	E	R	I	D
O	R	A	L	I	S	U
N	O	T	E	D	U	N

1.6

Abramelin Magic Squares: Configuration, Consecration, and Use

E	K	D	I	L	U	N
K	L	I	S	A	T	U
D	I	N	A	N	A	L
I	S	A	G	A	S	I
L	A	N	A	N	I	D
U	T	A	S	I	L	K
N	U	L	I	D	K	E

1.8

M	A	L	A	C	H
A	M	A	N	E	C
L	A	N	A	N	A
A	N	A	N	A	L
C	E	N	A	M	A
H	C	A	L	A	M

1.5

S	A	R	A	P	I
A	R	A	I	R	P
R	A	K	K	I	A
A	I	K	K	A	R
P	R	I	A	R	A
I	P	A	R	A	S

1.9

Conclusion and Insights About the Abramelin Lunar Ordeal

A	L	A	T	A	H
L	I	S	A	N	A
A	R	O	G	A	T
T	A	G	O	R	A
A	N	A	S	I	L
H	A	T	A	L	A

14.4

M	E	L	A	M	M	E	D
E	R	I	F	O	I	S	E
L	I	S	I	L	L	I	M
A	F	I	R	E	L	O	M
M	O	L	E	R	I	F	A
M	I	L	L	I	S	I	L
E	S	I	O	F	I	R	E
D	E	M	M	A	L	E	M

1.7

N	A	S	I
A	P	Y	S
S	Y	P	A
I	S	A	N

4.6

G	I	L	I	O	N	I	M
I	R	I	M	I	I	R	I
L	I	O	S	A	S	I	N
I	M	S	A	R	A	I	O
O	I	A	R	A	S	M	I
N	I	T	A	S	O	I	L
I	R	I	I	M	I	R	I
M	I	N	O	I	L	I	G

4.1

C	O	L	I
O	D	A	I
L	O	C	A
I	E	A	R

10.1

Conclusion and Insights About the Abramelin Lunar Ordeal

A	D	M	O	N
D	R	A	S	O
M	A	I	A	M
O	S	A	R	D
N	O	M	D	A

4.8

Z	O	G	E	O
O	S	O	N	E
G	O	L	O	G
E	N	O	S	O
O	E	G	O	R

20.5

S	A	L	O	M
A	R	E	P	O
L	E	M	E	L
O	P	E	R	A
M	O	L	A	S

19.11

M	O	R	E	H
O	L	O	G	E
R	O	F	O	R
E	G	O	L	O
H	E	R	O	M

24.3 (duplicate of 1.1)

I	P	O	M	A	N	O
P	A	M	E	R	A	M
O	M	A	L	O	M	I
M	E	L	A	C	A	H
A	R	O	C	U	M	I
N	A	M	A	M	O	N
O	M	I	H	I	N	I

7.3

S	E	G	I	L	A	H
E	R	A	L	I	P	A
G	A	R	E	N	I	L
I	L	E	M	E	B	I
L	I	N	E	R	A	G
A	P	I	L	A	R	E
H	A	L	I	G	E	S

16.5

Conclusion and Insights About the Abramelin Lunar Ordeal

L	O	S	I	T	O	S
O	R	A	K	I	R	O
S	A	R	O	P	I	T
I	K	O	N	O	K	I
T	I	P	O	R	A	S
O	R	I	K	A	R	O
S	O	T	I	S	O	L

20.9

A	L	L	U	P
L	E	I	R	U
L	I	G	I	L
U	R	I	E	L
P	U	L	L	A

1.11

BIBLIOGRAPHY

Achad, Frater. *XXXI Hymns to the Star Goddess Who is Not*. Will Ransom, 1923.

Assman, Jan. *Of God and Gods: Egypt, Israel, and the Rise of Monotheism*. University of Wisconsin Press, 2008.

"Augoeides." The Mystical Online Encyclopedia. Accessed December 24, 2023, from www.themystica.com/augoeides/.Banner, James, ed. *Ars Notoria: The Notory Art of Solomon the King*. Trident Books, 1997.

Barrabbas, Frater. *Transformative Initiation for Witches*. Crossed Crow Books, 2024.

—. *Sacramental Theurgy for Witches*. Crossed Crow Books, 2024.

—. *Elemental Power for Witches*. Llewellyn Publications, 2021.

—. *Spirit Conjuring for Witches*. Llewellyn Publications, 2017.

Betz, Hans Dieter, ed. *The Greek Magical Papyri in Translation; Including the Demotic Spells—Second Edition*. University of Chicago Press, 1996.

Bogdan, Henrik. *Ars Congressus Cum Daemone: Aleister Crowley and the Knowledge and Conversation of the Holy Guardian Angel*. University of Gothenburg, Entangled Religions 14.3. Accessed December 24, 2023, from er.ceres.rub.de/index.php/ER/article/view/10265/9934.

Davies, Owen. *Grimoires: A History of Magic Books*. Oxford University Press, 2009.

Dehn, Georg and Steven Guth, trans. *The Book of Abramelin: A New Translation*. Ibis Press, 2006.

Driscoll, Daniel J. *The Sworn Book of Honorius the Magician As Composed by Honorius through Counsel with the Angel Hocroell*. Heptangle Books, 1977.

Godwin, Joscelyn, and Adam McLean. *The Chemical Wedding of Christian Rosenkreutz*. Phanes Press, 1991.

Johns, June. *King of the Witches: The World of Alex Sanders*. Coward-McCann, 1969.

Mathers, S. L. MacGregor. *The Book of the Sacred Magic of Abramelin the Mage*. L. W. de Laurence Company, 1948.

Mead, G. R. S. *Pistis Sophia: A Gnostic Gospel*. Spiritual Science Library, 1984.

Menon, Sangeetha. "Advaita Vedanta." Internet Encyclopedia of Philosophy (IEP). Accessed on December 24, 2023, from iep.utm.edu/advaita-vedanta.

BIBLIOGRAPHY

Peterson, Joseph. The Sworn Book of Honorius Liber Juratus Honorii. Ibis Press, 2016.

Regardie, Israel, ed. Gems from the Equinox: Instructions by Aleister Crowley for his own Magical Order. Red Wheel/Weiser, 2007.

Robinson, James M., ed. *The Nag Hammadi Library*. Harper & Row Publishers, 1977.

Thakchoe, Sonam. "The Theory of Two Truths in India." Stanford Encyclopedia of Philosophy (SEP). Accessed on December 24, 2023, from plato.stanford.edu/entries/twotruths-india/.

Versluis, Arthur. *The Philosophy of Magic*. Arcana Paperbacks, 1996.

Wilber, Ken. The Atman Project: Collected Works, Volume II. Shambhala Publications, 1999.

Index

A

Absolute Self, 6
Air, 8–9, 11, 35, 37, 43–44, 47, 52, 54–55, 59–60, 65, 68, 80–81, 83, 85, 88–89, 91, 93, 96–97, 100–101, 115, 117, 129–131, 144–145, 159, 164–165, 177, 179, 188–189, 193–195, 201, 207, 219
Akephalos, 24–25
Alchemical Hieromany Rite of Union, 36–37, 135, 138
Alchemical Wedding, 55, 136
Archetypal Feminine, 44, 55, 136
Archetypal Gate, 7–9, 42, 46, 51, 57, 60, 73–74, 76, 92, 102, 174, 233
Archetypical Masculine, 55, 136
Ascension Gate, 9, 52, 102, 106
Assiah, 29, 50, 53–55, 90–91, 100, 111–112, 114, 203
Assmann, Jan, 23–25
Assumption of Great Powers, 11–12, 30, 36–37, 56–57, 135–136, 143, 152–153, 205
Atman, 6, 26, 132, 196, 204
Atziluth, 29, 50–51, 53–55, 57, 73–74, 76, 83–84, 90, 99, 111, 121, 123, 203
Augoeides, 6, 13–14, 145–146, 155, 200, 203–204
Autogenes., 22

B

Benediction, 8, 28, 31, 42, 48, 56, 61, 93, 103, 112, 143, 148–149, 153, 157–158, 174, 177, 183, 185, 188, 191, 197, 215
Berasheth, 24–25
Black Mirror, 32, 56, 153, 155–156, 158, 162–164, 221–225
Bornless One Invocation, 9–10, 15, 19, 27, 29, 31, 35–37, 42–43, 48, 53–57, 61, 63, 111–112, 138, 148, 152–153, 157–158, 180, 184, 193–195, 200, 202–203, 205, 207, 209–210, 213–215, 218, 223, 234
Briah, 50, 54–55, 90, 99, 118, 120, 196, 203

C

Cherubim, 8–9, 11, 37, 51–52, 57–59, 73–74, 88–89, 92–93, 96, 132, 171–172, 180–181, 194, 197, 203, 209, 216, 233
Crossroad, 31, 50–52, 55, 74, 76, 97, 136–137, 142, 147, 158, 197–198
Crowley, Aleister, 1, 6–7, 13, 15, 20–21, 23, 27, 54, 178
Crystal, 31–32, 43, 48, 54, 56, 71, 126–127, 157–159, 161, 178, 189

D

Daimones, 6
Death Delivering Stele, 31, 36, 56, 157–158, 165, 221–222, 225

E

Earth, 5, 8–9, 11, 15, 24–25, 35, 37, 44, 52, 54–55, 59–60, 65–66, 68, 70, 81–83, 85, 88–91, 93–95, 97, 100–101, 112, 114, 116, 126, 128–131, 139, 143–145, 149, 159, 161, 164–165, 172–175, 193–195, 198, 204, 207, 214–215, 232
Eastern Gateway, 9, 51–52, 74, 194
Egg, 8, 70, 99, 161, 184, 188
Element Godhead, 9–10, 35, 37, 46, 51–52, 61, 63, 73–74, 87, 92–93, 99, 101, 108, 144, 197, 209, 214–216, 223, 233
Enochian Star Temple, 63–64, 74, 93, 103
Envisioning, 11–12, 22–23, 31–32, 36–37, 56, 61, 105–106, 135–136, 138, 157–158, 160, 163, 197, 208, 213, 219–222, 234
Eye of Lucifer, 54, 71, 124, 126–127

F

Feast of the Tabernacles, 3, 5
Fire, 8–9, 11, 35, 37, 44, 52, 54–55, 58–59, 65, 69, 73–75, 77–78, 83, 85, 87–90, 93–94, 99, 101, 104, 109, 112–114, 117, 121, 123–126, 129–131, 142–146, 155, 159, 161, 165, 187–189, 191, 193–195, 197–198, 203, 207, 216, 230
Full moon, 5, 7, 9–12, 31, 35–37, 56, 157–158, 202, 208–209, 213–215, 221

G

Genius, 6, 14
Godhead, 6, 9–13, 15, 17, 21–22, 24–26, 29–32, 35–37, 42, 44, 46, 48, 50–55, 59–61, 63, 73–74, 77, 79, 81, 83–85, 87–93, 96–103, 106, 108, 128, 136–137, 144–149, 152, 158, 161, 171, 174, 178–182, 184–186, 188–189, 192–198, 201–204, 208–210, 213–216, 223–224, 233, 237
Godhead of Water, 35, 136, 193–194, 196–197, 209, 216
Golden Dawn, 6, 15, 19, 21–22, 24–25, 27, 29, 46–47, 54, 111, 229
Greater Abyss, 7, 54, 61
Greek Magical Papyri, 19–20, 24, 27–29, 34, 138, 148, 152, 157, 193. See also PGM

H

Hafiz, 186, 201, 204
Headless One, 18–19, 21, 23–24, 26–27, 50, 55, 204
Hidden Stele, 31, 36, 56, 157–158, 164, 221–222, 225
Hieromany Rite of Union, 135, 138
Holy Guardian Angel, 2–3, 6–7, 10–14, 16–19, 28, 41, 48, 50, 55, 69, 117, 124, 132, 169, 200–201, 203–206, 209, 211, 214–215, 217–219, 221–225, 232, 235, 237–238

K

K and C, 7, 15, 18–19, 169, 232, 237
Kabir, 186, 201, 204
Kerubiel, 35, 60, 89, 93, 95–96, 101, 185
Knowledge and Conversation, 14, 17, 200, 206

L

Lesser Abyss, 7, 54, 61, 236
Liber Samekh, 7, 15, 20, 23, 27
Liber VIII, 7, 27
Lunar Cycle, 3–7, 9–10, 18, 23, 34, 36, 138, 209

M

Mass, 7–8, 10–11, 28–29, 31, 36, 42, 48–49, 54, 56, 61, 91, 93, 100, 103, 107, 111–112, 118, 143, 148–149, 153, 157–158, 170, 173–174, 177, 179, 183, 185, 188, 191, 193–195, 197, 202, 208–209, 216, 218–219, 221–222, 225

Mathers, S. L. MacGregor, 1, 3, 5, 21–22, 25

Metatron, 35, 58, 87, 93, 96, 101, 145, 183–184, 188–189, 238

N

Nephilim, 42, 48, 65–66, 171, 233

New Moon, 5, 7, 11, 34–35, 170, 187, 193

O

Obligation, 16, 61, 171, 232, 236–238

Octagon, 9, 42, 50, 52, 54, 70, 92–93, 99, 114, 126, 149, 198

Ofaniel, 35, 60, 89, 93, 96, 101, 179–181

Ogdoadic Godhead Vortex, 10, 35, 37, 42, 48, 52, 92–93, 102–103, 196–197, 213–216

P

Paroketh, 54

Passover, 3, 5, 214, 216

Pearl, 184, 188–189

PGM, 15, 19, 21, 23–31, 34, 36–37, 48, 54–56, 138, 148, 152, 157–158, 221–223. *See also Greek Magical Papyri*

Pisces Cross, 46, 92, 97, 125

Powers of Sacramentation, 54

Q

Qabalistic World, 23, 29, 50–51, 53–55, 61, 73–74, 84, 90, 111, 203, 218, 233

R

Rikbiel, 35, 59, 88, 93–94, 101, 191–192

Rose Ankh, 31, 44, 46, 92, 98, 125, 136, 140, 142, 145, 158, 160–161, 222

Rose Cross, 44–47, 92, 98, 124, 128–129, 136, 138–140, 145

Rosenkreutz, Christian, 55, 135, 138, 211

Rumi, 186, 201, 204

S

Sacred Magic, 1, 3–4, 169, 231, 238

Sanders, Alex, 1

Seed, 70, 99, 128, 184, 186, 188–189, 238

Sep Tepy, 24–25

Seraphiel, 35, 58, 87, 93–94, 101, 188–189, 208

Seraphim, 8–9, 11, 37, 51–52, 57–58, 73–74, 85, 87, 92–97, 171–172, 180, 183, 194, 197, 203, 209, 216, 233

Spirit, 3, 9, 12, 14–16, 21–23, 26, 34, 44, 46, 50–52, 55, 65–66, 68–71, 73–88, 90–92, 98, 100, 103–105, 108–110, 112–127, 129–134, 136, 138–140, 143–147, 159, 161–165, 171–172, 174–175, 179–181, 183, 186, 188–189, 191–192, 194–195, 198, 204–205, 207, 209, 216, 219, 224, 230, 233, 236

Stele, 27, 31, 36, 56, 113, 157–158, 164–165, 221–222, 225

T

Tetrapatronis, 29, 43, 54–55, 111

Transfiguration, 7, 18, 41, 52, 61–62, 234–235

Transformation, 18, 41–42, 51–52, 55, 61, 75–76, 80, 90–91, 93, 100, 102–103, 109, 114–115, 121, 132, 136–138, 140–142, 145, 147, 199, 207, 235–236

Transmutar wand, 43, 68, 77–79, 81–82, 93, 106, 114, 127, 133, 138–140, 142, 149, 161, 223

Trapezoidal Cross, 45, 78–82, 103, 108–109, 132–133, 141, 145–146
Trigon Cross, 74, 83
Triple Tetrahedral Gateway, 10–11, 53

W

Watchtower, 9, 43, 47–52, 65, 73–82, 92–97, 101, 103–106, 108–109, 112, 114–118, 121, 125, 131–132, 134, 136, 138–142, 145–146, 149, 197, 211
Water, 8–11, 35, 37, 44, 52, 54–55, 58, 60, 64–69, 79, 83, 85, 87, 89–90, 93, 95–96, 99, 101, 104, 109, 118, 120, 129–131, 136, 142, 144–146, 148–149, 159, 161, 164–165, 182–185, 188, 193–198, 201, 207, 209, 216
Western Gateway, 9
Wilber, Ken, 195–196

Y

Yahoel, 35, 59, 88, 93, 97, 101
Yetzirah, 50, 54–55, 91, 100, 115, 117, 203
Yofiel, 35, 60, 89, 93, 95, 101, 172

Z

Zahariel, 35, 59, 88, 93, 95, 101, 172